Pose Du

TRANSNATI

'Transnationalism' refers to multiple ties and interactions linking people or institutions across the borders of nation-states. This book surveys the broader meanings of transnationalism within the study of globalization before concentrating on migrant transnational practices. Each chapter demonstrates ways in which new and contemporary transnational practices of migrants are fundamentally transforming social, political and economic structures simultaneously within homelands and places of settlement.

Transnationalism provides a much-needed single, clear and condensed text concerning a major concept in academic and policy discourse today. The book is for advanced undergraduate students, postgraduates and academics.

Steven Vertovec is Director of the Max-Planck Institute for the Study of Religious and Ethnic Diversity, Gottingen, Germany. He is co-editor of the journal *Global Networks* and editor of the Routledge book series 'Transnationalism'.

KEY IDEAS

Series Editor: PETER HAMILTON, The Open University, Milton Keynes

Designed to complement the successful *Key Sociologists*, this series covers the main concepts, issues, debates, and controversies in sociology and the social sciences. The series aims to provide authoritative essays on central topics of social science, such as community, power, work, sexuality, inequality, benefits and ideology, class, family, etc. Books adopt a strong 'individual' line, as critical essays rather than literature surveys, offering lively and original treatments of their subject matter. The books will be useful to students and teachers of sociology, political science, economics, psychology, philosophy, and geography.

Citizenship
Keith Faulks

Class
Stephen Edgell

Community
Gerard Delanty

Consumption
Robert Bocock

Globalization - second edition
Malcolm Waters

Lifestyle
David Chaney

Mass Media
Pierre Sorlin

Moral Panics
Kenneth Thompson

Old Age
John Vincent

Postmodernity
Barry Smart

Racism – second edition
Robert Miles and Malcolm Brown

Risk
Deborah Lupton

Sexuality – second edition
Jeffrey Weeks

Social Capital – second edition
John Field

Transgression
Chris Jenks

The Virtual
Rob Shields

Culture – second edition
Chris Jenks

Human Rights
Anthony Woodiwiss

Childhood – second edition
Chris Jenks

Cosmopolitanism
Robert Fine

Social Identity – third edition
Richard Jenkins

Nihilism
Bulent Diken

Transnationalism
Steven Vertovec

TRANSNATIONALISM

Steven Vertovec

Routledge
Taylor & Francis Group

LONDON AND NEW YORK

First published 2009
by Routledge
2 Park Square, Milton Park, Abingdon, Oxon, OX14 4RN

Simultaneously published in the USA and Canada
by Routledge
270 Madison Avenue, New York, NY 10016

Routledge is an imprint of the Taylor & Francis Group, an informa business

© 2009 Steven Vertovec

Typeset in Garamond and Scala by Swales & Willis Ltd, Exeter, Devon
Printed and bound in Great Britain by
TJ International, Padstow, Cornwall

British Library Cataloguing in Publication Data
A catalogue record for this book is available from the British Library

Library of Congress Cataloging in Publication Data
A catalog record for this book book has been requested

ISBN 10: 0–415–43298–7 (hbk)
ISBN 10: 0–415–43299–5 (pbk)
ISBN 10: 0–203–92708–7 (ebk)

ISBN 13: 978–0–415–43298–6 (hbk)
ISBN 13: 978–0–415–43299–3 (pbk)
ISBN 13: 978–0–203–92708–3 (ebk)

To Lia and Niko

Contents

ACKNOWLEDGEMENTS   ix

1 **Introduction: transnationalism, migrant transnationalism
   and transformation**   1
   Takes on transnationalism   4
   Migrant transnationalism   13
   What is transformation?   21

2 **Transnational social formations**   27
   Cross-fertilizing transnationalisms   27
   Some cross-cutting concepts   32
   Some transnational social formations   40

3 **Socio-cultural transformations**   53
   Cheap calls: the social glue of migrant transnationalism   54
   Dimensions of everyday transnationalism   61
   Transnationalism and integration   77

4 **Political transformations**   85
   Identities–borders–orders   86
   Dual citizenship/nationality   90
   'Homeland' politics   93

5 **Economic transformations**   101
   Trade and entrepreneurship   101
   Remittances   103
   Circular migration   119

6 **Religious transformations**   128
   Meanings of diaspora   128
   Religion, migration and minority status   137

Religion and diaspora   141
Religion and transnationalism   145

7   Conclusion: interconnected migrants in an
    interconnected world   156

    BIBLIOGRAPHY   164
    INDEX   201

ACKNOWLEDGEMENTS

This book marks the gathering of several overlapping strands of work over many years. So many years, in fact, that it is extremely difficult to flag and properly acknowledge the range of influences, encouragement, criticism and feedback that I have been fortunate to receive. Perhaps most of all, many ideas and background research for the book came through my experience directing the British Economic and Social Research Council (ESRC)'s national Research Programme on Transnational Communities. Between 1997–2003 the Programme entailed some 20 projects across numerous disciplines at different universities in the UK and abroad, directly engaged over 60 researchers, organized dozens of international conferences and produced dozens more books and other social scientific works (see www.transcomm.ox.ac.uk). I learned a great deal from all the TransComm colleagues and participants at events, from the Advisory Board members (Jeff Crisp, its Chair, is to be thanked most of all) and I am especially grateful to Anna Winton, Kay McLeary and Emma Newcombe – superb administrators without whom none of the TransComm activities would have happened or would have been so successful.

Some of these paths of learning continued through work at the ESRC Centre on Migration, Policy and Society (COMPAS) and the Institute of Social and Cultural Anthropology at the University of Oxford. Across these institutions and others at Oxford I have been fortunate to have excellent students and colleagues providing much support, insight and advice, particularly Roger Goodman, David Parkin, David Gellner, Frank Pieke, Ceri Peach, James Piscatori, Katharine Charsley, Susanne Wessendorf, Mette Berg, Hannah Gill, Alan Gamlen, Bridget Anderson, Nick Van Hear and Stephen Castles. In Oxford, special thanks must be made to my good friends and *Global Networks* co-editors Alisdair Rogers and Robin Cohen: they have profoundly stimulated, informed and channelled my interests in this topic over many years. Ali also gathered and edited the *Traces* news review for the TransComm programme, which provided a tremendous view into ongoing manifestations of transnationalism.

I wish to thank the Wissenschaftskolleg zu Berlin/Institute for Advanced Study, Berlin, where I spent an enjoyable year as Visiting Fellow working on the theme of transnationalism. I am also very grateful to the following colleagues who have offered helpful comments on earlier versions of the composite chapters, including: Alejandro Portes, Josh DeWind, Peggy Levitt, Ayse Caglar, John Eade, Nina Glick Schiller, Thomas Faist, Nancy Foner, Felicitas Hillman, Ruud Koopmans, Khalid Koser, Eva Østergaard-Nielsen, Ludger Pries, Werner Schiffauer, Tom Cheesman, Marie Gillespie, Ninna Nyberg Sørensen and Andreas Wimmer. I am also grateful to Heather Tinsley of TeleGeography, Inc. for her kind provision of data. In Vancouver, where I spent an enjoyable, albeit too brief, period as Visiting Scholar under the auspices of an ESRC fellowship, Dan Hiebert and David Ley acted as superb hosts and friends alongside their stimulating colleagues and students at Research on Immigration and Integration in the Metropolis (RIIM).

The chapters of this book represent reworked, interwoven and updated versions of several published articles, particularly Vertovec 1999a, 2003a, b, 2004a, b and 2006. I wish to thank the anonymous reviewers of those publications in the respective journals (you know who you are!). Remaining faults, despite constructive criticism, suggestions and correction, naturally remain mine.

Finally, and of course certainly not least, I am ever grateful to my wife Astrid and kids Lia and Niko for much tolerance (despite considerable eye-rolling) whenever the book was mentioned. I'm just sorry, especially to you, that it took so long to get off the desk.

Ljubljana, August 2008

1

INTRODUCTION

TRANSNATIONALISM, MIGRANT TRANSNATIONALISM AND TRANSFORMATION

Today transnationalism seems to be everywhere, at least in social science. That is, across numerous disciplines there is a widespread interest in economic, social and political linkages between people, places and institutions crossing nation-state borders and spanning the world. The expansion of transnationalism as a topic of study has been tracked by Gustavo Cano (2005). Cano examined publications that were keyworded 'transnational' or 'transnationalism' in the *Social Science Abstracts Database* and saw an increase from a mere handful of articles across the social sciences in the late 1980s to nearly 1,300 such keyworded articles by 2003; almost two-thirds were published between 1998–2003. As any current internet search will reveal, this expansion of interest is evident in a rapidly increasing number of publications, conferences and doctoral projects within the disciplines of sociology, anthropology, geography, political science, law, economics and history, as well as in interdisciplinary fields such as international relations, development studies, business studies, ethnic and racial studies, gender studies, religious studies, media and cultural studies. And as particularly detailed in the bulk of this book, such interest is growing in migration studies too.

It is not a coincidence that the growth of interest in transnationalism – or sustained cross-border relationships, patterns of exchange, affiliations and social formations spanning nation-states – parallels the growth of social scientific interest in globalization over the same period (see Guillén 2001). Facilitated, but not caused, by improved transportation, technology and telecommunications, globalization has entailed the increasing extent, intensity, velocity and impact of global interconnectedness across a broad range of human domains (Held *et al.* 1999). Enhanced transnational connections between social groups represent a key manifestation of globalization.

Of course there are numerous other ways of looking at aspects of globalization. These include new or modified uses of technology (such as the internet and mobile phones), the changing nature of the global labour force (surrounding de-industrialization and the rise of service industries in some places countered by industrial growth in others, feminization, 'flexibility', migration and outsourcing), the development of interconnected supply chains and markets, the growth and expansion of non-government organizations and social movements, and the changing capacity and roles of nation-states, multilateral agreements and international political frameworks (see *inter alia* Robertson 1992, Castells 1996, W.I. Robinson 1998, Held *et al.* 1999, Cohen and Kennedy 2000). Change within each of these spheres has implications for the transnational forms and activities of many kinds of groups and institutions.

Just as – contrary to the prediction of some observers – globalization itself has not produced a smooth, borderless, integrated global order, transnationalism has not entailed consistent kinds of social formations or practices. Reviewing James Rosenau's (2003) book *Distant Proximities*, John Urry (2003: 250) notes that rightly, from Rosenau's perspective, 'globalization is not viewed as essentially economic or political or socio-cultural or environmental. Rather, it is viewed as all of these, taking the form of multiple, complex, messy proximities and interconnections'. Just as transnationalism is a manifestation of globalization, its constituent processes and outcomes are multiple and messy too.

Some scholars have attempted to describe facets of 'globalization from above' (the sphere of large corporations, international agreements and so forth) as distinct from 'globalization from below' (entailing small-scale, non-state actors). Similarly a literature has developed suggesting a contrast between 'transnationalism from above' and 'from below'. While doubtless of some heuristic value, such conceptual binaries are ultimately not very satisfactory. The scales, spaces and mechanisms of globalization and transnationalism are just too entangled to allow such clear abstractions.

At least one conceptual clarification is worth underlining, to begin with. With regard to interactions between national governments (such as formal agreements, conflicts, diplomatic relations), or concerning the to-ing and fro-ing of items from one nation-state context to another (such as people/travel and goods/trade), we might best retain our description of these practices as 'inter-national'. When referring to sustained linkages and ongoing exchanges among non-state actors based across national borders – businesses, non-government-organizations, and individuals sharing the same interests (by way of criteria such as religious beliefs, common cultural and geographic origins) – we can differentiate these as 'transnational' practices and groups (referring to their links functioning across nation-states). The collective attributes of such connections, their processes of formation and maintenance, and their wider implications are referred to broadly as 'transnationalism'.

There are many historical precedents for and parallels to such patterns (see for instance Bourne 1916, Bamyeh 1993, Grant *et al.* 2007). Indeed, transnationalism (as long-distance networks) certainly preceded 'the nation'. Yet today these systems of ties, interactions, exchange and mobility function intensively and in real time while being spread throughout the world. New technologies, especially involving telecommunications, serve to connect such networks with increasing speed and efficiency. Transnationalism describes a condition in which, despite great distances and notwithstanding the presence of international borders (and all the laws, regulations and national narratives they represent), certain kinds of relationships have been globally intensified and now take place paradoxically in a planet-spanning yet common – however virtual – arena of activity.

As mentioned previously, transnationalism represents a topic of rapidly growing academic interest. While broadly remaining relevant to the description of 'transnationalism' offered above, however, most of this burgeoning work refers to quite variegated phenomena. We have seen increasing numbers of studies on 'transnational' communities, capital flows, trade, citizenship, corporations, intergovernmental agencies, non-governmental organizations, politics, services, social movements, social networks, families, migration circuits, identities, public spaces, and public cultures. These are obviously phenomena of very different natures, requiring research and theorization with different tools, on different scales and with different levels of abstraction. In the rush to address an interesting area of global activity and theoretical development, there has been much conceptual muddling.

It is a useful exercise, therefore, to step back at this point in order to review and sort out the expanding repertoire of ideas and approaches so as perhaps to gain a better view on how transnationalism has been discussed.

TAKES ON TRANSNATIONALISM

Below, the different 'takes' on the subject should not be considered exclusive; some rely on others. Nevertheless, the meaning of transnationalism has been variously grounded upon arguably distinct conceptual premises, of which six merit closer scrutiny. Therefore we will examine transnationalism as social morphology, as type of consciousness, as mode of cultural reproduction, as avenue of capital, as site of political engagement, and as (re)construction of 'place' or locality.

1. Social morphology

The meaning of transnationalism which has perhaps been gaining most attention among sociologists and anthropologists has to do with a kind of social formation spanning borders (see Chapters 2 and 3). Ethnic diasporas – what Kachig Tölölyan (1991: 5) has called 'the exemplary communities of the transnational moment' – have become a central focus for attempting to understand the shapes and dynamics of transnationalism. To be sure, diasporas embody a variety of historical and contemporary conditions, characteristics, trajectories and experiences, and the meaning of the term 'diaspora' itself has been interpreted widely by contemporary observers (see Chapter 6; also Vertovec 1998). One of the hallmarks of diaspora as a social form is the 'triadic relationship' between: (a) globally dispersed yet collectively self-identified ethnic groups; (b) the territorial states and contexts where such groups reside; and (c) the homeland states and contexts whence they or their forebears came (Sheffer 1986, Safran 1991, R. Cohen 1997).

Central to the analysis of transnational social formations are structures or systems of relationships best described as networks (see Chapter 2). This is a handle on the phenomena in line with Manuel Castells' (1996) analysis of the current Information Age. The network's component parts – connected by nodes and hubs – are both autonomous from, and dependent upon, its complex system of relationships. New technologies are at the heart of today's transnational networks, according to Castells. The technologies do not altogether create new social patterns but they certainly reinforce pre-existing ones.

Dense and highly active networks spanning vast spaces are transforming many kinds of social, cultural, economic and political relationships. Akhil Gupta and James Ferguson (1992: 9) contend that:

> Something like a transnational public sphere has certainly rendered any strictly bounded sense of community or locality obsolete. At the same time, it has enabled the creation of forms of solidarity and identity that do not rest on an appropriation of space where contiguity and face-to-face contact are paramount.

Further, Frederic E. Wakeman (1988: 86) suggests that the 'loosening of the bonds between people, wealth, and territories' which is concomitant with the rise of complex networks 'has altered the basis of many significant global interactions, while simultaneously calling into question the traditional definition of the state'.

In these ways the dispersed diasporas of old have become today's 'transnational communities' sustained by a range of modes of social organization, mobility and communication (see especially Guarnizo and Smith 1998). In addition to the long-standing ethnic diasporas and newer migrant populations which now function as transnational communities, many illegal and violent social networks also operate transnationally as well. For the United States Department of Defense, transnationalism means terrorists, insurgents, opposing factions in civil wars conducting operations outside their country of origin, and members of criminal groups (Secretary of Defense 1996). These kinds of cross-border activities involving such things as trafficking in drugs, pornography, people, weapons, and nuclear material, as well as in the laundering of the proceeds, themselves require transnational measures and structures to combat them (see for instance Stares 1996, Williams and Savona 1996, Castells 1998).

2. Type of consciousness

Particularly in works concerning global diasporas (especially within Cultural Studies) there is considerable discussion surrounding a kind of 'diaspora consciousness' marked by dual or multiple identifications. Hence there are depictions of individuals' awareness of de-centred attachments, of being simultaneously 'home away from home', 'here and there' or, for instance, British and something else. 'While some migrants identify more with one society than the other,' write Nina Glick Schiller, Linda Basch and Cristina Blanc-Szanton (1992b: 11), 'the majority seem to maintain several identities that link them simultaneously to more than one nation'. Indeed, James Clifford (1994: 322) finds,

> The empowering paradox of diaspora is that dwelling here assumes a solidarity and connection there. But there is not necessarily a single place or an exclusivist nation. ... [It is] the connection (elsewhere) that makes a difference (here).

Of course it is a common consciousness or bundle of experiences which bind many people into the social forms or networks noted in the section above. The awareness of multi-locality stimulates the desire to connect oneself with others, both 'here' and 'there' who share the same 'routes' and 'roots' (see Gilroy 1987, 1993). For Stuart Hall (1990), the condition of diaspora or transnationalism comprises ever-changing representations that provide an 'imaginary coherence' for a set of malleable identities. Robin Cohen (1996: 516) develops Hall's point with the observation that

> transnational bonds no longer have to be cemented by migration or by exclusive territorial claims. In the age of cyberspace, a diaspora can, to some degree, be held together or re-created through the mind, through cultural artefacts and through a shared imagination.

A wealth of personal and collective meanings and perspectives may subsequently be transformed, such that, as Donald M. Nonini and Aihwa Ong (1997) describe, transnationalism presents us with 'new subjectivities in the global arena'.

Further aspects of transnational or diasporic consciousness are explored by Arjun Appadurai and Carol Breckenridge (1989: i), who suggest that whatever their form or trajectory, 'diasporas always leave a trail of collective memory about another place and time and create new maps of desire and of attachment'. Yet these are often collective memories 'whose archaeology is fractured' (ibid.). Compounding the awareness of multilocality, the 'fractured memories' of diaspora consciousness produce a multiplicity of histories, 'communities' and selves – a refusal of fixity often serving as a valuable resource for resisting repressive local or global situations.

Finally, in addition to transformations of identity, memory, awareness and other modes of consciousness, a new 'transnational imaginary' (Wilson and Dissanayake 1996) can be observed reshaping a multitude of forms of contemporary cultural production.

3. Mode of cultural reproduction

In one sense depicted as a shorthand for several processes of cultural interpenetration and blending, transnationalism is often associated with a fluidity of constructed styles, social institutions and everyday practices. These are often described in terms of syncretism, creolization, bricolage, cultural translation, and hybridity. Fashion, music, film and visual arts are some of the most conspicuous areas in which such processes are observed. The production of hybrid cultural phenomena manifesting 'new ethnicities' (Hall 1991) is especially to be found among transnational youth whose primary socialization has taken place within the cross-currents of differing cultural fields. Among such young people, facets of culture and identity are often self-consciously selected, syncretized and elaborated from more than one heritage.

An increasingly significant channel for the flow of cultural phenomena and the transformation of identity is through global media and communications (see Chapter 3). Appadurai and Breckenridge (1989: iii) comment that

> Complex transnational flows of media images and messages perhaps create the greatest disjunctures for diasporic populations, since in the electronic media in particular, the politics of desire and imagination are always in contest with the politics of heritage and nostalgia.

Gayatri Spivak (1989: 276) describes 'the discourse of cultural specificity and difference, packaged for transnational consumption' through global technologies, particularly through the medium of 'microelectronic transnationalism' represented by electronic bulletin boards and the Internet.

Many other forms of globalized media are having considerable impact on cultural reproduction among transnational communities too, e.g. diasporic literature (for example, Chow 1993, King *et al.* 1995). Concerning television Kevin Robins (1998) describes aspects of deregulation affecting broadcasting regions that effect the emergence of 'new cultural spaces', necessitating a 'new global media map'. The expansion of satellite and cable networks has seen the spread of channels targeting specific ethnic or religious diasporas, such as Med TV for Kurds, Zee TV for Indians, and Space TV Systems for Chinese, Vietnamese, Japanese and Koreans. Viewing is not solely passive, and there are emerging multiple and complex ways in which these media are consumed (see for instance Gillespie 1995, Morley and Robins 1995, Shohat and Stam 1996).

4. Avenue of capital

Many economists, sociologists and geographers have seen transnational corporations (TNCs) as the major institutional form of transnational practices and the key to understanding globalization (see for instance Sklair 1995). This is due not least to the sheer scale of operations, since much of the world's economic system is dominated by the TNCs (Dicken 1992). TNCs represent globe-spanning structures or networks that are presumed to have largely jettisoned their national origins. Their systems of supply, production, marketing, investment, information transfer and management often create the paths along which much of the world's transnational activities flow (cf. Castells 1996).

Alongside the TNCs, Leslie Sklair (1998) proposes that there has arisen a transnational capitalist class comprising TNC executives, globalizing state bureaucrats, politicians and professionals, and consumerist elites in merchandizing and the media. Together, Sklair claims, they constitute a new power elite whose interests are global, rather than exclusively local or national, and who thereby control most of the world economy.

In addition to the Big Players in the global economy, however, the little players who comprise the bulk of transnational communities are making an ever greater impact. The relatively small amounts of money which migrants transfer as remittances to their places of origin now add up to at least $300 billion worldwide (IFAD 2007; see Chapter 5). Beyond what they mean to the families receiving them, for national governments remittances represent the quickest and surest source of foreign exchange. Indeed, a great number of national economies today, such as the

Philippines, Pakistan and many Latin American states, absolutely depend on monetary transfers of many kinds from 'nationals' abroad. This fact has prompted many countries to develop policies for the 'transnational reincorporation' of 'nationals' abroad into the home market and polity (Guarnizo and Smith 1998). One often-cited case is India, which provides a range of favourable conditions for 'non-resident Indians' (NRIs) to use their foreign-honed skills and capital to invest in, found or resuscitate Indian industries (Lessinger 1992; cf. *The Economist* 6 June 1998). Such policies have impacts beyond the economic dimension. As Katharyne Mitchell (1997b: 106) observes, 'the interest of the state in attracting the investments of wealthy transmigrants widens the possibilities for new kinds of national narratives and understandings'.

Resources do not just flow back to people's country of origin but to and fro and throughout the network. Robin Cohen (1997: 160) describes part of this dynamic; anywhere within the web of a global diaspora,

> Traders place order with cousins, siblings and kin 'back home'; nieces and nephews from 'the old country' stay with uncles and aunts while acquiring their education or vocational training; loans are advanced and credit is extended to trusted intimates; and jobs and economically advantageous marriages are found for family members.

The strategy is often one of spreading assets (particularly if one of the geographic contexts of activity – 'at home' or 'away' – is deemed unstable for reasons of political turmoil, racism, legal bureaucracy, shrinking labour market or simply bad business environment). While many transnational communities have found themselves dispersed for reasons of forced migration (van Hear 1998), others have largely spread themselves for economic reasons. Thus among the Chinese diaspora, Nonini and Ong (1997: 4) state that 'it is impossible to understand such transnational phenomena unless strategies of accumulation by Chinese under capitalism are examined, for such strategies penetrate these phenomena and are in turn affected by them'. Yet while economic objectives may be a catalyst for the formation of transnational groupings, such activities give rise to a host of others. Transnational activities are cumulative in character, Alejandro Portes (1998b: 14) notes, and 'while the original wave of these activities may be economic and their initiators can be properly labelled transnational entrepreneurs, subsequent activities encompass political, social, and cultural pursuits as well'.

5. Site of political engagement

'[T]here is a new dialectic of global and local questions which do not fit into national politics,' writes Ulrich Beck (1998: 29), and 'only in a transnational framework can they be properly posed, debated and resolved'.

Such a transnational framework – a global public space or forum – has been actualized largely through technology. Publishing and communications technologies make possible rapid and far-reaching forms of information dissemination, publicity and feedback, mobilization of support, enhancement of public participation and political organization, and lobbying of intergovernmental organizations (see Alger 1997, Castells 1997; see also Chapter 4). Certainly much needs to be done to realize the full civic potential offered by these, yet a considerable amount of political activity is now undertaken transnationally.

The most obvious and conventional forms of such activity are represented by international non-governmental organizations (INGOs), including the International Red Cross and various United Nations agencies. Their number has been rapidly increasing. The transnational dimensions are reflected in their ability to provide and distribute resources (especially from constituent bodies in wealthy countries to ones in poorer countries), facilitate complementary or cross-cutting support in political campaigns, and provide safe havens abroad for activities of resistance which are illegal or dangerous in home contexts. However many INGOs, Louis Kriesberg (1997) suggests, simply reflect the status quo of hierarchy and power. Transnational Social Movement Organizations (TSMOs), on the other hand, are INGOs that seek to change the status quo on a variety of levels. 'TSMOs,' according to Kriesberg (1997: 12) 'work for progressive change in the areas of the environment, human rights, and development as well as for conservative goals like opposition to family planning or immigration'. The issues which concern TSMOs themselves are transboundary in character, and they draw upon a 'planetization' of people's understandings (R. Cohen 1998). Jackie Smith (1997) observes that, among 631 TSMOs she examined, 27 per cent are explicitly concerned with human rights, 14 per cent with the environment, 10 per cent with women's rights, 9 per cent with peace, 8 per cent 'world order/multi-issue', 5 per cent with development, and 5 per cent 'self-determination/ ethnic'.

Transnational political activities are also undertaken by ethnic diasporas (Chapters 5 and 6). Robin Cohen (1995: 13) reasons that, 'Awareness of their precarious situation may also propel members of diasporas to advance legal and civic causes and to be active in human rights and social justice issues'. Yet the nature of much diasporic politics is contested. Katharyne Mitchell (1997a) deeply criticises the assumptions of many postmodernist theorists (especially Homi Bhabha 1994) who contend that hybrid, diasporic 'third space' standpoints are inherently anti-essentialist and subversive of dominant hegemonies of race and nation. Mary Kaldor (1996) points to the presence of both cosmopolitan anti-nationalists and reactionary ethno-nationalists within diasporas, and Arjun Appadurai (1995: 220) writes that among transnational communities,

> These 'new patriotisms' are not just the extensions of nationalist and counter-nationalist debates by other means, though there is certainly a good deal of prosthetic nationalism and politics by nostalgia involved in the dealings of exiles with their erstwhile homelands. They also involve various rather puzzling new forms of linkage between diasporic nationalisms, delocalized political communications and revitalized political commitments at both ends of the diasporic process.

The 'politics of homeland' engage members of diasporas or transnational communities in a variety of ways (Chapter 4). The relations between immigrants, home-country politics and politicians have always been dynamic, as Matthew Frye Jacobson (1995) and Nancy Foner (1997) remind us with regard to Irish, Italians, Poles and Jews in turn-of-the-century America. Yet now expanded activities and intensified links are creating, in many respects, 'deterritorialized' nation-states (Basch *et al.* 1993). Political parties now often establish offices abroad in order to canvass immigrants, while immigrants themselves organize to lobby the home government. Emigrants increasingly are able to maintain or gain access to health and welfare benefits, property rights, voting rights, or citizenship in more than one country (around half the world's countries recognize dual citizenship or dual nationality). Other forms of recognition have developed as well. For instance, in Haiti, a country that is politically divided into nine departments or states, during President Aristide's regime overseas Haitians were recognized as the Tenth Department complete with its own ministry (Basch *et al.* 1993). And in one of the strangest cases of transnational politics, the government of El Salvador provided free legal assistance to political refugees (fleeing their own regime!) in the

United States so that they could obtain asylum and remain there, remitting some $1 billion annually (Mahler 1998).

6. (Re)Construction of 'place' or locality

Practices and meanings derived from specific geographical and historical points of origin have always been transferred and regrounded. Today, a high degree of human mobility, telecommunications, films, video and satellite TV, and the Internet have contributed to the creation of trans-local understandings. Yet these are nevertheless anchored in places, with a variety of legal, political and cultural ramifications, not only for the practices and meanings, but for the places as well (cf. Kearney 1995, Hannerz 1996).

Some analysts have proposed that transnationalism has changed people's relations to space particularly by creating transnational 'social fields' or 'social spaces' that connect and position some actors in more than one country (see Glick Schiller *et al.* 1992a, Castells 1996, Goldring 1998, Pries 2001, Faist and Özveren 2004, Jackson *et al.* 2004, Levitt and Glick Schiller 2004). Appadurai (1995: 213) discerns that many people face increasing difficulties of relating to, or indeed producing, 'locality' ('as a structure of feeling, a property of life and an ideology of situated community'). This, he reckons, is due not least to a condition of transnationalism which is characterized by, among other things, 'the growing disjuncture between territory, subjectivity and collective social movement' and by 'the steady erosion of the relationship, principally due to the force and form of electronic mediation, between spatial and virtual neighbourhoods'. There have emerged, instead, new 'translocalities' (Appadurai 1995, Goldring 1998, R.C. Smith 1998).

Although invoked by a variety of observers and conveying a variety of meanings, 'transnationalism' provides an umbrella concept for some of the most globally transformative processes and developments of our time. The term's multi-vocality may actually prove to be advantageous: as Alejandro Portes (1998b: 2) points out,

> the concept may actually perform double duty as part of the theoretical arsenal with which we approach the world system structures, but also as an element in a less developed enterprise, namely the analysis of the everyday networks and patterns of social relationships that emerge in and around those structures.

Transnational networks and social relations are particularly evident among many migrants today, and therefore these have been subject to increasing social scientific attention.

MIGRANT TRANSNATIONALISM

Migrant transnationalism – a broad category referring to a range of practices and institutions linking migrants, people and organizations in their homelands or elsewhere in a diaspora – is a subset of a broader range of transnational social formations (Portes *et al.* 2007; also see Chapter 2 below). Although some early literature on migrant transnationalism in the early 1990s might have seemed to suggest such, it is not assumed that all migrants today engage in sustained social, economic and political engagement across borders. Indeed, modes or types of transnational contact and exchange may be selective, ebb and flow depending on a range of conditions, or develop differently through life cycles or settlement processes.

A number of works trace the rise of the transnational perspective on migration (such as Smith and Guarnizo 1998, Portes *et al.* 1999, Portes 2001a, 2003, Kivisto 2001, Levitt 2001b, Vertovec 2001a, Levitt *et al.* 2003). It is fair to say that the whole transnational paradigm shift across the multidisciplinary field of migration studies was catalyzed by certain key anthropological works (especially Georges 1990, Grasmuck and Pessar 1991, Rouse 1991, Glick Schiller *et al.* 1992a, Basch *et al.* 1993; see also Kearney 1995).The prominence of this topic now goes far beyond anthropology; indeed, in recent years transnationalism has become one of the fundamental ways of understanding contemporary migrant practices across the full range of social sciences (Levitt and Jaworsky 2007). Surprisingly, even policy makers have gradually adopted the term and perspective too (Vertovec 2006).

While the term 'transnationalism' is fairly new and currently *en vogue*, sociologists of migration have long recognized that migrants maintain some form of contact with family and others in their homelands, especially through correspondence and the sending of remittances. From the 1920s until recent times, however, most migration research focused upon the ways in which migrants adapted themselves to their place of immigration rather than upon how they continued to look back to their place of origin. Since the early 1990s 'the transnational turn' has provided 'a new analytic optic which makes visible the increasing intensity and scope of circular flows of persons, goods, information and symbols triggered by international labour migration' (Caglar 2001: 607; cf. Levitt and Sørensen 2004). Christian Joppke and Ewa Morawska (2003: 20) acknowledge that 'Although not a new phenomenon in the history of international migration, contemporary immigrant transnationalism, of course, is not an exact replica of the old, but a different configuration of circumstances'.

What's 'old' about migrant transnationalism? Social patterns and practices of migrants to the Americas in the late nineteenth and early twentieth centuries, for example, attest to the following kinds of transnational connections (see for instance Morawska 1999, Glick Schiller 1999, Foner 2000):

- families were split between the countries of origin and destination, yet strong emotional ties were maintained;
- a considerable number of migrants returned to their homeland, or undertook some kind of movement back-and-forth between the two contexts over extended periods of time;
- strong long-distance networks were created and maintained, facilitating chain migration;
- ongoing communication between migrants and families in homelands was maintained, particularly through letters;
- migrants sent remittances to families in the homeland, which were spent on both consumption and investment;
- migrant associations were established, sometimes collecting money to send for projects in home towns (such as repairing churches);
- some migrants established businesses in both home and host countries, sometimes linking their activities through imports and exports;
- many migrants sustained political interests in their homelands, including the organization of political rallies, lobbying and funding for political parties;
- some migrant-sending countries formally exhibited concern over the welfare of their nationals abroad.

What's 'new' about migrant transnationalism, then? Current research reveals some distinct contemporary developments (detailed throughout this book), including the facts that:

- while migrants continue to retain strong bonds of emotion, loyalty and affiliation with families, traditions, institutions and political organizations in their homelands, advances in the 'technology of contact' have powerfully affected the extent, intensity and speed at which they can do so. Cheap telephone calls, faxes, email and Internet sites, satellite TV, ubiquitous print media and inexpensive and frequent modes of travel have allowed for continuous and real-time communication within global migrant networks;

- forms of migrant transnationalism both draw upon and contribute to other processes of cultural, economic, political and technological globalization;

- the speed and intensity of communication between home and away has created in many contexts a 'normative transnationalism' in which migrants abroad are ever more closely aware of what is happening in the sending context and vice-versa. Research demonstrates how even those who have never themselves moved from the home context are powerfully affected by events, values and practices among their transnationally connected relatives and co-villagers abroad;

- the sheer scale of remittances represents both a quantitative and qualitative shift. Currently global remittances officially exceed $300 billion per year. Now many countries are wholly reliant on remittances for a significant share of their national economies, including for example the Philippines, Pakistan, Egypt, and practically every country in Central America;

- advances in telecommunications have facilitated wider, more intensive and increasingly institutionalized forms of political engagement with homelands, including party politics and electioneering, lobbying, mass demonstrations, post-conflict reconstruction, support for insurgency and support of terrorism;

- migrant hometown associations have recently grown in number and extent of activity, now often organizing large sums of collective remittances for development, including the construction of infrastructure (roads, water works, schools, sports facilities) and equipment (ambulances, medical and educational supplies) for their localities of origin;

- government outreach programmes for emigrants have been established or embellished, including special banking and investment schemes to attract foreign capital, special government offices to observe the welfare of nationals abroad, and the introduction of legislation to allow dual citizenship to migrants who wish to naturalize in their host country;

• in many Western countries 25 years of identity politics (around anti-racism and multiculturalism, indigenous peoples, regional languages, feminism, gay rights, and disability rights) have created a context in which migrants feel much more at ease when publicly displaying their transnational connections. In this way, compared to earlier times, transnationalism has 'come out of the closet' (Morawska 1999).

Questions as to 'what's old' and 'what's new' about transnational migrant practices are still debated by migration scholars. Yet Alejandro Portes (2001b: 19) recalls Robert Merton's notion of "the fallacy of adumbration": that is, once a social scientific idea has been formulated, it is easy to find historical anticipations of it. This does not dismiss the idea. As Robert Smith (2003: 725) says, 'if transnational life existed in the past but was not seen as such, then the transnational lens does the new analytical work of providing a way of seeing what was there that could not be seen before'. Further, it might be true to say that long-distance connections maintained by migrants 100 years ago were not truly 'transnational' – in terms of one contemporary sense of regular and sustained social contact; rather, such earlier links were just border-crossing migrant networks that were maintained in sporadic fashion as best as migrants at that time could manage.

The 'what's old/new' question is but one of a number of doubts or criticisms that have challenged the transnational turn in migration studies. Gathered from a variety of published articles, conference sessions and workshop debates concerning the transnational lens on migrant communities, a recurrent set of criticisms – 'the usual suspects' – are evident. I call these 'the usual suspects' by way of two meanings: (a) the same criticisms are persistently repeated (often without taking account of how they have actually been addressed by a variety of scholars throughout a now massive range of literature), and (b) although purporting to critique 'the transnationalism literature', critics (such as Kivisto 2001, Fitzgerald 2002, Waldinger and Fitzgerald 2004) most often focus on a limited number of works by a small set of authors (especially Glick Schiller, Basch and Szanton-Blanc, the contributors to M.P. Smith and Guarnizo 1998, and various works by Portes).

The 'usual suspect' criticisms usually entail one or more of the following issues:

- *Conceptual conflation and overuse:* 'transnationalism' is often used interchangeably with 'international', 'multinational', 'global' and 'diasporic'. There is also the problem of suggesting that all migrants engage in transnationalism.
- *Oldness/ newness:* questions abound as to whether transnational activities among migrants are new, and to how, or to what extent, they are new.
- *Sampling on the dependent variable:* researchers have looked for transnational patterns and found them. What about the cases in which transnationalism doesn't develop, or what conditions give rise to particular forms of transnationalism?
- *Trans-what?:* research and theory have not adequately problematized the difference between trans-*national*, trans-*state* and trans-*local* processes and phenomena.
- *The nation and nationalism in transnationalism:* it is sometimes suggested that the transnational approach privileges 'the nation' and, rather than moving beyond the nation-state model in social science, serves to reinforce it.
- *Transnationalism vs. assimilation (vs. multiculturalism):* a false dichotomy/ trichotomy between these terms has been posited, rather than a robust account of their inter-relationship.
- *Technological determinism:* are contemporary forms of migrant transnationalism merely a function of today's modes of real-time communication and cheap transportation?
- *Not all migrants are transnational:* even within specific groups or local communities, there is great variation in migrants' border-crossing practices: how many? how 'much'? what type?
- *Generational limitation:* are current patterns of transnational participation among migrants going to dwindle or die with the second and subsequent generations?

To call the above criticisms 'the usual suspects' is not to underestimate their importance, despite the fact that that sometimes such criticism of transnationalism often comes by way of tiresome conceptual nit-picking. Made recurrently since the mid-1990s in publications, seminars and conferences, the critical assessments outlined above do indeed represent important caveats, problematics and grounds for theoretical correction. Yet none of these critiques, contrary to some critics' own beliefs, delivers a knock-out blow. And to be sure, such criticisms have been fully engaged and responded to by a wide variety of social scientists – including the most criticized authors (see especially Glick Schiller and Levitt 2006).

It is clear that much more conceptual and empirical work remains to be done with regard to sharpening the transnational approach to migration research and analysis. One way to do this is by better disaggregating and characterizing types and levels of transnational activity (cf. Levitt 2001a, Riccio 2001, R.C. Smith 2001, Fitzgerald 2002). There is need for this despite the fact that, as Alejandro Portes (2003) points out, 'it has been recognized from the start that transnational activities are quite heterogeneous and vary across immigrant communities, both in their popularity and in their character.' And, if it still needs saying, most scholars recognize that not all migrants develop transnational practices, and many do so only in one sphere of their lives (Faist 2000).

The development of migrant transnationalism as a theoretical focus has entailed considerable conceptual tuning concerning modes, levels, extents and impacts of transnationalism. For example, theorists have formulated typologies such as:

- transnationalism 'from above' – global capital, media, and political institutions; and 'from below' – local, grassroots activity (Smith and Guarnizo 1998);
- 'narrow' – institutionalized and continuous activities; and 'broad' transnationalism – occasional linkages (Itzigsohn *et al.* 1999);
- 'great' – of state and economy; and 'little' transnationalism – of family and household (Gardner 2002);
- 'linear' – based on affective ties to others in a place of origin; 'resource-dependent' – opportunities and constraints surrounding labour market position and accumulation of necessary economic and other resources that can enable cross-border practices; and 'reactive' transnationalism – especially based on discrimination and loss of status in the receiving context (Itzigsohn and Giorguli-Saucido 2002, 2005);
- 'broad' – including both regular and occasional activities; and 'strict' transnationalism – regular participation only (Portes 2003);
- 'core' – patterned and predictable around one area of social life; and 'expanded' transnational activity – occasional practices in a wider array of spheres (Levitt 2001a, b).

Such types of transnationalism are variably manifested among different groups of people depending on a range of factors including geographical proximity of sending and receiving contexts, histories of interdependence between nation-states and localities, patterns of migration and processes of settlement.

Another way of refining transnational theory is through categorizing kinds of transnational migrants themselves. Here, such proposed categories of people involved in transnational activity comprise those whose quests for work or 'mobile livelihoods' (Sørensen and Olwig 2001) involve them in transnational migration circuits (Rouse 1991) or patterns of circular migration (Duany 2002; Chapter 5). In addition to the majority of cases described in much literature involving unskilled labour migrants, other categories increasingly relevant to the transnational approach include: undocumented migrants (Hagan 1994), return migrants (Thomas-Hope 2003), retirement migrants (King *et al.* 1998), forced migrants (Castles 2003), refugees and asylum seekers (Koser 2002), religious specialists servicing migrants (Riccio 1999), highly skilled workers generally (Vertovec 2002), information technology workers employed through global 'body shopping' (Xiang 2001) and trained occupational specialists drawn back from diasporas to contribute to the development of their homelands (J.B. Meyer and Brown 1999).

A further means of typologizing transnationalism focuses on degrees of mobility relating to transnational practice and orientation. In this way observers differentiate transnationalism among people (a) who travel regularly between specific sites, (b) who mainly stay in one place of immigration but engage people and resources in a place of origin, and (c) who have never moved but whose locality is significantly affected by the activities of others abroad (Mahler 1998, Levitt 2001b, Golbert 2001).

Identifying types, specificities and differences surrounding migrant transnationalism is perhaps a conceptually burdensome task, but it is an arguably necessary one. Differentiation provides clearer ways of describing the infrastructures, conditions or contexts of transnational relations. Transnational infrastructures and their impacts among migrants vary with regard to a host of factors, including family and kinship organization, transportation or people-smuggling routes, communication and media networks, financial arrangements and remittance facilities, legislative frameworks regarding movement and legal status, and economic interdependencies linking local economies.

Despite theoretical developments, the field of migrant transnationalism is still faced with certain methodological challenges. For instance:

- What are the proper or best scales (such as global/national/urban/local) or levels of analysis (macro-, meso-, micro-) to focus upon in order to gauge processes, their development and their impacts? How can we best conceive of relations between scales and levels? Until these questions are clarified, we will continued to be faced by the situation described by Nicholas DeMaria Harney and Loretta Baldassar (2007: 190) in which,

  > While many researchers use the concept of transnationalism to name or analyse processes, patterns, and relations that connect people or projects in different places in the world, its macroscalar associations do have their interpretive limits, obscuring and eliding different scales, networks and manifestations of connections, which, as a result, diminish its clarity as a conceptual tool.

- How can social scientists best move beyond methodological nationalism, 'the assumption that the nation/state/society is the natural social and political form of the modern world' (Wimmer and Glick Schiller 2002: 301), while recognizing the continuing centrality of nation-states in conditioning modes of migrant transnationalism? Or, as Kevin Robins and Asu Aksoy (2004: 183) depict the contemporary study of migrant cultural forms,

  > there always seems to be a rather conservative undertow to this transnational cultural analysis. In the end, one is left with the sense that, actually, there are no meaningful changes in the way that transnational cultures can imagine and organize themselves. The analysis of transnational media remains grounded in the conventional ideal of community bonding and the sharing of a common culture. For, in the end, in spite of all the evocations of the possibilities inherent in global flows and mobilities, there seems to be a basic inability to move on from the core ideas and concepts of the national imagination. In the discussion of transnational futures, the fundamental reference point continues to be the stubborn and insistent idea of 'imagined community'.

- What is the best or most appropriate 'unit of analysis' for studying migrant transnationalism? The field has seen a confusing mix of research focusing on groups based on criteria of nation-state ('Mexicans', 'Turks', etc.), region ('Oaxacans', etc.), ethnic group ('Kurds', etc.), village or locality and family. Each criteria has a different story to tell, of course, but – as in any social scientific study – we have to be aware of certain kinds of 'methodological ethnicism' which assumes ethnic groups as natural units.

A decade or more of social scientific attention to migrant transnationalism has produced, among other things, elaborate typologies of border-crossing social practices and networks. Given that migrant transnationalism and its consequences take so many forms, how can we begin to think about possible broader transformations stemming from migrant transnationalism?

Notwithstanding certain criticisms and analytical challenges, the transnational lens on migrant activities shows that some significant things are happening across a spectrum of human activities across the world. It is clear that many migrants today conduct activities and orientations that link them with significant others – family, co-villagers, political comrades, fellow members of religious congregations – who dwell in nation-states other than those in which the migrants reside. What kinds of changes are stimulated by these connections? In what spheres of life? How deep are the changes and how long-lasting? These are high among the analytical questions begged by transnational takes on migrant dynamics. It is these kinds of questions that this book addresses by way of assessing kinds and sites of transformation brought about by migrant transnationalism.

WHAT IS TRANSFORMATION?

Most studies of migrant transnationalism describe facets of social organization. That is, social scientists in this field of migration studies tend to research the nature and function of border-crossing social networks, families and households, ethnic communities and associations, power relations surrounding gender and status, patterns of economic exchange, and political institutions. Social change, in migrant transnationalism studies, tends to be gauged by the ways in which conditions in more than one location impact upon such forms of social organization and the values, practices and structures that sustain them. Another way of looking at this is to observe how 'the transnational migrant links the different contexts and contributes to changes in both' (Schuerkens 2005: 534).

In other fields of study concerning global interconnections, though, some theorists attempt to understand broader – indeed, global – enduring, structural shifts in social, political and economic organization. Such shifts are often referred to as forms of 'transformation' rather than mere (localized) change. To be sure, a common theme in the study of globalization is transformation. As James Rosenau (2003: 19) puts it,

> Few dissent from the proposition that advances in transportation and electronic technologies, and especially the Internet, have resulted in a transformation, a compression if not collapse, of time and distance, as well as altered conceptions of hierarchy, territory, sovereignty, and the state.

This is in distinction from change occurring only in one locality, level or scale. 'Stated more strongly,' Rosenau (2003: 23) says, 'change that occurs only at the micro level of people or only at the macro level of collectivities, rather than at both levels, is likely to be more a momentary fad than an enduring transformation.' While 'fad' might be a bit too dismissive, the point is taken: there is a world of difference between change in specific domains and change sweeping entire social structures and systems.

For instance, in contrast to social change affecting specific institutions, Kenneth Wiltshire (2001: 8) suggests that 'transformation ... describes a more radical change, a particularly deep and far-reaching one which within a relatively limited time span modifies the configuration of societies'. Neil Smelser (1998) points to profound social transformations that develop out of both individual and collective short-term actions within immediate environments: these accumulate in often unexpected ways to constitute fundamental changes in societies. Ulf Hannerz (1996) explicitly links the contemporary study of social transformation to the analysis of transnational connections affecting national societies, local communities and individuals. As Stephen Castles (2001: 14) puts it,

> The point is that global change and the increasing importance of transnational processes require new approaches from the social sciences. These will not automatically develop out of existing paradigms, because the latter are often based on institutional and conceptual frameworks that may be resistant to change, and whose protagonists may have strong interests in the preservation of the intellectual status quo. If classical social theory was premised on the emerging national-industrial society of the nineteenth and early twentieth centuries, then a renewal of social theory should take as its starting point the global transformation occurring at the dawn of the twenty-first century.

In their impressive volume, *Global Transformations*, David Held and his colleagues (1999) advocate the 'transformationalist' thesis or view of the long-term changes wrought by the intensification of interconnections known as globalization. Such a perspective stresses how a variety of conditions and parallel processes combine to bring about large-scale patterns of transformation. Their book especially concentrates on the following dimensions that can be analysed both quantitatively and qualitatively: (1) 'the extensiveness of networks of relations and connections', or the stretching of social relationships 'such that events, decisions and activities in one region of the world can come to have significance for individuals and communities in distant regions of the globe'; (2) 'the intensity of flows and levels of activity within these networks' that are not occasional or random, but somehow regular or patterned; (3) 'the velocity or speed of interchanges' of resources and information that provide immediate feedback, often in real time. These are all dimensions of transformation to be found in modes of migrant transnationalism.

Furthermore, it is inherent to the views of Held *et al.* (1999) that large-scale patterns of transformation come about through a constellation of mutually conditioning factors and parallel processes. Such an approach to transnationalism and cumulative societal transformation is exemplified by the work of Manuel Castells (especially 1996, 1997) as he describes the joint impacts of various kinds of enhanced computer-mediated communication on work patterns, collective identities, family life, social movements and states. Such mutually conditioning factors and parallel processes leading to broader transformations are to be found within patterns of migrant transnationalism too.

What's *not* transformative in migrant transnationalism? The widening of networks, more activities across distances, and speeded-up communications might be important forms of transnationalism in themselves. But they do not necessarily lead to long-lasting, structural changes in global or local societies. We are back to the 'what's old/new?' critique: migrants have historically maintained long-distance social networks, and the fact that messages or visits take less time does not always lead to significant alterations in structure, purpose or practice within the network.

But sometimes the matter of degree really counts. The extensiveness, intensity and velocity of networked flows of information and resources may indeed combine to fundamentally alter the way people do things. Patricia Landolt (2001: 220) suggests, with regard to migrant transnational activities, that there are times when 'a quantitative change results in a qualitative difference in the order of things'. In this field of study we can sometimes observe – following Smelser – how transformation is brought about by numerous individual and collective short-term actions within social environments that span distance locales. As portrayed by Portes (2003):

> Despite its limited numerical character, the combination of a cadre of regular transnational activists with the occasional activities of other migrants adds up to a social process of significant economic and social impact for communities and even nations. While from an individual perspective, the act of sending a remittance, buying a house in the migrant's hometown, or travelling there on occasion have purely personal consequences, in the aggregate they can modify the fortunes and the culture of these towns and even of the countries of which they are part.

In this cumulative way migrant transnational practices can modify the value systems and everyday social life of people across entire regions (see for instance Shain 1999, Kyle 2000, Levitt 2001b).

There is a point to be emphasized in analyzing the impacts of migrant transnationalism: while not bringing about substantial societal transformations by themselves, patterns of cross-border exchange and relationship among migrants may contribute significantly to broadening, deepening or intensifying conjoined processes of transformation that are already ongoing (and often subsumed by the overarching concept of globalization). This is what I argue by way of the conventional categories of socio-cultural patterns, politics, economics and religions in respective chapters of this book.

Each chapter is based on the recognition that specific practices and processes across borders have effects on: how people think about and position themselves in society both here-and-there; how they undertake aspects of their everyday activities while taking account of their multiple connections across borders; and how they organize themselves collectively according to multiple criteria and participate within encompassing contexts and scales – within or spanning specific localities – politically and economically. When such processes accumulate to alter fundamentally some key societal structures, we can designate them as forms of significant transformation.

In order to better equip ourselves theoretically to understand transnational phenomena, Chapter 2 first focuses upon a number of social scientific concepts which, it is suggested, are conceptually useful. These include notions of social networks, social capital, and embeddedness. A variety of transnational social formations – transnational social movements, transnational business networks, cybercommunities and transnational migrant groups – are subsequently discussed in terms of these key concepts. The study of each one of these types of transnational social formation throws up further concepts that are valuable for the study of the field as a whole.

Chapter 3 is devoted to examining migrant transnationalism, particularly how certain kinds of socio-cultural transformation and transnational lives are fostered by long-distance, cross-border connections among migrants. As the chapter details, such transformations are especially facilitated by the advent of cheap telephone calls. Everyday transnational practices are shown to have lasting impacts on families, on gendered social structures, and – drawing on Pierre Bourdieu – on the *habitus* of persons by way of conditioning their dispositions, orientations and patterns of social action. Following this discussion of *habitus* and the kinds of attributes it might entail, the mechanisms through which transnational lives give rise to 'cosmopolitan competence' and 'modes of managing multiplicity' are also considered in this chapter. The ways in which migrants conduct their transnational lives and maintain their long-distance attachments also have implications for one of the burning contemporary questions in many places: that is, how well transnationally connected migrants are 'integrating' into their host societies. The chapter rounds off with a look at several studies which, on the whole, demonstrate that such migrants are indeed able to 'integrate' and stay transnationally engaged on a number of dimensions.

Questions of migrant 'integration' beg the question 'Integration into what?' The answer usually entails some notion of nation-state society. The conventional model of the nation-state as a bounded, sovereign whole has been challenged by numerous processes surrounding globalization. Transnational processes and practices are themselves produced by, and contribute to, globalization. In Chapter 4 we look at migrant transnationalism and resultant forms of political transformation – particularly affecting the model of the nation-state and its encompassing conceptual complex or 'analytical triad' of 'identities–borders–orders'. Such transformations are witnessed most explicitly with the growth of dual citizenship and enhancement of a variety of 'homeland' political activities among migrants and 'diaspora engagement policies' created by governments.

Economic transformations stimulated by migrant transnationalism are the subject of Chapter 5. New initiatives for trade and entrepreneurship have emerged alongside migrants' enhanced transnational connectivity, but it is the astounding growth of global remittances that has especially received the attention of academics and policy-makers. This chapter examines flows, impacts and other issues regarding the transformative power of remittances, either sent by individuals or by hometown associations. Whereas the contemporary world migration order and its concomitant patterns of transnationalism are based on the premise of migrants moving to work and sending remittances home, there are currently high-level calls to create (or renew) alternative transnational systems of circular migration that would see the orderly, regularized mobility of workers between sending-and-receiving contexts. These are also assessed in Chapter 5.

While religious membership, activity and organization represents one of the oldest spheres of long-distance connectivity, modern migrant transnationalism arguably brings new phenomena that are, or have the potential to be, transformative with respect to age-old traditions. Yet religious change is subject to numerous conditions and processes, and in order to clarify and distinguish just what might be taking place through migrant transnationalism, Chapter 6 outlines differential or overlapping kinds of change within religious beliefs, practices and institutions that are brought about by conditions of diaspora (following a closer look at the term itself); by migration processes and ensuing situations of minority status; and by transnational connections. Numerous examples are given from a range of traditions, especially Hinduism and Islam.

Chapter 7 concludes the book with a discussion of some of the ways in which patterns of migrant transnationalism have become widely acknowledged if not accepted. The chapter emphasizes how contemporary migrants and migration processes both depend on and contribute to the increasing interconnectedness of people and societies around the world. Some possible long-term effects are speculated upon, particularly the potential for patterns of migrant transnationalism to contribute toward a globally shared, cosmopolitan future.

2

TRANSNATIONAL SOCIAL FORMATIONS

The studies of various social and political formations have embraced transnational perspectives. Can insights from the study of one kind of transnationalism have uses toward the social scientific understanding of another?

The following chapter examines a number of research fields and topics in order (a) to review briefly a set of sociological concepts and to suggest that they have a kind of core bearing across the study of various transnational social formations, and (b) to outline some ideas and perspectives drawn from work concerning other kinds of transnationalism that might have some theoretical purchase if applied to the analysis of migrant forms of transnationalism. It is proposed that conceptual borrowing might prompt insights into global processes of social transformation as well as specifically shine further light on ways that contemporary migrants create, maintain and make use of modes of exchange and relationship that span considerable distances and nation-state borders.

CROSS-FERTILIZING TRANSNATIONALISMS

Global activities among individuals, groups and organizations today take a wide variety of forms. Although these activities share the adjective 'transnational', it is uncommon to find theoretical attempts to span them.

In terms of transnational studies, Robert Keohane and Joseph Nye's (1971) edited volume *Transnational Relations and World Politics* arguably represents a kind of landmark. The book's contributors probed a set of transnational activities surrounding numerous kinds of border-crossing contacts, coalitions and interactions that are not controlled by organs of government. As a whole the volume raised important questions about a prevailing state-centric view of international relations. It emphasized the importance of 'global interactions' (defined as movements of information, money, objects and people across borders) and their impacts on interstate politics (see Nye and Keohane 1971). With such a broad view, contributing chapters addressed a breadth of transnational relations among multinational businesses, revolutionary movements, non-government organizations (NGOs), trade unions, scientific networks and the Catholic Church. Obviously these comprise highly diverse phenomena that operate on dissimilar scales. However, Keohane and Nye's volume attempted a cross-cutting approach in order to suggest possible common functions and effects surrounding different kinds of transnational social structures. While this amounted to 'a fundamentally different perspective on world affairs', the book and its project 'failed to gain much ground' (Orenstein and Schmitz 2006: 483).

About a decade later, another significant milestone in the field was represented in a collection of essays by James Rosenau (1980). This book highlighted tendencies toward the 'transnationalization' of world affairs through the rise of new global relations and associations among private individuals and groups, from students and tourists through NGOs and corporations. Rosenau emphasized how such non-state transnational connections could radically transform modes of collective action and global political interdependence. Among other things, he posed still-significant questions surrounding the implications of transnationalism for building a new civics in 'an era of fragmenting loyalties'. Indeed more recently, Peter Koehn and Rosenau (2002: 106) observe, 'The explosion of interpersonal interactions across territorial boundaries provides the energy that drives the transformative efforts of civil-society networks'.

By now, many years later and prompted by a growing and widespread interest in notions of globalization (especially as fostered by technological change), there has been a proliferation of literature concerning many types of transnational collectives. In the Introduction to a special issue of the journal *Global Networks*, Alejandro Portes (2001a) distinguishes between various kinds of cross-border organizational structures and activities that are, in much literature, confusingly (since they are sometimes interchangeably) called international, multinational and transnational. Portes cuts a path through the terminological jungle by delimiting each concept with reference to differentiated sources and scales of activity. In his reckoning, 'international' pertains to activities and programmes of nation-states, 'multinational' to large-scale institutions such as corporations or religions whose activities take place in multiple countries, and 'transnational' to activities 'initiated and sustained by non-institutional actors, be they organized groups or networks of individuals across borders'. Such a typology is useful to avoid terminological uncertainty and to facilitate more rigorous analysis in each sphere.

While there is certainly an acute need to distinguish terms and concepts within an increasingly messy academic arena, there is still much to be gained by occasional exercises in cross-disciplinary and cross-field theorizing. There are many kinds of transnational activity today, and many rich areas of social scientific inquiry surrounding them (cf. W.I. Robinson 1998). Yet there are few Keohane and Nye- or Rosenau-style attempts to learn from, or through, approaches and analyses from one transnational domain to another. This is likely one major consequence of years of increasing specialization in the social sciences. Notable exceptions include Sarah Mahler's (1998) discussion of different activities attributed to transnationalisms 'from above' and 'from below', and Michael Peter Smith's (2001) call for 'comparative transnationalisms'.

Ultimately, each transnational field of study – whether concerning corporations, NGOs, religions, migrants or other social groups – share a kind of common goal: to examine empirically, and to analyse, transnational activities and social forms along with the political and economic factors that condition their creation and reproduction. To do this, we should be able to utilize, draw from or be intellectually stimulated by all of the concepts and methods available (while recognizing, and then perhaps bracketing, the specific meanings they hold in their respective academic fields).

Although there are a number of limitations to such an exercise, the application of terms and concepts from other fields of study can be an activity akin to looking at one's own material with borrowed glasses: usually much will become more blurry but on occasion perhaps one or two things might become clearer. The usefulness of such attempts at conceptual cross-fertilization can be judged, as J. Clyde Mitchell (1974: 279) put it, by 'the utility of the terms and concepts to which they refer for representing regularities in field data which otherwise might escape attention'. The search for more evocative terminology and concepts, while certainly not a replacement for the process of theorizing itself, can be a stimulating and sometimes revealing activity – even if only by sharpening the cognizance of how and why certain terms, concepts and sociological phenomena studied in one area of social science really *don't* compare well to others.

The following review represents an attempt to rouse further thinking in the field of transnational migration studies by suggesting potentially useful approaches and ideas from other relevant fields of social scientific research. Below, I draw on selected works concerning the study of transnational social movements, transnational business networks and so-called cybercommunities. These are but a few areas of inquiry among several that could be drawn upon by way of parallel transnational social formations. We could alternatively conduct such an exercise concerning: ethnic diasporas (e.g. R. Cohen 1997), worldwide terrorist networks (Hoffman 1998a), transnational organized crime (Williams and Savona 1996), transnational policing activities (Sheptycki 2000), religious organizations (Rudolph and Piscatori 1997a), the so-called 'transnational capitalist class' of corporate executives, state bureaucrats, professionals and other elites (Sklair 2001), or globalized occupational groups such as domestic workers (B. Anderson 2000), seafarers (Lane *et al.* 2001) or sex workers (Kempadoo and Doezema 1998). Indeed, depending on how and just how far we wish to define transnational social formations, we also could include:

> tourism, charter flight *hajj* and other modern pilgrimages, invisible colleges in science, exchange students, au pair girls, foreign pen pals as part of growing up, transcontinental families, international aid bureaucracies, summer beach parties of backpacking Interrail-passholders from all over, and among voluntary associations everything from Amnesty International to the European Association of Social Anthropologists. It is these dispersed institutions and communities, groupings of people regularly coming together and moving apart, short-term relationships or patterns of fleeting encounter, which offer the contexts in which globalization occurs as the personal experience of a great many people in networks where extremely varied meanings flow. These networks are indeed denser in some parts of the world than in others, but they are hardly now a feature only of Western industrial society.
>
> (Hannerz 1992a: 46–7)

The suggestion that we might gain insight into one kind of transnational social formation by looking at another should not be very surprising, not least because it is increasingly recognized that participation in one transnational social formation might indeed lead to, or overlap with, another. Such crossing is observable in the activities of female domestic workers, whose work as individual transnational migrants is transformed transnationally when they become organized worker-activists (Anderson 2001). Another example is that of overseas Chinese families whose kinship and personal relationships are reshaped into powerful (and eventually less Chinese network-dependent) transnational business operations (Olds and Yeung 1999). Yet another is represented by Mourides, Senegalese Sufis whose networks within Europe and between Europe and Senegal function to circulate important religious figures, maintain patterns of moral conduct, and provide crucial information for small trading (Riccio 1999, 2001).

In undertaking an exercise in drawing upon other areas of study, I am by no means arguing that migrant transnational communities are *like* these other kinds of transnational social formation. Rather, I merely wish to suggest that it may occasionally prove useful to think through some of the concepts and terminology used to describe the other formations. Resonant with Mitchell's suggestion above, such concepts and approaches might serve as potentially useful devices for re-ordering or seeing alternative patterns in data concerning specific transnational migrant groups. In this way, the essay represents an attempt at conceptual cross-fertilization between parallel fields of study.

Similar cross-fertilizations have already occurred within some of the parallel fields that I survey in this chapter. Glenn Morgan (2001) suggests ways in which recent studies of transnational migrant groups have bearing on business studies, while Saskia Sassen (2000, 2001) places the study of transnational migrants in a kind of mutual interaction with attempts to understand global transformations of urban structures, national politics and international economies. Adrian Favell (2001) critically reviews how many current theories of globalization have latched onto migration as a metaphor for broader changes in society. Jörg Flecker and Ruth Simsa (2001) juxtapose the structures and practices of transnational businesses and globalized non-profit organizations. So it is perhaps about time for transnational migration scholars, too, to rummage the conceptual coffers of our colleagues who study other kinds of transnational groups.

I raise a further couple of caveats. By extrapolating from these subjects together I am not suggesting that transnational social formations are of a common type or function. Nor is this an attempt to build a single overarching theory of transnational social formations. Instead, again, in this chapter I selectively draw upon a diverse set of literatures to extract some key ideas, terms and approaches that seem to overlap or resonate with different areas of study. Here the aim is to suggest that the conceptual tools from parallel fields might provide insights and help to better structure ongoing research, analysis and theory concerning transnational migrant communities.

SOME CROSS-CUTTING CONCEPTS

First, it is important to realize how the process of conceptual and termi-nological borrowing from one or another sociological domain has already significantly benefited the study of international migration. This is espe-cially evident with three key terms (each representing a wealth of episte-mological and methodological insights) chosen for brief discussion here: *social networks*, *social capital* and *embeddedness*. These terms are discussed below not just to recap their basic meanings and to demonstrate that key-words from various realms of sociology have been utilized in migration studies. The purpose is also to flag them as fundamental concepts that run through or underpin studies and approaches to what I am calling parallel transnational social formations.

Social Networks

Ulf Hannerz (1980: 181) long ago suggested that social network analysis 'probably constitutes the most extensive and widely applicable frame-work we have for the study of social relations'. As a method of abstraction and analysis, the social network approach sees each person as a 'node' linked with others to form a network. The advantage of the social net-work perspective lies in its ability to allow us to abstract aspects of inter-personal relations which cut across institutions and the boundaries of aggregated concepts such as neighbourhood, workplace, kinship or class (Rogers and Vertovec 1995). This perspective fosters empirical research 'as a way of revealing *de facto* active networks rather than *a priori* assump-tions of community solidarity' (Bridge 1995: 281).

Network analysis provides a vocabulary for expressing the social envi-ronment as patterns or regularities in the relationships among actors

(Wasserman and Faust 1994). However, it would be a mistake to suggest network analysis is of one method. Drawing upon earlier views of Ronald S. Burt (1980), Mustafa Emirbayer and Jeff Goodwin (1994: 1414) describe network analysis as a kind of a paradigm or perspective, 'a loose federation of approaches' rather than a singular predictive 'social theory'. Network analysts seek to operationalize research concepts such as social structure, social distance, cohesion and network itself. Many other sociologists, it should be recognized, use such terms simply as descriptive metaphors.

Looking at the world as a series of networks has many potentially serious drawbacks, of course. Network analysis itself has been a 'much abused concept' (Dicken *et al.* 2001: 92). Already in the early 1970s, the anthropologist J.A. Barnes – largely recognized as one of the first to employ the concept of social networks in the (1954) analysis of a Norwegian fishing community – complained that the notion of social networks had created a 'terminological jungle, in which any newcomer may plant a tree' (in J.C. Mitchell 1974: 279). Nitin Nohria (1992: 3) observed ten years ago that the 'indiscriminate proliferation of the network concept threatens to relegate it to the status of an evocative metaphor, applied so loosely that it ceases to mean anything'. This proliferation continues today, including some rather new permutations. For instance, during the 1990s and through the present we have witnessed the development of actor-network theory (ANT), a rather esoteric perspective arising out of poststructuralism and the sociology of science, in which humans, objects, practices, semiotic systems of discourses and rules, and environments are all conceived to be linked in a mutually conditioning configuration (see for instance Murdoch 1998, Law and Hassard 1999).

Going back to the roots of social network analysis, however, we can ground the perspective's contribution to the study of social relations. Barnes described the idea of network analysis as investigating how the 'configuration of cross-cutting interpersonal bonds is in some unspecified way causally connected with the actions of these persons and with the social institutions of their society' (in J.C. Mitchell 1974: 282). This conceptualization was almost unabashedly an extension of classical structural-functionalism in anthropology. However, the basic idea was, and is, that network structures provide both opportunities and constraints for social action. Network ties also function by way of channelling the flow of material and non-material resources (Wasserman and Faust 1994). The nature of relational ties between actors might concern: evaluation (e.g. friendship), transfer of material resources (e.g. lending), affiliation (e.g. membership in a club), behavioural interaction (e.g. sending messages), movement between places (e.g. migration), formal relations (e.g. authority) or perceived biology (e.g. kinship or descent) (ibid.).

All of these ideas obviously have bearing for the study of transnational social formations. This is because, not least, 'Global networks increasingly give organizational expression to corporations, ethnic diasporas, professional bodies, non-governmental organizations, criminal groups, terrorists, and social and political movements' (Rogers *et al.* 2001: iv).

Though not without its problems and critics, social network analysis has operationalized many terms and concepts that researchers of transnational social formations would do well to bear in mind when collecting, analysing and describing data. These include: network *size* – the number of participants in a network; *density* – the 'extent to which everyone of ego's contacts know each other' (J.C. Mitchell 1969: 15); *multiplexity* – 'the degree to which relations between participants include overlapping institutional spheres. For instance, individuals who are work associates may also be linked by family ties, political affiliations, or club memberships' (Portes 1995: 9–10); *clusters* or *cliques* – a specific area of a wider network with higher density than that of the network as a whole; *strength of ties* – the 'relative frequency, duration, emotional intensity, reciprocal exchange, and so on which characterize a given tie or set of ties' (Emirbayer and Goodwin 1994: 1448–9), which are often described on a continuum from 'strong' to 'weak' (see Granovetter 1973); *durability* – a function of time, since relationships might come into being, disappear, or remain potential (J.C. Mitchell 1969); *reachability* (or *mesh* or *compactness*) – 'the extent to which links radiating out from some given person though other persons eventually return to that same person' (J.C. Mitchell 1987: 304); *frequency* – regularity of contact within a social network; and *content* – 'the actor's construction of the meaning of that relationship to him in terms of his understanding of the other person's expectation of his behavior' (J.C. Mitchell 1974: 294). Mitchell consistently emphasized that 'the determination of the content involves knowing what meaning the actors in any situation are attributing to the cues, signs and symbols being presented in the interaction' (ibid.: 296) and that this calls ideally for ethnographic research (see J.C. Mitchell 1966, 1969, 1987). Content might include economic exchange or assistance, kinship obligation, religious cooperation, friendship and gossip.

Manuel Castells, although largely employing the concept of network as a way of describing the dominant organization form of the informational/ global economy (and therefore not immediately of interpersonal relationships), nevertheless underlines two network-related terms that sit well with those listed above. In talking broadly of network forms, Castells observes,

> The components of the network are both autonomous and dependent vis-à-vis the network, and may be a part of other networks, and therefore of other systems of means aimed at other goals. The performance of a given network will then depend on two fundamental attributes of the network: its *connectedness*, that is its structural ability to facilitate noise-free communication between its components; its *consistency*, that is the extent to which there is sharing of interests between the network's goals and the goals of its components.
>
> (1996: 171; emphasis in original)

Although all of the above terms and concepts define (and may be used to quantify) various aspects of social ties, it remains clear that such ties are not fixed. As well as being reproduced, networks are constantly being socially constructed and altered by their members (Nohria 1992).

Social networks don't just concern how people are connected: they also affect the *circulation of resources*, which can be defined as anything that allows an actor or group to 'control, provide or apply a sanction to another social actor: money, facilities, labor, legitimacy, group size, discretionary time, organizing experience, legal skills, even violence' (Knoke and Wisely, in Bosco 2001). Especially relevant here are Mark Granovetter's (1973) seminal notions of '*weak*' and '*strong*' *ties* in social networks. While the latter lend themselves to greater group cohesion, the former may be far more useful by way of the distribution of resources. The 'weak ties' thesis suggests ways in which a person's indirect social connections are often important channels through which ideas, influences or information are reached.

The general social networks perspective is not short of critics. Among problems identified by a number of social scientists, it is often pointed out that the structure of a network in itself says very little about the qualitative nature of relationships comprising it – not least concerning the exercise of power (cf. Doreen Massey 1993, 1999, Dicken *et al.* 2001). Emirbayer and Goodwin (1994) are critical of the problems that the social networks perspective has with questions of cultural content and individual agency.

Too often, Emirbayer and Goodwin suggest, network analysis can tend to reify social relationships and to suggest a kind of structural determinism.

It is important to underscore, as J.C. Mitchell (1974) did, the difference between using network terminology to describe social situations, on the one hand, and on the other hand undertaking rigorous network analysis. The former involves descriptive and metaphoric usage, while the latter involves specific methods of collecting data and often sophisticated mathematical analysis including algebraic procedures, graph theory, functional mapping and so forth. In other words, one can productively use network terms and concepts to order the research process and to elucidate data significantly without going all the way to engaging bipartite graphs, *n*-clans and Lambda sets (see Wasserman and Faust 1994).

Social capital

A concept that is closely related to social networks (though much harder to quantify), with particular regard to their substance and impact, is 'social capital'. Portes (1995: 12), drawing especially on Pierre Bourdieu (1980) and James Coleman (1988), defines social capital as the 'capacity of individuals to command scarce resources by virtue of their membership in networks or broader social structures. ... The resources themselves are *not* social capital; the concept refers instead to the individual's *ability* to mobilize them on demand' (emphasis in original; see also Burt 1992, Portes and Sensenbrenner 1993, Portes 1998a). That is, social capital is not a property inherent to an individual, but rather it exists in, and is drawn from, that person's web of relationships. By extension, the concept has been applied to collective groups, communities and even large political structures (most famously by Putnam 1995; see Portes and Mooney 2002).

Social capital – itself a metaphoric, shorthand notion – can provide privileged access to resources or restrict individual freedoms by controlling behaviour (Portes 1998a). It is based on collective expectations affecting an individual's behaviour (Portes and Sensenbrenner 1993), including general shared values, normative reciprocity and 'enforceable trust' – or the mode by which loyalty and morality is monitored and safeguarded within a social network. Enforceable trust mainly functions, and is reproduced, by more classical sociological notions concerning social rewards and sanctions. Social capital is maintained, for example, by visits, communication by post or telephone, marriage, participation in events and membership in associations. There is a certain amount of debate as to what degree, and how, social capital is convertible to other forms of capital, namely financial and human (see Faist 2000).

Embeddedness

A full appreciation of both social networks and social capital in any case-study requires an awareness of the forms and conditions of their 'embeddedness'. Granovetter (1985, 1992) has emphasized how, essentially like all actions, economic action is socially situated and cannot be explained wholly by individual motives. Such actions are not simply carried out by atomized actors but are embedded in ongoing networks of personal relationships. '"Embeddedness"', he says, 'refers to the fact that economic action and outcomes, like all social action and outcomes, are affected by actors' dyadic (pairwise) relations *and* by the structure of the overall network of relationships' (1992: 33; emphasis in original).

Portes (1995) develops Granovetter's ideas by describing two kinds of embeddedness. The first, *relational* embeddedness, involves actors' personal relations with one another, including norms, sanctions, expectations and reciprocity. The second, *structural* embeddedness, refers to different scales of social relationship in which many others take part beyond those actually involved in an economic transaction. Specific exchanges of an actor can be identified with respect to either or both kinds of embeddedness in order to interpret relevant sets of conditioning factors. Thomas Schweitzer (1997) also suggests two facets of embeddedness akin to Portes's types. Schweitzer describes a kind of 'vertical' facet represented by hierarchical linkages through which local actors are connected to broader or extra-local levels of the larger society, culture, economy and polity (in much the same meaning as structural embeddedness described by Portes). He also proposes a 'horizontal' facet of embeddedness referring to the ways economic transactions, social relations, political activities might overlap in a particular (culturally conditioned) system (cf. Burt 1992, Granovetter 1985).

In each case, Schweitzer stresses, a social networks approach to embeddedness is the most advantageous for empirical and theoretical analysis. This is echoed in the methodology of many other scholars. The embedded social networks view is relevant, for instance, to Doreen Massey's (1993, 1999) notion of 'power-geometry' whereby social relations are viewed as geographic and networked at a variety of scales from household to the international arena. The kind and degree of power individuals have relies on how they are variously embedded in networks of relations found at these various scales. It is highly significant, too, for transnational studies, since border-crossing social networks entail multiple forms of embeddedness that are not easily reconciled. As Peter Dicken and his colleagues (2001: 96) point out, 'A network link that crosses international borders is not just another example of "acting at a distance", it may also represent a *qualitative disjuncture* between different regulatory and socio-cultural environments' (emphasis in original).

... and transnational migration

The study of transnational practices surrounding migration has provided a prime topic for the utilization of all three general sociological concepts outlined above (see especially Faist 2000). This builds upon a much broader use of the concepts in migration studies. A considerable number of works over the past few decades use, in one way or another, a social networks perspective for the study of migration (see among others Kearney 1986, Grasmuck and Pessar 1991, Portes 1995, D.S. Massey *et al.* 1999, Vertovec and Cohen 1999a, Brettell 2000). This is not surprising since networks, according to a long-standing view, provide the channels for the migration process itself. In his historical overview of immigration into the United States, Charles Tilly (1990) emphasizes that 'networks migrate'. 'By and large', Tilly (ibid.: 84) says, 'the effective units of migration were (and are) neither individuals nor households but sets of people linked by acquaintance, kinship, and work experience'. Monica Boyd neatly sums up much of the network approach to migration, stating:

> Networks connect migrants across time and space. Once begun, migration flows often become self-sustaining, reflecting the establishment of networks of information, assistance and obligations which develop between migrants in the host society and friends and relatives in the sending area. These networks link populations in origin and receiving countries and ensure that movements are not necessarily limited in time, unidirectional or permanent.
>
> (1989: 641)

It is often pointed out that for migrants, social networks are crucial for finding jobs and accommodation, circulating goods and services, as well as for psychological support and continuous social and economic information. Social networks often channel migrants into or through specific places and occupations. Local labour markets can become linked through specific networks of interpersonal and organizational ties surrounding migrants (Poros 2001). By way of example, such patterns and processes of network-conditioned migration were extensively and comparatively examined in 19 Mexican communities and confirmed by Douglas Massey, Luin Goldring and Jorge Durand (1994). Indeed, Alejandro Portes and Robert Bach (1985: 10) propose that migration itself 'can be conceptualized as a process of network building, which depends on and, in turn, reinforces social relationships across space'. Migration is a process that both depends on, and creates, social networks.

Of course, dimensions of social position and power, such as the class profile of the network, have been shown to have considerable conditioning impact on migration processes. This has been demonstrated for instance by Janet Salaff, Eric Fong and Wong Siu-lun (1999). Following the insights of Bott (1957), Salaff and her colleagues demonstrate how middle-class emigrants from Hong Kong, in contrast to working-class ones, used different kinds of networks for different kinds of purposes in arranging their movement and resettlement abroad during the period of British handover of the colony to China. Such studies, among many, point out the varieties of relational and structural embeddedness in migrants' networks (cf. Portes 1995).

Opportunities and constraints in the migration process arise from aspects of social capital in networks, too (see among others Grasmuck and Pessar 1991, D.S. Massey *et al.* 1994, Portes 1998a). Significant studies here are exemplified by Bruno Riccio's (1999) research on Senegalese Mouride traders in Europe, showing how a kind of enforceable trust exists in these networks simultaneously conditioning business advantages and behavioural restrictions, and by Pnina Werbner's (1990) description of a complex economy of gift exchange among Pakistanis in Manchester that links individuals, households and entire extended families in Britain and Pakistan.

Methodological approaches and theories surrounding social networks, social capital and embeddedness have had considerable analytical power in migration studies. These three key ideas are being valuably adapted within emergent approaches to transnational connections among migrants as well: indeed, at least two significant studies – by David Kyle (2000) on modes of Ecuadorian migrant transnationalism and by Patricia

Landolt (2001) on patterns of Salvadoran economic transnationalism – centrally utilize and interweave all three concepts.

With the rise and spread of cross-disciplinary interest in transnational processes and practices, the conceptual value of social networks, social capital and embeddedness can be found in the study of parallel transnational formations as well. Yet of course, in addition to adopting such pre-existing sociological terms, each field of study concerning different transnational formations has developed a variety of their own useful concepts and approaches.

SOME TRANSNATIONAL SOCIAL FORMATIONS

In this section I briefly and selectively review some thinking around the study of transnational social movements, transnational business networks and cyber communities. A few key ideas and concepts from each field are highlighted by way of suggesting their relevance to understanding migrant forms of transnationalism.

Transnational social movements

Since the 1970s, the expression 'social movements' has gone in and out of fashion in sociology and political science (Cohen and Rai 2000). The field, which has largely been stimulated by the writings of prominent sociologists such as Touraine, Melucci, Castells, and Tilly, concerns forms of direct political activity outside the state that usually cut across class lines. One prominent theorist, Sidney Tarrow (1998a: 4), broadly defines social movements as 'collective challenges, based on common purposes and social solidarities, in sustained interaction with elites, opponents, and authorities'. He stresses that a key characteristic of social movements, so defined, is the mounting of *contentious* challenges through disruptive direct action. For such purposes collective action is mobilized 'to mount common claims against opponents, authorities, or elites' based on 'common or overlapping interests and values' or by tapping 'more deep-rooted feelings of solidarity or identity' (ibid.: 6).

The study of social movements over the past decade represents a field that has 'gone transnational' (see J. Smith *et al.* 1997, Keck and Sikkink 1998, Tarrow 2000, 2005). The 'new transnationalism' in this field 'studies the regular interactions between state and non-state actors across national boundaries aimed at shaping political and social outcomes at home, abroad, and in an emerging global sphere of governance' (Orenstein and Schmitz 2006: 482).

Transnational social movements themselves are nothing especially new. The 1833–65 Anglo-American campaign to end slavery in the United States and the 1888–1928 international suffrage movement to secure voting rights for women are just two examples of this kind (Keck and Sikkink 2000; cf DeMars 2005). Yet Robin Cohen and Paul Kennedy (2000), drawing upon both Tilly (1978) and Hegedus (1989), describe a fairly recent 'planetization' of social movement activities that entails a widening repertoire of techniques for mobilizing support and waging campaigns. The transnational repertoire of social movements includes: networking activities over long distances; enhancing possibilities for pooling resources; intensifying processes of coalition-building; empowering people 'at the base' and connecting them directly to people 'at the top'; and augmenting a 'multiplier process whereby flows of pressure feed into each other on a cumulative and mutually reinforcing basis' (Cohen and Kennedy 2000: 320).

Scholars of transnational social movements are divided with regard to the role and importance of such NGOs and networks (see Lux 2006): some believe these are increasingly significant players in world affairs, others think their global influence is rather limited.

Despite the singular title of his book *The New Transnational Activism*, Tarrow (2005) emphasizes that there is not one united form of transnational activism but many. David Stark and his colleagues (2006) build upon Tarrow's insights to distinguish seven overlapping forms of, or possibilities for, transnational connection between local civic organizations and foreign bodies. Such organizations can: (1) *communicate with* foreign agencies; (2) *receive money* from them; (3) *receive non-monetary resources* (such as information or skills) from them; (4) have *formal partnerships*; (5) be involved in *international activities* together; (6) *take foreign actors into account* in their own decision-making; and (7) *formally report* to foreign organizations.

With regard to factors and processes of social formation, Tarrow (1998b: 235) observes that transnational social movements take root among pre-existing social networks that shape trust, reciprocity and collective identity (that is, factors relevant to social capital). Doug McAdam, John McCarthy and Mayer Zald (1996) suggest three broad sets of factors conditioning the emergence and shape of social movements: the structure of political opportunities and constraints, the kinds of formal and informal organization available for mobilization, and 'framing processes'.

Migration scholars might benefit by pondering, through analytic analogy, how such factors might condition repertoires of activity among transnational migrant communities as well.

1. Political opportunity structures

Following McAdam *et al.* (1996), social movement scholars have demonstrated how the shape and activities of social movements are formed in light of the constraints and possibilities posed by the political characteristics existing in given national and local contexts. Such characteristics include the openness or closure of formal political access, the stability of alignments within a political system, and the presence or absence of influential allies. In any assessment of political opportunity structures, one needs to recognize a 'dialectics of scale' regarding differential connections and influences of local, national and international arenas (Miller 1994).

Concerning migrant communities, examples of analyses enlisting the concept of political opportunity structures include both Patrick Ireland's (1994) and Yasemin Soysal's (1994) comparative studies of local and national conditions and policies shaping immigrant groups' organization and mobilization. The approach is at the heart of the analysis of Kurdish transnational political activity in Germany and the Netherlands undertaken by Eva Østergaard-Nielsen (2001), while the differential effects of political opportunity structures can also be seen in the study of community developments among Colombians in New York City and Los Angeles carried out by Luis Guarnizo, Arturo Ignacio Sánchez and Elizabeth Roach (1999). Aihwa Ong's (1999) work on the relationship between overseas Chinese entrepreneurs, states and markets can also be read as an example of a transnational group creatively engaging opportunity structures.

Just as the above studies have contributed to our understanding of how migrants shape their practices in light of varying contexts, the study of transnational migration will benefit by explicitly and rigorously examining the ways in which transnational social structures and practices have emerged in light of what we can call opportunity structures – in both 'sending' and 'receiving' contexts – and how they factor into migrants' own desires and strategies for conducting their lives transnationally. However in adopting such a framework of analysis, Østergaard-Nielsen (2001: 277) points out, researchers must bear in mind that opportunity structures 'are embedded in a normative definition of migrants' place and role in receiving country politics'; just how migrants engage such normative definitions and structures while also negotiating the norms and policies of their sending states remains a salient question for the political science of migrant transnationalism.

While needing to recognize, as in studies of social movements, a 'dialectics of scale' (involving structures encompassing national, regional and local contexts), such transnationalism-conditioning opportunity structures might include: national asylum regimes; provisos around visas, citizenship, voting, residency, naturalization and other aspects of legal status; sources of and access to bodies of information on migrant incorporation; frameworks for taxation (and for avoiding it); pension policies (especially whether and how one can collect it abroad); education, insurance and health care provisions; housing availability and assistance; access to legal representation; business assistance schemes; banking systems and modes of financial transfer, terms of mortgages and loans, labour union membership and activity, and the organization of local ethnic or hometown associations for migrant assistance. Of course, such opportunity structures differentially condition, and are engaged by, the transnational activity of migrants in relation to gender, class, occupational type, educational level and legal status.

2. Mobilizing structures

What social movement sociologists call mobilizing structures represent 'those collective vehicles, informal as well as formal, through which people mobilize and engage in collective action' (McAdam *et al.* 1996: 3). Resource mobilization theory has been influential in describing such structures and processes of social movement formation. This body of theory concerns how the presence or absence of available resources, generally defined, intervenes in the success or failure of mobility strategies of social movements (see for instance McCarthy and Zald 1977). With particular value for analyzing the course of development of any social movement, Bert Klandermans and Dirk Oegema (1987) outline four aspects of mobilization: formation of potentials, activation of recruitment networks, arousal of motivation to participate, and removal of barriers to participate.

The utility of such analytic devices may be valuable in migration studies too. The relevance of a mobilizing structures concept to transnational migrant communities is evident, for instance, in the model developed by

Nadje Al-Ali, Richard Black and Khalid Koser (2001) to describe factors influencing both the capacity and desire of Bosnian and Eritrean refugees to participate transnationally in the reconstruction of their countries of origin. Al-Ali *et al.* demonstrate how the availability and modes of use surrounding resources channel the degree, form and extent of refugees' transnational activities. Research on collective practices (including association meetings, the pooling of funds, visits by delegations, and community development projects) – such as Rob Smith's (2006) on Mexican villagers in New York and Mexico, and Peggy Levitt's (2001a) on Dominican villagers in Boston and the Dominican Republic – exemplifies an important approach to migration studies that underscores the role of what arguably might best be call mobilizing structures in shaping transnational practices.

There is much need for further study into the ways migrants collectively manage resources over long distances for purposes of community development in areas of origin (such as supplying water systems or building healthcare centres, sports facilities or places of worship). Klandermans and Oegema's (1987) four aspects of social movement mobilization structures, noted above, suggests but one useful set of conceptual tools that might be drawn from this area of research and adapted for researching and analysing transnational migrant collective activities.

3. Framing

As defined by McAdam *et al.* (1996: 2), the concept of social movement framing addresses 'the collective process of interpretation, attribution, and social construction that mediates between opportunity and action'. That is, framing refers to processes of negotiating conscious, shared meanings and definitions with which people legitimate, motivate and conduct their collective activities. Fernando Bosco (2001) reinforces the concept by discussing 'conscious and strategic efforts by groups of people to fashion shared understandings of the world and of themselves that legitimate and motivate collective action'. The recognition of such processes is urged as a way of 'bringing culture back in' to social movement studies (McAdam *et al.* 1996: 6).

The framing process is certainly no stranger to students of international migration. This is so because, in this field, it seems to describe the core process of ethnic community formation whereby groups in migration/minority situations self-consciously reflect upon their identities, symbolically define ethnic group boundaries, and organize themselves for the purpose of political empowerment. A substantial body of literature is concerned with these processes.

In the study of transnational migrant groups there is a growing set of work concerning the ways in which the negotiation of identity both shapes, and is shaped by, embeddedness in more than one location and one social order (see for instance Heisler 2001, Vertovec 2001a). It is clear that the study of transnational migrant groups has much to gain from further, specific attention to what social movement sociologists call the framing process. It has special significance with regard to transnational migrant communities, not least because such processes of negotiation are often undertaken within and across highly variegated contexts. Transnational migrants often embark on a process of 'making values from two worlds fit' (Levitt 2001a: 97). Such negotiations of meaning can raise fundamental questions among groups as to: who we are, who is not part of us, and how we (perhaps differentially our men, our women, our children) are to act properly or morally or politically in relation to the perceived conditions of location A or B.

The social scientific study of social movements has adapted its own concepts and methodological tools to 'go transnational'. The transnational interest in social movements focuses mainly on activist networks that connect a range of actors sharing common values, discourse and information. The emergence of transnational social movements is often explained with reference to changing (i.e. globalizing) political opportunity structures and avenues of resource mobilization (especially electronic modes of communication and financial transfer). As noted early in this chapter, interests in and explanations of contemporary migrant transnationalism seem to share many of these very similar bases. In a similar way, the study of business organizations and business networks has also 'gone transnational'.

Transnational business networks

Many social scientists have drawn from research on processes and practices surrounding transnational corporations (TNCs) in order to broadly understand the nature and dynamics of transnationalism and globalization (e.g. Dicken 1992, Sklair 1995, Castells 1996). Concomitant with the examination of TNCs, researchers on management, organizational and business practices have become increasingly interested in the shape and functions of transnational business networks, supplier commodity chains, production networks, and innovative networks (see for instance Yeung 2000, Dicken *et al.* 2001).

Henry Wai-chung Yeung (1998: 3–4) discusses how, for most large businesses and corporations, networks have become 'an all-embracing organizational structure for transnational activities'; hence, 'the network form of organization has come to dominate today's world of international business'. Yeung (ibid.: 65) describes a business network as 'an integrated and coordinated structure of ongoing economic and non-economic relations embedded within, among and outside business firms'. In his analysis of the geographical spread and structural transformation of Hong Kong Chinese firms – and representing another instance of conceptual cross-fertilization – Yeung draws specifically on Granovetter's ideas concerning embeddedness.

> The concept of 'embeddedness' helps revitalize network analysis by injecting social and historical dimensions into the study of transnational production systems in their time-space contexts. By recognizing the cultural and social *embeddedness* of the function of network relations and economic transactions, we can better understand the nature of production systems prevailing in different societies and localities.
>
> (Yeung 1998: 59; emphasis in original)

In other words, transnational corporate networks are empirically embedded in their structural contexts as well as in ongoing business and personal relationships.

Yeung (ibid.: 65f.) importantly suggests that participants and agents in transnational business networks benefit from an 'economics of synergy' through which they can achieve what is otherwise impossible were an individual to attempt a specific mode of action alone. The 'economics of synergy' becomes manifest in information sharing, pooling of resources (capital, labour and technology), mutual commitments and reciprocity regarding personal favours. These ideas are resonant with the notion of social capital. And similar to other core facets of social capital, Yeung underscores the importance of trust and mutual understanding within a network in order to avoid opportunism and to promote the general welfare of the network.

It can also be said that social capital is relevant to the ways in which business networks mobilize different forms of knowledge, skill and competence. This is evident in what Ash Amin and Patrick Cohendet (1999) describe as tacit versus codified knowledge in globalized companies. Codified knowledge, which is formally taught to employees, is naturally of high significance to the running of large, decentralized firms. Yet it is tacit knowledge (of operations, strategies, competitors, markets) which is often critical in gaining competitive advantage. This is imparted particularly through face-to-face contacts and the high degree of mutual trust and understanding they sustain. Further, Amin and Cohendet point to the potential benefits of the network as a 'nexus of competences' drawn from the experience and expertise of its members.

Amin and Cohendet also derive their analysis from Granovetter, here with reference to notions of strong and weak ties in networks and especially regarding processes of learning and adaptation within organizations. Within business networks, they say,

> What matters most, however, is not the presence of ties of association, but their nature. For example, ties which are too strong and long-standing – for instance those involving dependent subcontractors to networks of interests jealously guarded by dominant players – might actually prevent renewal and innovation by encouraging network closure and self-referential behaviour. In contrast, where economic agents have the option of participating in many competing networks on the basis of loose ties, reciprocal relations, and independent intermediaries, the prospect for innovative learning through interaction seem to be enhanced.
>
> (ibid.: 92)

An 'economics of synergy', tacit knowledge, a 'nexus of competences', and the idea of disadvantageous network closure versus advantageous looseness are concepts that may be revealing when applied to transnational migrant social formations. The concepts might stimulate researchers to look into, or re-evaluate data concerning, specific aspects of migrants' transnational practices. For instance, the notion of an 'economics of synergy' might prompt migration scholars to think further about the modes and impacts of close-knit or pooled economic exchanges within transnational migrant networks. Analyses surrounding disadvantageous network closure versus advantageous looseness may be important for trying to understand why some migrant networks stagnate and others flourish, and why some forms of transnationalism remain 'broad' and others 'narrow' (Itzigsohn *et al.* 1999). Research on the content, management and reproduction of tacit knowledge and the exploitation of a 'nexus of competences' within migrant networks might have significance for analysing patterns in the rise of, and discrepancies of success among, transnational migrant entrepreneurs (Portes 2001b).

Cybercommunities

A final parallel field of transnational social formation research that also relies heavily on network concepts, among others, is that of 'virtual' or 'cyber-' communities. Networks and communities formed around computer-mediated communication (CMC) have aroused the suspicion of many sociologists. As Tarrow (1998b: 241) describes it,

> The growing web of e-mail networks that are traversing the world may excite the attention of those with easy access to computers because of their obvious capacity to reduce transaction costs and transmit information quickly across national lines, but they do not promise the same degree of crystallization, of mutual trust and collective identity, as do the interpersonal ties in social networks.

However – fuelling much current debate – there is an increasing number of academic works arguing that on-line networks and relationships do indeed constitute communities comparable to face-to-face ones, and that there are pressing needs to develop the field of cybercultural studies (see for instance Escobar 1994, Jordan 1999, Dutton 1999, M.A. Smith and Kollock 1999, Bell and Kennedy 2000, Wilson and Peterson 2002).

In a study highly uncharacteristic of anthropologists, Daniel Miller and Don Slater (2000) have written a detailed ethnographic study of how Trinidadians, at home and in diaspora, make use of the Internet. Miller and Slater are critical of the often conventional approach that treats Internet 'cyberspace' as a kind of placeless place. Such a view, Miller and Slater say, presupposes 'online' communication takes place in a space *apart from* the rest of 'offline' social life. The notion of 'virtuality', too, only suggests people treat computer-mediated relationships 'as if' they are real. While such approaches may be valuable in certain instances, Miller and Slater argue, they are not a good point of departure for studying the actual use of the Internet by a number of kinds of communities.

Miller and Slater (ibid.: 5) propose that we need to treat Internet media as 'continuous with and embedded in other social spaces' and that

Internet-mediated communications 'happen within mundane social structures and relations that they may transform but that they cannot escape into a self-enclosed cyberian apartness'. The authors (ibid.: 6) found that their informants themselves made little distinction between, for instance, 'e-commerce and other commerce, playground chat and ICQ chat, religious instruction face-to-face or by email'. The prevailing view of their informants is rather that these are simply complementary forms of communication and information alongside the newspaper, telephone and television. Miller and Slater conclude that it is fruitless to separate offline and online life: computer-mediated communication forms a *part of* everyday life for many people. Therefore we should not underestimate the Internet's importance or seriousness for transforming aspects of social life (cf. Castells 1996).

Such potential social transformation is suggested by what Barry Wellman (1999) calls 'computer supported social networks (CSSNs)'. These networks form around electronic mail, electronic bulletin-boards, newsgroups and multi-user dungeons (MUDs) or virtual chat rooms. 'Such groups,' Wellman (ibid.: 336) suggests, are 'a technologically supported continuation of a long-term shift to communities organized by shared interests rather than a shared place (neighborhood or village) or shared ancestry (kinship group).' CSSNs can offer important non-material social resources akin to face-to-face relationships, including psychological and emotional support, companionship, and a sense of belonging. Like face-to-face networks, cybercommunities can exhibit facets of social capital and reciprocity as well.

> Such norms typically arise in a densely knit community, but they appear to be common among frequent contributors to distribution lists and newsgroups. People having a strong attachment to an electronic group will be more likely to participate and provide assistance to others.
>
> (ibid.: 343)

Wellman also insists that rather than remaining wholly anonymous online (through their 'avatars' or Internet pseudonym identities), people often do bring important aspects of their offline selves to cybercommunication: gender, age, stage in life cycle, cultural milieu and socio-economic status. For example, this might be the case for computer-mediated groups formed around such situations as drug addicts, people with specific physical handicaps or mental illnesses, or the victims of sexual abuse. Yet '[t]he limited evidence available suggests that the ties people develop and maintain in cyberspace are much like most of the "real-life" community ties: intermittent, specialized, and varying in strength' (ibid.: 353). Computers accelerate the ways people operate in and manipulate networks. Through cyber-networks, people now have an 'enhanced ability to move between relationships' (ibid.: 356).

In a similar manner, David Elkins (1999) outlines the rise of 'virtual neighbourhoods' in which affinity among electronically connected 'neighbours' is based on voluntary participation by interest rather than proximity. However, Elkins warns against the danger of such neighbourhoods becoming 'virtual ghettos' in which people only communicate with others who share the same interests or views.

There is a good deal of interest in the ways electronic and computer-mediated communication links transnational migrant communities, channels information between home and away, and enhances coherent identities (see Rai 1995, Miller and Slater 2000, Mandaville 2001). Surely a grasp of certain concepts and debates in the social scientific study of cybercommunities will be an asset in studying transmigrant uses of technology.

Addressing the question of how globalization and migration interact to affect social change, Adrian Favell (2001: 397) believes,

> it will be necessary to systematically take the daily structures of everyday life in the old bounded world of the nation-state-society – one thinks of family structures, the structures of professions, social mobility, the life-cycle, etc. – and, via the empirical study of individuals whose lives have crossed boundaries, see how and where these structures are being transformed.

Implicit in Favell's advice concerning the importance of 'structures' is, by extension, the importance of studying networks. '[T]he network remains useful as a root metaphor,' Hannerz (1992a: 51) insists,

> when we try to think in a reasonably orderly way (without necessarily aiming at rigour of measurement) about some of the heterogeneous sets of often long-distance relationships which organize culture in the world now – in terms of cumulative change or enduring diversity.

Other such advantages of a social networks perspective are described by Thomas Schweitzer (1997: 739):

On the one hand, network tools are very specific and thus ideally suited to the investigation of embeddedness in depth. On the other hand, the concepts, procedures, and hypotheses of social network analysis have a general formal core that facilitates productive comparisons across cases and thereby addresses the problem of theoretical synthesis.

Of course, as argued strongly by Bruno Riccio (2001), we must try to avoid the reification of social networks in the study of transnational migrant communities. Instead, Riccio proposes, we might focus on the ongoing processes of networking or network formation by which they are actively reproduced, maintained, transformed and extended.

This chapter has surveyed and summarized some key terms and concepts drawn from the study of transnational social formations parallel to those of migrant groups. The purpose has been to suggest notions that it may be 'good to think with' when collecting and interpreting material regarding transnational communities. A recap of some of these terms and concepts includes:

- *social networks:* which includes attention to the number and reach of social ties, their density, multiplicity, normative content, connectedness, consistency, and the implications of weak versus strong ties;
- *social capital:* around which we have seen the importance of notions such as normative reciprocity, loyalty, rewards, sanctions and 'enforceable trust';
- *embeddedness:* which includes the differentiation of relational and structural types alongside vertical and horizontal facets;
- *social movements:* representing a field in which processes and forms are shaped by political opportunity structures, mobilizing structures, the notion of framing, resource mobilization, the scope for enhancing organizational possibilities for pooling resources, and the development of transnational repertoires of action;
- *business networks:* which also represent a broad field of study within which we have highlighted the usefulness of concepts such as the economics of synergy, tacit knowledge, a nexus of competences, and network closure versus innovation;
- *cybercommunities:* another far-reaching category within which studies have underlined the significance of issues like on-line versus off-line ties, people's enhanced abilities to move quickly between different

kinds of relationships, the recognition of the rise of computer-mediated communication as forming a part of everyday life, and the meaning of terms such as virtual neighbourhoods versus virtual ghettos.

Such an exercise of employing borrowed concepts should not remain simply one of trying on hats. As Adrian Favell (2001) emphasizes, 'doing theory' is not merely a matter of adopting and adapting new metaphors. The usefulness of any concepts brought into a field of study should be observed in the ways they can shape the gathering and analysis of empirical and ethnographic data.

The study of transnational processes and practices is arguably rather new to three fields discussed in this piece: migration, social movements and business. By way of fashioning an appropriate language, analytical concepts and methodological approaches, social scientists in all three fields are still finding their way around. Obviously certain sociological notions – such as social networks, social capital, and embeddedness – have been adopted and have had important bearing on conceptualization and theoretical analysis in each one of these fields. Especially since the study of these topics is still partially nascent, further conceptual cross-fertilization – between these fields of transnational study or from elsewhere in the social sciences – will likely prove as fruitful.

3

SOCIO-CULTURAL TRANSFORMATIONS

'More persons than ever before', observe Peter Koehn and James Rosenau (2002: 106), 'in more places around the world are opting to pursue transnational lives'. Wide-ranging contemporary experiences of the transnational lives of individuals have been entertainingly described by journalists such as Gregg Zachary (2000) in *The Global Me* and Pico Iyer (2001) in *The Global Soul.* Just how transnational lives are shaped among individuals, and how they impact social spheres, can be approached from a wide variety of angles and levels. That is to say, transnational individual and social lives are certainly not of one kind, and their effects are inconsistent, patchy in one place or another, good for some – bad for others, short-term or long-term in their ramifications. However, transnational lives are not boundless in their scope either. They are rather, as Guarnizo and Smith (1998: 10) describe them,

> bounded in two senses – first, by the understandings of 'grounded reality' socially constructed within the transnational networks that people form and move through, and second, by the policies and practices of territorially-based sending and receiving local and national states and communities.

Throughout this book, such a dual perspective is also emphasized, seeking to take account of people's grounded realities and meanings as well as the contextual conditioning factors, opportunities and constraints within and through which transnational lives are lived. This chapter begins with one of the most commonplace – yet surely one of the most significant – infrastructures fostering and shaping transnational lives: the telephone network. Telephones (especially mobiles), their extension and the decreasing costs of international calling have enabled the most fundamental social aspects of transnational life, namely everyday communication across long distances and around the world. Following a look at the phenomenon and impact of cheap calls, we will have a brief look at transformations across an exemplary range of socio-cultural dimensions surrounding transnational life: these include families, gender structures and roles, the 'habitus' or worldviews shaped by living here-and-there, and what we might call inter-cultural behavioural competences (otherwise described as cosmopolitanism). The chapter concludes with a discussion of migrant transnationalism in relation to one of the hottest topics in most migrant-receiving countries, that of so-called immigrant integration or assimilation.

CHEAP CALLS: THE SOCIAL GLUE OF MIGRANT TRANSNATIONALISM

As discussed in Chapter 1, globalization is now commonly characterized as the world-spanning intensification of interconnectedness. Commencing in the mid-1990s, there was a rush among social scientists to describe globalization's contours and mechanisms, especially by way of the impacts of new technologies. This rush witnessed numerous studies concerning email and the Internet, electronic bulletin boards, satellite television and other hi-tech developments. Yet arguably nothing has facilitated processes of global linkage more than the boom in ordinary, cheap international telephone calls. This is especially the case among non-elite social groups such as migrants.

The proliferation of cheap international telephone calls has coincided with other processes of globalization. The overall volume of international telephone calls climbed massively from 12.7 billion call minutes in 1982 to 42.7 billion call minutes in 1992 and further to 154 billion by 2001 (Held *et al.* 1999: 344). This rise has become a particularly salient feature in recent years through at least two developments: the significant increase in the carrying capacity of the long-distance network and the dramatic fall in the cost of international telephone calls (see Cairncross 1997).

The introduction of fibre-optic cable in the 1980s and, more recently, low-orbiting satellites and new techniques for re-routing or piggy-backing calls have technologically facilitated the ease, efficiency and cost-effectiveness of providing for millions of telephone connections simultaneously. The 1990s witnessed plummeting prices and surging international telephone traffic. Driven by a highly competitive market, in many cases calls abroad that used to cost several dollars per minute eventually came to cost only a few cents per minute. People around the world, given access to an ever-expanding telephone network, could make low-cost calls that were previously unaffordable. The number of calls made to other countries from the USA alone increased from 200 million in 1980 to 6.6 billion in 2000, and almost a quarter of all international calls are placed from the USA (FCC 2002). Conversely, more people now phone the USA: international telephone traffic has increased significantly over the past decade, but so has the centrality of the USA within the global system of telephone traffic (Barnett 2001, Louch *et al.* 1999).

The growth of international telephony is also displayed in the development of the Global System for Mobile Communications (GSM), the most popular global standard for mobile phones. GSM is now used by 2.29 billion people across over 200 countries and territories – 80 per cent of which are developing countries (PR Newswire 2006). Latin America and the Caribbean lead in the percentage growth rate (adding 74 million users in one year alone to March 2006), with the Middle East and Africa having the next highest growth rates. The ten fastest growing telecommunications markets between 2000–2005 were Nigeria, Ecuador, India, Pakistan, Kuwait, El Salvador, the United Arab Emirates, Bolivia, Senegal and Venezuela; in all these countries mobile phones have outnumbered landline phones (TeleGeography 2006). While it took 12 years to sell the first billion GSM phones, it took only two and a half years to sell the next billion. In Kenya, for example, there were 15,000 mobile phone users in 1999; by 2007 there were 8 million out of a population of 25 million (Rice 2007).

Cheap telephone calls have impacted enormously and variously on many kinds of transnational communities. One of the most significant (yet under-researched) modes of transnational practice affecting migrants' lives is the enhanced ability to call family members. Whereas in previous eras migrants had to make do with exorbitantly expensive calls or slow-paced post, they are now able to communicate with their families abroad on a regular, if not day-to-day, basis. This obviously has considerable impact on domestic and community life, intergenerational and gender relations, religious and other cultural practices, and local economic development in both migrant-sending and migrant-receiving contexts. Marital and family relationships across long distances had previously been severely strained by slow communication such as letters (Mahler 2001). The real-time communications allowed by cheap telephone calls now serve as a kind of social glue connecting families and other small-scale social formations across the globe (see especially Horst 2006).

Migrants' increased use of cheap international calls can be inferred from national statistics in specific migrant-sending and migrant-receiving countries. The telecommunications consultancy TeleGeography, Inc. surveys statistical research on global telephone traffic. By comparing the company's data between 1995 and 2001 – one of the key growth periods – through looking at minutes of voice teletraffic (i.e., omitting fax and internet services) we can see a remarkable growth in traffic between specific countries with strong migration connections. This therefore suggests intensifying patterns of transnationalism via telecommunication. In practically all countries examined, the total volume of all international calls originating from that country roughly doubled (i.e. rose 100 per cent) during this period. International calls from Germany to Turkey increased 54 per cent while calls from Turkey to Germany increased by 35 per cent, Turkey to the Netherlands rose 58 per cent and Turkey to Belgium by 80 per cent. Calls from Pakistan to the UK increased by 123 per cent, by 141 per cent to Saudi Arabia, and by 556 per cent to Canada. Calls from the UK to India swelled by 439 per cent, to Pakistan by 390 per cent, and to Hong Kong by 292 per cent. Calls from Mexico to the USA – the destination that comprises over 80 per cent of all Mexican calls abroad – grew by 107 per cent. In turn, calls from the USA to Mexico now account for the largest destination of all outgoing American telecommunications, having increased 171 per cent between 1995 and 2001. In this same period calls from the USA to the Philippines increased 452 per cent, to India 408 per cent, to Brazil 206 per cent, to the Dominican Republic 189 per cent, to Jamaica 127 per cent, to China 93 per cent, and to Colombia 95 per cent.

The TeleGeography figures are highly indicative of the massive expansion marking patterns of transnational communication between specific countries. Of course, we cannot account for the proportion of calls actually made by migrant families; a considerable number of the international calls will have been, for instance, within the business market. Yet it is highly likely that the number of telephone calls between members of migrant families comprises a significant share, and reflects the same extraordinary scale of increase, in each set of international telephone calls.

An important factor contributing to the expansion of international telephoning, particularly among migrants, has been the development and spread of pre-paid telephone cards. With, say, a $10 pre-paid card one can make a three-hour phone call from many cities in the USA to various places in Latin America. Use of these cards – which are easily available at petrol stations, newsagents and convenience stores in urban areas in most Western countries – doubled between the years 2000 and 2002 alone (Wolfe 2002). Over half of all traffic carried via phone cards is international (Brown 2003). Moreover, industry analysts state that:

> It is well known that the main users of prepaid calling cards are first gener-ation immigrants. Their desire to stay connected with family at home, strong networks within their US-based community, and the ability to pass the news of a well-priced product help drive the competition among providers. These ethnic markets, also known as 'bodega' markets, require different marketing strategies for different cultural groups. Although pro-ducers of prepaid cards have responded to this by creating various pricing patterns in their cards that attract certain ethnic users, success still lies in their placement. Proper distribution is the main factor in their sale.
>
> (Mensah and Smith 2002)

One phone card distributor interviewed for a corporate study in the USA claimed to sell almost exclusively to 'the ethnic markets', saying most of his prepaid cards are currently being sold to Brazilians, then Chinese, Dominicans, various ethnicities from Africa (especially Ugandans, Ghanaians and Nigerians) and the Middle East (mainly from Lebanon, Syria and Egypt). Other distributors now target specific immigrant com-munities, such as Chinese in the Pacific Northwest, Israelis in New York, Indians in Silicon Valley and Cubans in Florida (de la Cruz 2002). Telephone companies have appealed to such niches by printing national symbols on specific phone cards (Gill 2004).

The 'ethnic market' for long-distance calls is substantial elsewhere, too. In Germany, for instance, Deutsche Telekom lost 190,000 Turkish cus-tomers – whose telephone bills are twice as high as the average German household due to calls abroad – to the telephone company Otelo; this has prompted fierce competition in Turkish-speaking marketing between the two companies (Caglar 2002).

New technologies around telephoning are having an impact in less developed contexts where migrants' families remain. One example is a recently unveiled service that will allow Mexican-Americans to pay for communications services or facilities for family and friends in Mexico. Another product is a 1-800 service that allows friends and family in Mexico to call the United States at rates significantly cheaper than collect calls. A growing trend in the prepaid telephone card industry involves sales of international origination cards that allow people to purchase telephone time for relatives and friends in other countries.

Telecommunications infrastructure is developing in poor areas, too, largely on the back of transnational migration practices. In many places one can witness the increasing use of public telephones in village centres, reduced-rate telephone cards and mobile phones, even fairly remote villages. The Dominican Republic – locus of intense transnational practices of exchange between resident families and emigrant kin – represents one case of recent advances in communications infrastructure. Currently the 'teledensity' (lines per capita) of mobile phones in the Dominican Republic is higher than that of mainline phones (Intelecard 2003). This represents a trend particularly in developing countries, where the costs of building infrastructure are far more conducive to wireless than wired telephones. Another current is witnessed in Bangladesh, where the innovative micro-finance institution Grameen Bank has created a telecommunications branch and 'village phone' programme providing infrastructure and 950 mobile phones in village and urban areas that give telephone access for 65,000 people (Richardson *et al.* 2000). By far, most of the uses of the village phones are to talk with migrant relatives overseas – and particularly to discuss remittances.

The personal, real-time contact provided by international telephone calls is transforming the everyday lives of innumerable migrants. Among transnational Salvadorans, for example, new telecommunications infrastructures mean that 'times have changed; they are still physically distanced, but they can now feel and function like a family' (Mahler 2001: 584). Whereas throughout the world non-migrant families commonly have discussions across a kitchen table (e.g., can we buy a refrigerator? what do we do about the teenager's behaviour? who should take care of grandmother?), now many families whose members are relocated through migration conduct the same everyday discussions in real time across oceans. Cheap telephone calls have largely facilitated this. For a single family to be stretched across vast distances and between nation-states, yet still somehow functioning for collective gain, is now common.

There is still a grossly uneven distribution of telecommunications infrastructure in the world. Since the 1970s a clear hierarchy of telecommunications structures has emerged (Barnett 2001). In recent years there has arisen a growing gulf between countries that make and receive a lot of calls and those that make and receive few. 'Developing countries are either marginal to international communications or linked via asymmetrical relationships to a group of richer nations' (Louch *et al.* 1999: 96). Only certain countries have increased their telephone contact with each other, while the USA remains at the centre of the clique. Statistics show that among those countries that have markedly increased voice telecommunications with each other (like USA–Mexico, UK–India and others mentioned above), most are not coincidentally bridged by transnational migrant groups.

With regard to such country comparisons, however, Hugh Louch and his colleagues (1999: 97) raise an important point that bears further analytical and methodological consideration: such nationally categorized data infers the attributes of actions made by individuals to countries. Instead, social scientists should recognize that '[t]he real network we are describing is one among 5 billion individuals, not 200 countries' (ibid.)

There are many technological advances that have assisted and continue to drive processes of globalization. Cheap telephone calls represent one of the most significant forms of globalizing technology. As Frances Cairncross (1997: 27) puts it, 'The death of distance will be driven by the plummeting price of long-distance and international calls'. Following a sustained period of tremendous expansion, growth in the volume of international calls slowed to only 10 per cent in 2001 – suggesting perhaps that the rapid gains resulting from low costs may have reached saturation point. The slowest growth was reported in North America, the fastest in Asia (see www.telegeography.com). Yet while the volume of calls may be levelling off despite decreasing costs, a broadening of the global telephone network – especially driven by wireless technologies surrounding both telephone and internet services – is continuing apace. The tele-linking of the world is expanding into more rural and remote areas, especially throughout developing countries. The needs of nationally internal and international migrants will continue to drive much of the telephone industry's use and growth.

Everyday cheap international telephone calls account for one of the main sources of connection among a multiplicity of global social networks. For many of today's migrants, transnational connectivity through cheap telephone calls is at the heart of their lives. For migrants and their kin in distant parts of the world, telephone calls can only provide a kind of punctuated sociality that can heighten emotional strain as well as alleviate it. This mode of intermittent communication cannot bridge all the gaps of information and expression endemic to long-distance separation. Nevertheless, cheap international telephone calls join migrants and their significant others in ways that are deeply meaningful to people on both ends of the line.

The telephone represents just one rapidly developing infrastructure of transnational life. Because of needs in trying to maintain communication and information, migrants are often at the cutting edge of technology adoption (Karim 2003, Panagakos and Horst 2006a, b). Since the mid-1990s migrants have been able to socially capitalize (i.e., build their social capital) by way of communication media such as diasporic websites (McClure 2000, van den Bos and Nell 2006), electronic bulletin boards (Rai 1995), email (Miller and Slater 2000), video-teleconferencing (Benítez 2006), film-making and consumption (Naficy 2001) and satellite and cable television (Robins and Aksoy 2004).

Raelene Wilding (2006), for instance, describes the use of information and communications technologies (ICTs) for maintaining everyday social life at a distance, particularly involving families and their mundane but crucial activities like the remembrance of birthdays and anniversaries, providing care to the aged and advice to new mothers. Nevertheless, Wilding (ibid.: 137) says, 'although ICTs serve to maintain transnational relationships, different forms of communication have different consequences for the family relationships they sustain'. That is, the letter, telephone, email and website are used in a variety of ways for various purposes by individuals, often also reflecting aspects of gender, generation, locality, class and cultural group (see especially Miller *et al.* 2005). Heather Horst and Daniel Miller (2006: 86–97) note how the boom in communications technologies has had profound impacts not just on the ability of families to maintain relationships at a distance, but to transform such relationships as well, for good or bad (e.g. through intensifying expressions of love and support or by manifesting gradual estrangement among family members). Horst and Miller also underline the phenomenon of 'link-up' – that is, how mobile phones are often used not to convey information but simply to maintain and develop social networks through brief but regular contact.

What is particularly remarkable, we might add, is certainly not that migrants make use of ICT to shape their transnational lives; rather, what is of note is the way that such technologies have both enabled and fit in with the everyday nature of maintaining transnational ties, making regular – indeed, in many cases, daily – contact with family and associates overseas a routine or commonplace occurrence.

DIMENSIONS OF EVERYDAY TRANSNATIONALISM

There has been a considerable amount of social scientific research that has detailed 'the emergence of transnational social practices and institutions that create a field of sociability and identification among immigrants and people in the country of origin' (Itzigsohn and Giorguli-Saucido 2002: 788). In the following section we have a look at just a few of the most significant institutions and aspects of social life affected by transnational ties.

Families

The provenance of most everyday migrant transnationalism is within families. In many cases family life has been extensively modified in light of transnational practices (see Goulbourne 1999, Fouron and Glick Schiller 2001, Herrera Lima 2001, Bryceson and Vuorela 2002, Gardner and Grillo 2002). Guarnizo (1997) proposes that changes in family and household organization can be approached by way of transnational residential arrangements, budget management and intergenerational cultural reproduction. Yet there are other dimensions of transnational family life that need attention, too, such as the nature of parenting and the experience of children.

'Long-distance parenthood' linking 'fractured families and geographically dispersed homes' is a common feature characterizing much contemporary migrant experience (Lobel 2003). Within dispersed family structures – practically regardless of the cultural origins of migrants – it is transnational life among female migrants which 'radically rearranges mother–child interactions and requires a concomitant radical reshaping of the meanings and definitions of appropriate mothering' (Hondagneu-Sotelo and Avila 1997: 557). Some migrant mothers have had to undertake the nurturing of their children through text messaging, phone calls and letters (Parreñas 2005). Such rearrangements are known to cause considerable emotional distress, anxieties, sacrifices, financial pressures and difficult negotiations with caregivers who must often fill-in for distant parents (cf. Mahler 2001). The fact remains that many women who leave to work across borders remain deeply embedded in family life (Hondagneu-Sotelo and Avila 1997).

Indeed, shifting work and travel arrangements mean that today more than ever, circularly migrating parents often rotate periods of migration to ensure that one of them remains with the children while the other works abroad (Orellana *et al.* 2001). The difficulties of juggling the responsibilities of parenting is also related to phenomena surrounding so-called 'global care chains' (Hochschild 2000) in which women from developing countries migrate to take care of other people's children while financially supporting, and needing to find caregivers for, their own children. These and other patterns of transnational family life have necessitated new forms of managing and coping with mixed motivations, strategies and emotional tribulations among parents with regard to their children 'left behind' (Orellana *et al.* 2001). Such patterns entangle parents' anxieties over their children's welfare with the desire to improve the possibilities for their future.

Emotional entanglements do not just relate to children 'left behind'; they pertain also to children who accompany their migrant parents and to 'parachute kids' – such as Chinese or Korean children sent to the USA or Canada to attend school with the hope of eventually gaining admission to North American universities (Zhou 1997b). In each case there is often a feeling of being 'caught between two nations, educational systems, and ways of growing up, [that] conveys one of the risks of transnational childhoods – feeling marginal in both places' (Orellana *et al.* 2001: 583). Similarly, Cecilia Menjívar (2002) found that Guatemalan '1.5 generation' (born abroad, migrated young) children in the USA only partially absorbed the transnational orientations of their parents. This was compounded by the inability to travel to Guatemala (given the undocumented status of their parents), by poor linguistic competence and by a dearth of community institutions to foster and sustain transnational links.

> This does not imply that the children's lives are played out independent of their communities of origin, because important decisions in their lives often involve families in both places. The children's ties with the parental

homeland, however, depend on the parents' activities and interests, and the children themselves cannot always make sense of the parents' efforts to keep them oriented to home.

(Ibid.: 547)

The disjuncture between parents' transnational orientations and children's local ones may lead to exasperation. Marjorie Faulstich Orellana and her colleagues (2001: 581), researching among Mexicans, Koreans and Yemenis, found that '[p]arents expressed frustration that their children [in the USA] didn't appreciate the things their children back home would never have, and they thought about "sending kids back" to give them another perspective on life'. Using 'back there' as a reference point for values and behaviour, 'transnational disciplining' serves as an important strategy for some parents to control children's behaviour. But as Guarnizo (1997: 301) points out, when followed through this strategy often backfires because of the wearing down of kin support – a migrant's 'most valuable asset in the country of origin' – and the occasional unwilling return of mothers to take care of forcibly repatriated children.

From the children's perspective, Diane Wolf (2002) describes 'emotional transnationalism' among Filipino youth whose lives entail struggles between their own experiences and expectations and those of their parents and grandparents spanning California and the Philippines. Among other things, such struggles have resulted in particularly high rates of depression and despair, especially among young women. Her study underscores the point that 'Although families create the ties that bind and bond, they can also be sites of intense conflict and contradiction' (ibid.: 284-5) – a truth that may intensify when the families are maintained transnationally.

These developments do not always entail a clash of social worlds, however. Drawing upon a detailed ethnography of Mexicans living between Mexico and New York City, Fernando Herrera Lima (2001: 91) suggests that 'the transnational family is buffered by its extensive social networks, allowing the transnational experiences to form a fluid continuum, rather than a radical divide compartmentalizing life into two separated worlds'. Such networks surrounding transnational families allow for the circulation of people, goods, jobs, and information as well as for the re-creation and modification of cultural values and practices.

Through socialization within the family, individuals acquire and put to use some of their basic orientations, dispositions and social practices.

When socialization and family life take place across two or more settings (which usually entail differing social positions and structures), ever more complex processes and components arise in building the personal repertoires of *habitus* (see below). The practices, outlooks and points of reference of one context might displace, compete or merge with those of the other context. In this way, to adopt the view of Herrera Lima (2001: 91), 'Transnational families are therefore vehicles – better yet, agents – for both material exchanges and the creation, re-creation and transformation of cultures'. Indeed, for many migrants, living a transnational life itself entails a distinct kind of culture or set of norms.

Gender

The 'everyday routinized activities and practices' within transnational families have obvious significance for gender relations (Al-Ali 2002: 250). Transnational families demonstrate how culturally constructed concepts of gender operate within and between diverse settings. In various related ways, the position of women in households – and thereby daily gender relations – may be fundamentally altered and liberating, especially when it is the wives and daughters who have migrated to become the breadwinners for the families who have stayed (Hondagneu-Sotelo 1994). In other cases a patriarchal grip on women within families may be reinforced due to the perceived threats, posed by transnational existence, to cultural notions of feminine virtue. It should be stressed that the significance of gender also manifests in numerous spheres outside family and household, of course, especially in transnational community associations, religious congregations and places of work (see among others Goldring 2001, Mahler and Pessar 2001, Salih 2003).

Citing a number of studies, José Itzigsohn and Silvia Giorguli-Saucedo (2005: 896) note that

> men and women participate differently in transnational social spaces. Men appear to be more committed to the maintenance of public and institutionalized transnational ties than are women, while women appear more committed to participating in the life of the receiving country.

Such findings tally with the broader, gendered approach to migration (see Pessar 1999a, b, Willis and Yeoh 2000, Pessar and Mahler 2003). Such migration studies often find that irrespective of cultural background, women's social status – in the household and community (local and transnational) – generally improves through the migration process, mainly through access to employment and a certain degree of control over income and material resources. In numerous studies, evidence also suggests that conversely, men often lose status – potentially threatening their gender identity (cf. Charsley 2007).

> Their low occupational status might satisfy the needs within the household, but it weakens traditional gender roles and does not award public recognition. As a result, men desire to return home in order to regain the status and privileges that their migration has challenged. Men also attempt to reinforce their own values and norms as a way of reassuring their identity in an environment that is strange to them.
>
> (Itzigsohn and Giorguli-Saucedo 2005: 897)

Here research suggests that '[m]en's transnational involvement is more likely to be of the reactive type, related to the difficulties or the discrimination they encounter in the incorporation process. Women's transnational participation is more likely to be resource dependent' (ibid.: 916).

At other times gender structures are entrenched or strengthened by migration and transnational life. In a study of families spread across Canada and India, for instance, Margaret Walton-Roberts (2004) observed how the disadvantaged position of women in the 'private' sphere is reproduced within transnational households. This included impacts on women's decisions on marriage, family movements and fertility practices. Marisa Alicea (1997), who focused on how Puerto Rican women make important decisions about the use of household resources across national boundaries, found that although transnational practices provide women with possibilities for creating strong identities and resisting racial and class oppression, 'patriarchal domination' is not undermined through such long-distance engagement. Yet another pattern was revealed among Filipino transnational households by Rhacel Salazar Parreñas (2005). She noted how various gender transgressions ensued with the separation of migrant parents, with mothers becoming key income earners while leaving children behind, and fathers taking on nurturing roles in the absence of mothers. Yet rather than transforming gender structures, Parreñas concludes, gender norms are often reinforced through socialization of conventional gendered role expectations in children. In this way, Filipino children in transnational families learn that fathers are for discipline and mothers are for nurture.

Gender relations and family forms are fundamental features of cultural institutions that are generated by sets of outlooks and values inculcated through social practices and experiences. One concept that is useful for gaining a better understanding of the form, content and workings of such outlooks and values – and how they might be transformed through transnationalism – is *habitus*.

Habitus

Pierre Bourdieu's (1977, 1990) concept of *habitus* refers to a socially and culturally conditioned set of durable dispositions or propensities for certain kinds of social action. This set or repertoire is internalized by individuals in the course of their life experiences and in relation to their social positions. The dispositions of *habitus* selectively generate everyday social practices immediately and in the context of specific social fields. As a set of neither wholly conscious nor wholly non-conscious perceptions, outlooks, points of reference, *habitus* guides personal goals and social interactions.

> The power of the *habitus* derives from the thoughtlessness of habit and habituation, rather than consciously learned rules and principles. Socially competent performances are produced as a matter of routine, without explicit reference to a body of codified knowledge, and without the actors necessarily 'knowing what they are doing' (in the sense of being able adequately to explain what they are doing).
>
> (Jenkins 1992: 76)

Most practices, according to Bourdieu (1990: 56), can only be accounted for by relating them between 'the social conditions in which the *habitus* that generated them was constituted, to the social conditions in which it is implemented'. This relation between partially or non-conscious dispositions and contextualized action makes *habitus* a more useful concept than the older, related anthropological concept of 'worldview' – described as a kind of cognitive map or complex of motivations, perceptions and beliefs (see for instance Jones 1972). Although they are abstract concepts, both *habitus* and worldview manifest themselves in individual narratives and directly observable, daily practices and social institutions.

How does the concept of *habitus* relate to migrant transnationalism? A number of scholars bring this or similar notions into play to describe the nature and impact of transnational outlooks and experiences of migrants. Rob Smith (2001), for example, invokes such a meaning when he describes the practices and relationships linking home and abroad as a 'transnational life' among immigrants and their descendants. Guarnizo (1997) suggests we might think of a transnational *habitus* as entailing:

> a particular set of dualistic dispositions that inclines migrants to act and react to specific situations in a manner that can be, but is not always, calculated, and that is not simply a question of conscious acceptance of specific behavioural or sociocultural rules. ... The transnational *habitus* incorporates the social position of the migrant and the context in which transmigration occurs. This accounts for the similarity in the transnational *habitus* of migrants from the same social grouping (class, gender, generation) and the generation of transnational practices adjusted to specific situations.
>
> (Ibid.: 311)

Guarnizo (ibid.) further writes of how Dominicans retain 'a dual frame of reference' through which they constantly compare their situation in their 'home' society to their situation in the 'host' society abroad. Roger Rouse also described the 'bifocality' of people's daily rhythms and routines of life joining localities in Michoacán and California. 'Their bifocalism,' thought Rouse (1992: 46), 'stemmed not from transitional adjustments to a new locale, but from a chronic, contradictory transnationalism'. Sarah Mahler (1998) takes up Rouse's notion, emphasizing ways in which researchers need to look at the nature of transnational migrants' 'lived reality' to determine whether or how they might be 'bifocal' with regard to their social ties and personal outlooks.

The complex *habitus* of migrant transnationalism has been described in other, related ways. In a transnational community spanning 'OP' – Oaxaca and Poughkeepsie, New York – Mountz and Wright (1996: 404) describe how members 'act daily in pursuit of shared objectives and with an acute awareness of events occurring in other parts of [OP]'. Aspects of life 'here' and life 'there' – whether perceived from the migrant's starting or destination point – are perceived as complementary (cf. Salih 2002). This relation is clearly conveyed in Katy Gardner's (1993a, 1995) accounts of the interplay between notions of *desh* (home) and *bidesh* (foreign contexts) among Sylhetis in Britain and Bangladesh. While in everyday discourse, *desh* is associated with the locus of personal and social identity and religiosity, *bidesh* conveys material bounty and economic opportunity. Gardner (1993a: 1–2) describes a kind of cognitive tension among Sylhetis that likely characterizes the predicament of a great many migrants around the world:

> The economic dominance of families with migrant members has meant that *bidesh* is associated with success and power, which *desh* is unable to provide. Statements concerning *bidesh* are therefore part of a discourse about the insecurity of life in Bangladesh and the continual economic struggle which villagers face. ... Individual opportunism and enterprise are therefore channelled towards attempting to go abroad, leading to dependency on something which for many is no more that a fantasy, a dream-land, which few villagers will ever see.
>
> Co-existing, sometimes uneasily, with this set of images and ideals is the centrality of *desh* to group identity, and the spiritual powers with which it is linked. There is therefore a constant balancing of the two views, between the economic and political power of *bidesh*, and the fertility and spirituality of *desh*. This continual ambivalence, and negotiation of what might appear to be oppositional presentations of the world, is an integral part of migration and the contradictions which it involves.

Ambivalence and negotiation around *desh–bidesh* are expressed and reproduced in a variety of ways, including the exchange of goods, images and ideas between the two settings. Gardner (ibid.: 5) further describes *desh–bidesh* not as polar opposites, but as sites in 'local mental maps [that] involve a geography of power, in which locations are points along a continuum, with different types of empowerment to be found at each'.

The effects of transnationalism for changing meanings, attitudes and experiences both 'here' and 'there' are relevant to recent studies concerning migrants and transformations of the meaning of 'home' (Rapport and Dawson 1998, Al-Ali and Koser 2002). An illustration of this is provided by Ruba Salih (2002, 2003), who details how Moroccan women in Italy engage in material practices representing the two countries. Whether in Italy or Morocco, the women buy, consume, display and exchange commodities from their 'other home' in order to symbolize their ongoing sense of double belonging.

Once such a kind of *habitus* of dual orientation is constructed and reproduced by migrants, it might have further impacts. For one, it is hard to dismantle. David Kyle (2000: 2) discusses at least one informant who foresees 'no clear exit strategy from the binational life he had built over eleven years of shuttling back and forth' between New York City and his village in Ecuador. Another consequence concerns the transformation of outlook and practice among those closely associated with the transnational migrant. Here, through the experiences of his informants, Kyle came to think of the links between these distinct places 'as more of an emergent transnational social reality, involving migrants and nonmigrants alike, than simply an international movement of labor' (ibid.: 9). The point about nonmigrants is significant: such a transnational social reality incorporates and infuses what we can call the *habitus* of many people 'left behind' but whose lives are still transformed by the transnational activities and ideologies among those who actually move (cf. ibid.: 202).

Relatedly, Rebecca Golbert (2001) documents the case of young Ukrainian Jews who have developed 'transnational orientations from home' towards the Ukraine, Israel and other Jewish communities in the USA, Germany and elsewhere. She describes how young Ukrainian Jews undertake the evaluation of everyday experiences, the past, and the future with 'a double consciousness' garnered from transnational links and a transnational conception of self. 'Their daily reality', Golbert (ibid.: 725) observes, 'is embedded in a transnational frontier of intersecting ideas, relationships, histories and identities; at the same time, transnational practices are localised through intimate and shared experiences'. Recounting narratives and the sharing of experiences – particularly regarding Israel – Golbert shows how returnees have had a powerful impact even on the transnational orientations of those who have never left the Ukraine. They, too, have a *habitus* re-oriented to more than one locality.

By conceptualizing transnational experience through the idea of *habitus*, social scientists might better appreciate how dual orientations arise and are acted upon. The notion also shines light upon the ways in which transnational life experiences may give rise not only to dual orientations but also to a personal repertoire comprising varied values and potential action-sets drawn from diverse cultural configurations.

Cultural competence/cosmopolitanism

Indeed, as Donald Nonini (1997) observes among Malaysian Chinese, labour migrants often develop 'new forms of *habitus*' allowing them to cope with a range of cultural differences encountered in their travels and transnational lives. Such *habitus* includes experiences, skills, information, abilities and orientations characteristic of individuals who 'familiarize themselves with other cultures and know how to move easily between cultures' (Werbner 1999: 20). Such attributes are often associated with 'cosmopolitanism' (see Vertovec and Cohen 2002) – here, not necessarily as 'openness toward difference and otherness' (Roudometof 2005) but rather more practically as a kind of cultural competence, 'a built-up skill in maneuvering more or less expertly with a particular system of meanings and meaningful forms' (Hannerz 1990: 239).

Although there is not much research on the kinds of attributes and skills that are wrought by transnational lives, Steffan Mau and his colleagues have conducted empirical surveys on this question and have indeed found 'a positive correlation between the transnationalization of life worlds and the cosmopolitanization of attitudes and values' (2008: 16–17). In addition to attitudes and values, Koehn and Rosenau have sought to elaborate just what kind of skills or competences are acquired through transnational experiences that enable individuals to 'participate effectively in activities that cut across two or more national boundaries' (2002: 114). These are reproduced in Table 3.1.

Table 3.1 Dimensions of transnational competence

Analytic competence	• Understanding of the central beliefs, values, practices, and paradoxes of counterpart culture(s) and society(ies) – including political and ethnic awareness;
	• Ability to link counterpart-country conditions to one's own circumstances and vice versa;
	• Number and complexity of alternative cultural paths assessed;
	• Ability to discern effective transnational strategies and to learn from past successes and failure.
Emotional competence	• Motivation and ability to open oneself up continuously to divergent cultural influences and experiences;
	• Ability to assume genuine interest in, and to maintain respect for, different (especially counterpart) values, traditions, experiences, and challenges (i.e. intercultural/ transnational empathy);
	• Ability to manage multiple identities;
	• Sense of transnational efficacy.

Creative/imaginative competence	• Ability to foresee the synergistic potential of diverse cultural perspectives in problem solving;
	• Collaborative ability to articulate novel and shared transnational synthesis;
	• Ability to envision viable mutually acceptable alternatives;
	• Ability to tap into diverse cultural sources for inspiration.
Behavioural competence: Communicative facility	• Proficiency in and use of counterparts' spoken/written language;
	• Skill in interpretation and in using an interpreter;
	• Proficiency in and relaxed use of interculturally appropriate nonverbal cues and codes;
	• Ability to listen to and discern different cultural messages;
	• Ability to engage in meaningful dialogue; to facilitate mutual self-disclosure;
	• Ability to avoid and resolve communication misunderstandings across diverse communication styles.
Functional (project/task) adroitness	• Ability to relate to counterpart(s) and to develop and maintain positive interpersonal relationships;
	• Ability to apply/adapt understanding, sensitivity, and imagination in transnational interactions;
	• Flexible ability to employ extensive and nuanced range of transnationally accommodative organizational strategies and interaction paths;
	• Ability to overcome problems/conflicts and accomplish goals when dealing with transnational challenges and globalization/localization pressures.

Source: Koehn and Rosenau 2002: 110

Of course, not all of these attributes are developed or utilized at once; rather, '[a]ctors possess components of the several skills in varying degrees and in different mixes' (Koehn and Rosenau 2002: 114). Therefore, these kinds of cosmopolitan competences might best be understood along a continuum from incapable to proficient (ibid.). With regard to the persons who acquire and develop such competences,

Koehn and Rosenau generally have in mind the global elite of business professionals. However, most if not all of these skills are also gained by 'working class cosmopolitans,' including labour migrants, through their own transnational experiences (cf. Werbner 1999). This is what some scholars have also referred to as modes of 'actually existing cosmopolitanism' (B. Robbins 1998), 'everyday cosmopolitanism' (Ang *et al.* 2002) and 'tactical cosmopolitanism' entailing 'a mish-mash of rhetoric and organizational strategies' through which new migrants 'attempt to negotiate partial inclusion in society without becoming bounded by it' (Landau and Haupt 2007: 4).

The notion of cosmopolitan cultural competences produced by transnational lives resonates with the range of concepts that researchers in sociology and cultural studies have invoked better to convey a sense of openness and mutability in the cultural practices of migrants and ethnic minorities. These includes notions of translation, creolization, crossover, cut 'n mix, hyphenated identity, bricolage, hybridity, syncretism, third space, multiculture, multiple cultural competence, transculturation and diasporic consciousness (see among others Hannerz 1987, Hebdige 1987, Gilroy 1987, 1993, Ålund 1991, Robins 1991, Bhabha 1994, Back 1996, Werbner and Modood 1997, Vertovec and Rogers 1998). Another way of conceiving the capacities and practices by way of which people routinely engage cultural differences is as the 'pragmatic manipulation of multiplicity' (Amit-Talai 1995) or – following Hannerz's (1992b) approach to culture as modes of managing meaning – to consider them as modes of managing multiplicity.

What is the mechanism of managing multiplicity? One way of approaching this is through considering culture as a kind of 'toolkit', advocated by Ann Swidler (1986). Here, cultural attributes drawn from a number of sources throughout one's life are understood as a set of resources from which people can construct diverse strategies of action day-to-day, situation-by-situation (echoing Bourdieu's concept of *habitus* as discussed above). This means, according to Swidler (ibid.: 281), that people engage in their everyday activities by 'selecting certain cultural elements (both such tacit culture as attitudes and styles and, sometimes, such explicit cultural materials as rituals and beliefs) and investing them with particular meanings in concrete life circumstances'.

The selective use of cultural practices, or enactment of meanings and values drawn from an overlapping set of sources, is sometimes described as a process akin to language use among people competent in more than one language. This is especially relevant to what is called code-switching in linguistics (see especially Rampton 1995). For example, with regard to young Asians in Britain, Roger Ballard (1994) underlines the analogy between cultural and linguistic practice: 'Just as individuals can be bilingual', Ballard (ibid.: 31) emphasises, 'so they can also be multicultural, with the competence to behave appropriately in a number of different arenas, and to switch codes as appropriate'. Further, he says,

> If we are [...] usefully to probe the analogy of cultural and linguistic practice, especially surrounding ideas of code-switching and code-mixing, we must recognise that sometimes the process is due to purposeful selection and emphasis, and sometimes it is non-conscious or inadvertent.

However, if social scientists are better to comprehend the dynamics of transnational repertoires, cosmopolitan competence, code-switching processes and the like, it should be emphasized that their capacities are not without considerable constraints. Ayse Caglar (1994: 34) points this out (with reference to the practices of German Turks) by stating that:

> [T]he debris of our past experiences are not immediately usable, since they are already embedded in structures in which they have meanings. These limit their immediate use in producing new arrangements. The ability to take what seems fitting and to leave out the rest is the outcome of a particular set of conditions. To be able to take elements and structures out of their context and create new arrangements with ones from different sources, certain conditions need to be fulfilled. Moreover, these juxtapositions and bricolage are not random, nor do they represent a chaotic jumble of signs. In their hybridity, they still tell a story. They have an organizing principle or principles. The objective is then first to identify the conditions that enable this drastic uprooting of elements and practices from very different sources, and second to explain the organizing principle(s) of their recombination and resetting ... .

Caglar's points provide a significant corrective to perspectives toward hybridity, cosmopolitanism, multiple identities and similar concepts surrounding modes of managing multiplicity which often suggest an unbridled horizon of cultural appropriation and enactment available to diasporic subjects and others leading transnational lives. Importantly, she reminds us that – as we have considered in Chapter 2 – social actors' actions are embedded in a constellation of relations and structures, and that actions of transnational actors are, indeed, multiply embedded.

Norms and identities

Over a decade ago Arjun Appadurai observed that 'few persons in the world today do not have a friend, relative, or coworker who is not on the road to somewhere else or already coming back home, hearing stories and possibilities' (1996: 4). This is arguably even more evident today.

Within many families whose lives are stretched across migrant sending and receiving contexts, transnational patterns of everyday activity, communication and exchange have become normative (Portes *et al.* 1999b, Faist 2000). Such norms of transnational life coincide with the conscious and non-conscious dispositions of *habitus*. They involve what Patricia Landolt (2001: 217) calls 'circuits of transnational obligations and interests.' Transnational social patterns variously condition people's everyday expectations (about potentials for migration, work, household development and individual life course), moral obligations (for disseminating information to friends and kin, engaging in reciprocal exchange of resources and enlisting of mutual support), institutional structures (including how best to organize or participate in religious communities and hometown associations) and relations to the state (fashioning practices to manipulate it, contest it or avoid it altogether).

Such norms are often embedded in a transnational moral economy of kin. This is underlined in Carmen Voigt-Graf's (2002) study of Punjabis, Kannadigas and Indo-Fijians in Australia. 'Given that kinship is the organising principle of Indian transnationalism', she observes (2002: 286), 'the type and regularity of transnational flows depends primarily on what happens within the extended family rather than on the economic or political situation in the home or host country'. Migration and transnational communication within extended families involve tactics for collective upward mobility, while marriages are arranged to extend a family's kinship networks strategically. In this way the social capital of families can be transformed into economic possibility if the need arises (see Ballard 2003a).

On the whole, one of the strongest sets of sustained – and indeed embellished – norms surrounding migrant transnationalism is that concerning migration itself. It is now a rather well-known dictum that, at least for a period, migration leads to more migration: migrants find jobs and send money back, encouraging and facilitating others to migrate. Now many nation-states expect, or indeed encourage, migrants to stay abroad and to send money home (see Chapter 5). Rapid and real-time communication fuels anticipation among would-be migrants. Information about living conditions, job opportunities and people's experiences circulate widely throughout immediate and expanded social networks. These usually underscore local perceptions in migrant-sending areas that 'in order to move up you need to move elsewhere' (Sørensen 2000: 3). Hence, in an increasing number of local communities in developing countries, it is expected that certain members of the family will emigrate using pre-existing transnational social networks. The timing and nature of migration depends on numerous variables (the season if regarding agricultural work, pooled money available, access to travel brokers and contacts along the migration route or in the destination point, etc.; such migration variables are often highly gendered as well); a further crucial factor is that '[m]igrants' desire and ability to participate transnationally also varies across the life cycle' (Levitt 2003: 183). Norms around migration and emergent transnational life naturally overlap with, or mutually reinforce, the kinds of social practices already described by way of telephone calls and family concerns.

The norms that manage and sustain migrant transnationalism do not determine individual behaviour nor do they ensure social cohesion within the migrant group and its extended network in the place of origin. Such norms may in fact stimulate new social tensions, fragmentation and disarticulation within families and local communities. Alison Mountz and Richard Wright (1996) describe how, within a Mexican transnational community, both cultural traditionalists in the home village and a variety of 'dissenters' abroad oppose a number of emergent transnational norms (the latter set includes *los irresponsables* – the irresponsible ones – who fail to communicate with or send money to families, and 'practical questioners' who wish to pursue their own goals independently of family and community). Within many transnational families, perhaps the greatest concern over 'dissenters' – or at least potential ones – surrounds the orientations and practices of members of the second and subsequent post-migration generations.

High among questions and criticisms regarding the transnational lens on migration are issues as to how members of second and subsequent generations are affected by transnationalism. There is one common view that transnational practices among second-generation youth are currently minimal and likely to dwindle further in the course of time. However, another view – and one in line with an understanding on how a transnational *habitus* is shaped and acted upon – suggests that there exist

> strong influences in the transnational social fields in which the second generation is embedded. This view stresses the importance of the sending-country individuals, resources, and ideas that are a constant presence in the lives of the second generation and holds that even selective, periodic transnational practices can add up.
>
> (Levitt and Waters 2002: 4)

Recent research suggests that there are patterns of intensive transnational activism at particular life-stages among the second generation (Levitt 2002, R.C. Smith 2002). Further, and not surprisingly, there appears to be a considerable variety of patterns and kinds of transnationalism among different groups of second-generation youth (Kasinitz *et al.* 2002). In each case the interplay is apparent of parents' transnational *habitus*, an array of local conditioning factors, and second-generation youth's own hybrid or multicultural *habitus*. Thus among young Indian-Americans, Sunaina Marr Maira (2002: 23) observes that

> second-generation youth culture becomes a site of struggles to define notions of authenticity that, while drawing on transnational imaginings of 'India', also work to position these youth in relation to hierarchies of race, class, gender, and nationalism that mark them as 'local'.

Such studies suggest that even though specific transnational orientations and practices of communication and exchange may not be sustained in strong forms by second and subsequent generations, the process of being socialized within a milieu of such transnational orientations and practices will often have a substantial influence on longer-term configurations of outlook, activity and – perhaps especially – identity.

A massive body of social and social psychological theory addresses the ways in which people conduct their everyday lives in terms of their identities. According to most prevailing theories (neatly summarized by Richard Jenkins (1996), who draws especially upon George Herbert Mead, Erving Goffman and Fredrik Barth), identities are seen to be generated in, and constructed through, a kind of internal (self-attributed) and external (other-ascribed) dialectic conditioned within specific social worlds. This holds for both personal and collective identities, which should be understood as always closely entangled with each other (while recognising the serious theoretical problems debated around notions of self, personhood and collectivity; see for example Rouse 1995).

It follows, then, that '[s]ince the salience and intensity of the identity/ ies enacted can vary across situations, collaborators, and/or time, transnational actors must be flexible and skilled at managing multiple counterpart identities' (Koehn and Rosenau 2002: 112). Another way of looking at this situation is through what Hannerz (1996), describes with respect to people who live in diverse 'habitats of meaning' that are not territorially restricted. The experiences gathered in these multiple habitats accumulate to comprise people's cultural repertoires, which in turn influence the construction of identity – or indeed multiple identities. Each habitat or locality represents a range of identity-conditioning factors: these include histories and stereotypes of local belonging and exclusion, geographies of cultural difference and class/ethnic segregation, radicalized socio-economic hierarchies, degree and type of collective mobilization, access to and nature of resources, and perceptions and regulations surrounding rights and duties (cf. Meyer and Geschiere 1999).

Together the multiple contexts create what some have called a 'transnational social field' (Glick Schiller *et al.* 1992b), 'transnational social space' (Pries 1999), 'transnational village' (Levitt 2001a) or 'translocality' (Appadurai 1995). However termed, the multi-local life-world presents a wider, ever more complex set of conditions that affect the construction, negotiation and reproduction of social identities. These identities play out and position individuals in the course of their everyday lives within and across each of their places of attachment or localities of perceived belonging.

TRANSNATIONALISM AND INTEGRATION

Much of twentieth-century scholarship on migration was devoted to ways through which migrants adapted to new contexts, a process variously named assimilation, integration, settlement, insertion or incorporation (see among others Alba and Nee 2003, Castles *et al.* 2003, and Waters and Jiménez 2005). Early discussions of migrant transnationalism tended to suggest that sustained, cross-border connections represented an alternative to assimilation (cf. Appadurai 1990, Basch *et al.* 1993, Faist 2000); ensuing debates pondered whether 'there had emerged in the modern world an alternative form of adaptation of immigrants to receiving societies that was at variance from what these traditional concepts suggested' (Portes *et al.* 2002: 279).

What are the implications of sustained transnational connections for migrants' integration? There are various answers to this question, various modes of transnationalism and integration that can be examined, and various studies that have attempted to measure or interrogate related processes and phenomena.

The degrees to and ways in which today's migrants maintain identities, activities and connections linking them with communities outside their places of settlement are unprecedented. Of course, not all migrants maintain the same level or kinds of transnational engagement, socially, culturally, economically or politically. Much of this will be largely conditioned by a range of factors including migration channel and legal status (e.g. refugees or undocumented persons may find it harder to maintain certain ties abroad), migration and settlement history, community structure and gendered patterns of contact, political circumstances in the homeland, economic means and more. That is, transnational practices among immigrants are highly diverse between and within groups (whether defined by country of origin, ethnicity, immigration category or any other criteria; cf. Vertovec 2007).

Many migrants develop and maintain strong modes of community cohesion – but not necessarily with others in their locality. The strongest senses of cohesion or belonging may remain with others in a homeland or elsewhere in a diaspora. However, this needn't mean they are not becoming integrated in their places of settlement. Belonging, loyalty and sense of attachment are not parts of a zero-sum game based on a single place. That is, the 'more transnational' a person is does not automatically mean he or she is 'less integrated', and the 'less integrated' one is does not necessarily prompt or strengthen 'more transnational' patterns of association.

Instead, with regard to transnationalism and integration – or assimilation, in American parlance – numerous works have come to underline their 'concurrent and intertwined' nature (Itzigsohn and Giorguli-Saucedo 2005), 'interconnectedness' along with 'their both/and rather than either/or character' (Kivisto 2005: 311), 'simultaneity' and the emergence of 'complex amalgam structures and dispositions that combine elements of assimilation and transnationalism' (Joppke and Morawska 2003: 3). Indeed, Ewa Morawska (2003) suggests more than 40 factors that shape different forms and combinations of transnationalism and assimilation. However, drawing on extensive fieldwork among Mexicans in

New York, Robert Smith (2006) demonstrates how transnationalism and assimilation are aspects of a single social process. Many immigrants, such as those with whom Smith worked, cross borders several times, negotiating identities and involvements in both the 'old' and 'new' countries continuously.

The insight that transnationalism does not hinder integration also pertains to the concept of segmented assimilation. This key notion in the American literature recognizes that migrants might follow differing trajectories and outcomes reflecting the dynamics of race/ethnicity and class (and to some degree, geography). Segmented assimilation theory sees at least three possible paths for migrants' socio-economic mobility: upwards into White, middle-class society, downwards into the broadly excluded or low-income working class, or into an ethnic or racialized community characterized by its own economic and cultural patterns (Portes and Zhou 1993, Zhou 1997a, Portes and Rumbaut 2001; cf. Waldinger and Feliciano 2004). This important approach emphasizes that a linear process based on White, middle-class norms is not the only measuring stick for integration; indeed, the segmented assimilation thesis argues that processes of incorporation may mean greater – rather than lesser – social distance between immigrants and White Americans (Itzigsohn and Giorguli-Saucedo 2005). What's more, '[e]ach of these different trajectories of integration into the host society can coincide with the maintenance of different forms of identificational and participatory transnationalism' (Joppke and Morawska 2003: 25; see also Morawska 2004).

Empirical research has demonstrated the complex relationships between modes of transnationalism and integration. For instance, the Comparative Immigrant Entrepreneurship Project (CIEP) provided robust data on Colombians, Dominicans and Salvadorans in five major US cities between 1996 and 1998. Its findings, analysed and published by a variety of academics, demonstrate that across a range of variables and correlations, modes of transnational participation have compound interplays with processes of integration. Economic transnational practices are positively associated, 'accelerating rather than retarding the long-term integration of contemporary immigrants' (Portes *et al.* 2002: 294). Using the CIEP data, Alejandro Portes (2003) shows that many forms of transnational participation increase with levels of human capital including years of education, occupational status and extent of experience in the US. In another study based on the same dataset (Guarnizo *et al.* 2003), the authors find a similar correlation with regard to political transnationalism; that is, education level, amount of time in the US and citizenship do not reduce interest in homeland politics – indeed, they may facilitate it since 'A US passport enables former migrants to travel back and forth without restrictions; greater time in the United States is usually associated with economic stability and more resources to invest in favoured political causes [in the homeland]' (ibid.: 1229). Mariano Sana's (2005) CIEP analysis shows a different picture: that the prominent transnational practice of remitting money correlates strongly with renting a home, the lack of citizenship and lack of language fluency – which are all evidence of limited migrant integration or incorporation. Another CIEP study by Itzigsohn and Giorguli-Saucedo (2005) concludes that:

> The same factors that promote incorporation – i.e., exposure to American life, increased socio-economic status – also promote transnational participation. On the other hand, factors that hinder the process of incorporation, namely the encounter with the American racial systems, also push immigrants toward transnational participation.
>
> (Ibid.: 916)

In addition to realizing that the relationship between transnationalism and integration is not a zero-sum game, it is important to understand that neither concept is of a piece; that is, various modes or components can be selectively combined by migrants. Here, Peggy Levitt (2003: 194) has highlighted such a selective nature of participation (whether in 'host country' or transnational/'home' spheres) by relating the experience of one of her informants, Pratik, a Gujarati engineer living in Boston:

> Pratik, then, successfully combines selective assimilation and transnational involvements to advance in both settings. He is not interested in participating in Indian or US politics. He has assimilated into mainstream economic life in the US but rejects membership in its cultural and religious institutions. And at the same time, he is active in the economic and religious life of his sending community. He purposefully picks and chooses where and what he will be involved in, so far achieving mobility in both contexts.

In a study of 300 immigrants in the Netherlands from six Western and non-Western countries of origin Erik Snel, Godfried Engbersen and

Arjen Leerkes (2006) also examined multiple kinds and extents of transnational involvement alongside measures of integration. They included an attitudinal dimension, marked by the degree of identification with both sending and 'host' contexts as well as with others in diaspora. Their analysis found considerable variation between all these factors among the groups in question. 'Transnational activities occur both among migrants with good and with marginalized social positions (in terms of educational level and labour market participation) in the host society', it was observed (ibid.: 300). Their intriguing results show that the 'least structurally integrated' respondents (Moroccans and Antilleans) identify strongly with their countries of origin but do not develop notable transnational activities.

> Transnational activities are not confined to particular migrant groups or to a particular type of migrant. [...] transnational *identifications* weaken the longer the migrants live in the Netherlands. However, involvement in transnational *activities* hardly diminishes with increased length of stay, which suggests that these occur in part for reasons other than transnational identification (for example, because of familial obligations).
>
> (Ibid.: 303, emphasis in original)

The Dutch study further underlines the point that transnational involvement itself does not impede integration, nor is there a direct correlation between social position and transnational activities.

Comparing patterns among Oaxacans in the USA and Kurds in Germany, Jeffrey Cohen and Ibrahim Sirkeci (2005) describe both costs and benefits of transnational engagement with regard to integration processes. Sustained transnational activity, they suggest, can lead to concentrated and segmented communities in settlement societies, and such ethnic enclaves may mitigate integration through limiting interaction with non-community members. However, Cohen and Sirkeci also note how transnational identities can and do assist migrants to cope with new settings. So, again, we are left with coexisting – competing? – processes.

In a recent study on new migrants and community cohesion in Britain (Jayaweera and Choudhury 2008), informants were asked about a range of possible transnational engagements (surrounding family contact, sending money, owning property, political involvement, etc.) as well as about the various local spaces in which they did or did not regularly

meet and talk with people from different ethnic and/or religious backgrounds (homes, workplaces, streets, markets, schoolgates, associations,
places of worship, GP surgeries, etc.). It was hypothesized that the higher
the number of such engagement-spaces (up to 22 in this survey), the
greater the capacity for social integration. Among 199 new immigrants –
that is, people with less than five years' residence in the UK – it was
found that

> interviewees who demonstrated the greatest number of types of transna-
> tional involvement (four or more) were the most likely to: be employed,
> have a perception of financial stability, have voted in the 2005 general elec-
> tion and meet people of a different ethnicity and religion in more spaces on
> average.
>
> (Ibid.: 100)

The reasons for such patterns are not clear, but one might be a matter of
confidence in relation to overall engagement activity: when immigrants
feel thoroughly engaged in a field of interactions whether in the UK or
spanning a place of origin, this may well provide a sense of confidence to
engage yet other people and spaces. If, on the contrary, exclusion from
interaction – in the UK or place of origin – is felt, this may work to dis-
courage inclinations to engage further.

The incontestable fact is that with regard to either processes of transnationalism or integration, migrants adapt. Sustained and intensive
patterns of transnational communication, affiliation and exchanges can
profoundly affect manners of migrant adaptation – including practices
associated with positive or limited integration – through the maintenance
of a particularly strong sense of connection or orientation to the people,
places and senses of belonging associated with the place of origin. As in earlier eras, migrants feel powerfully bound to homelands and communities
elsewhere – and now they can variously express and enhance this attachment. At the same time, new immigrants clearly are getting on with
developing a new life, livelihood, social ties and political interests in their
places of settlement.

Stephen Castles (2002: 1158) postulates that '[i]t is possible that
transnational affiliations and consciousness will become the predominant
form of migrant belonging in the future. This would have far-reaching
consequences.' One possible approach to understanding such a
process and its consequences is to consider how patterns of migrant

transnationalism entail the re-orienting of people's *habitus* towards 'bifocality'. The structure and workings of *habitus* are certainly hard to 'measure', but they are arguably discernible in social practices and conveyed in narratives. The dispositions and practices generated by a transnational *habitus* are not, moreover, evenly spread within a group or family. Yet these are nonetheless not to be underestimated, because such dispositions and practices have substantial impact on individual and family life course and strategies, individuals' sense of self and collective belonging, the ordering of personal and group memories, patterns of consumption, collective socio-cultural practices, approaches to child-rearing and other modes of cultural reproduction. These latter functions particularly concern ways in which the re-orienting of first generation *habitus* conditions that of second and subsequent generations.

A re-orientation of *habitus* takes place in the course of any person's relocation and integration into a new social system. That is necessary since the process involves the negotiation and competent selection of actions in respect to immediate, local systems of structured relationships. Broadly, the transnationally influenced re-orientation of *habitus* arguably contributes to a more widespread process of transformation affecting many Western societies, namely the public recognition of multiple identities.

More than 25 years of consciousness-raising activities around anti-racism and multiculturalism, indigenous peoples, feminism, gay rights, disability rights, regional languages and other civil identity issues has effected the transformation of the public sphere. Compared to conditions before this period, there is now much more public recognition, in a variety of forms (legal reform, political representation, positive media images, etc.), surrounding people's claims to difference and multiple identities (see for instance Young 1990, The Runnymede Trust 2000, Hall 2002). By the late 1990s,

> Pluralist understanding of persisting diversity, once a challenge to the conventional wisdom, had *become* the conventional wisdom, not only in the US and other classic countries of immigration such as Canada and Australia, but also in much of northern and western Europe.
>
> (Brubaker 2001: 531, emphasis in original)

The fact that many migrants feel powerfully bound to elsewhere – and that they now variously express it – is both legitimated by and contributes to this broader trend of public transformation (cf. Glick Schiller 1999, Foner 2000, Levitt 2001b). Interestingly, something else happening to the public sphere parallels this trend and is also deeply affected by transnationalism: namely, the reconceptualization of the model of the nation-state, a theme addressed in the next chapter.

4

POLITICAL
TRANSFORMATIONS

There is a widespread, long-standing model of the nation-state that por-
trays it as the combined legal and institutional structures governing the
people, economy, and political processes contained inside a recognized
border. Within a now very large body of literature, scholars debate
whether, or how, processes of globalization have affected the conventional nation-state model (see for instance W.I. Robinson 1998, Scholte
2000, Guillén 2001). For example, Martin Albrow (1997) sees the model
as an outdated form of social and political organization; Susan Strange
(1996) describes the 'declining authority of states' while Saskia Sassen
(1996) asserts that economic globalization is leading to a fundamental
redefinition of nation-state sovereignty and territoriality; Martin Carnoy
and Manuel Castells (2001) depict a dramatic decline in the autonomy of
nation-states and their growing dependence on globalized processes of
production and trade, on other states, and on lower levels of the state.
And in probing the concept of 'cosmopolitanism', a variety of authors –
including Craig Calhoun, David Held, Ulrich Beck, Rainer Bauböck and
Mary Kaldor (all in Vertovec and Cohen 2002) – describe how assorted
inter-state, intra-state and ultra-state practices test the viability of a conventional model of the nation-state and the international system based
around it.

In some quarters the arguments around globalization and political
change have gone to extremes, suggesting we are witnessing the 'death of

the nation-state'. Others point to the continuation, if not strengthening, of the legitimacy and capacity of states to enforce their laws and policies. Whether they are sceptics, hyper-globalists or transformationists (Held *et al.* 1999), most observers agree that the nation-state has been radically challenged, at least, by processes and phenomena surrounding such things as the emergence of complex global economic patterns, massive and instantaneous international financial flows, an array of regional pacts and multilateral agreements (on trade, the environment, crime and terrorism, etc.) and 'humanitarian' military interventions – all things which seem to upset long-standing notions of cultural and political sovereignty. While not necessarily dying, the nation-state is transforming into a type of political organization or apparatus involving more multiple and overlapping jurisdictions, sets of identities and social orders no longer really contained by borders (cf. Beck 2002).

There has been considerable discussion among sociologists, political scientists and political philosophers regarding the challenges to the nation-state specifically posed by immigration (e.g., Bauböck 1994, Soysal 1994, Sassen 1998, Joppke 1998, 1999). While debates over globalization and political change, immigration and the nation-state continue, we can see that migrant transnationalism does not itself bring about transformations of the nation-state. Such transformations are happening anyway, due to a confluence of processes within the global political economy. But forms of migrant transnationalism make an important contribution to such significant shifts affecting the nation-state model. In what ways is this happening?

IDENTITIES–BORDERS–ORDERS

Within the field of International Relations, one current way of attempting to understand broad contemporary political challenges is through the 'analytical triad' or 'dynamic nexus' between the concepts of 'identities–borders–orders' (Albert *et al.* 2001). The idea here is that, in order to appreciate changes happening in any one of these three conceptual domains, it must be assessed in relation to the other two. Yosef Lapid (2001: 7) writes:

> Processes of collective identity formation invariably involve complex bordering issues. Likewise, acts of bordering (i.e., the inscription, crossing, removal, transformation, multiplication and/or diversification of borders)

invariably carry momentous ramifications for political ordering at all levels of analysis. Processes of identity, border and order construction are therefore mutually self-constituting. Borders, for instance, are in many ways inseparable from the identities they help demarcate or individuate. Likewise, they are also inseparable from orders constituted to a large extent via such acts of individuation and segmentation. Thus, in any specific case, if we want to study problems associated with any one of our three concepts, we can richly benefit from also considering the other two.

In other words, as with the conventional model of the nation-state, some sense of identity is presumed to characterize a people; this identity/people is believed to be contiguous with a territory, demarcated by a border; within the border, laws underpin a specific social and political order or system; this social order – which is conceived to be different from orders outside the border – both draws upon and reinforces the sense of collective identity. 'Identities–borders–orders' are legitimated and reproduced through a system of narratives, public rituals and institutions, formal state bureaucracies and informal social relationships, written and unwritten regulations, sets of assumptions and expectations of civility and public behaviour (Schiffauer *et al.* 2003).

Various processes of globalization and the rise of regional, global or 'cosmopolitan' structures of governance assail essential components of national 'identities–borders–orders' by compounding identities, ignoring borders and over-ruling orders. Migration itself confronts 'identities–borders–orders'. 'One reason migration enters political agendas with greater frequency and salience now', suggests Martin Heisler (2001: 229), 'is that, at least in some host societies, it *disturbs the sense of boundedness*' (emphasis in original).

> The ability to change countries of residence with relative ease and the possibility of reversing the move can vitiate the need to make lasting identitive commitments. Identities can thus be partial, intermittent, and reversible in the modern Western democratic state. Order no longer depends on unalloyed loyalty stemming from immutable national identity – identity for which there is no plausible or legitimate alternative. Countries' borders are not seen as coextensive with a comprehensive political community.
>
> (Ibid.: 236)

Nowadays, Heisler (ibid.: 237) concludes, 'migration tends to attenuate territorial sovereignty, monolithic order, and identitive solidarity'. In various ways, some of which are described below, the political dimensions of migrant transnationalism inherently involve questions of identity (Vertovec 2001a) and often raise contentious issues concerning civic order and the cohesiveness of 'host' societies (Vertovec 1999b).

With regard to the *'identities'* part of the analytical triad, politicians contribute to senses of 'peoplehood' by enacting laws of membership, determining who is included, who is excluded, and determining what are their respective rights and duties (Pickus 1998). This need not be monolithic of course; recent trends in broadening such a national sense of identity can be seen in contemporary citizenship tests for immigrants and policies crafting multiculturalism. However, what such 'peoplehood' means is also affected by concurrent policies in many states extending and withholding rights, voice and welfare access to immigrants. These effectively create a multiple tiered sense of membership (Motomura 1998).

With regard specifically to migrant transnational practices, David Fitzgerald (2000: 10) observes that transnational migrants challenge nation-state ideals of belonging in both sending and receiving countries. They do this not least by moving back and forth between states, sometimes circumventing state controls over borders and taxes. 'Transnational migrants often live in a country in which they do not claim citizenship and claim citizenship in a country in which they do not live,' he points out (ibid.: 10). 'Alternatively, they may claim membership in multiple polities in which they may be residents, part-time residents, or absentees.' This phenomenon is witnessed in examples of immigrants – even naturalized ones – going 'home' from Germany or the USA to vote in Turkey or the Dominican Republic.

Such trends run counter to orthodox assimilation theories that assumed immigrants would be less likely to continue involving themselves in the political concerns of their nation-state of origin. Instead, for many migrants with transnational networks and lifestyles, 'the country of origin becomes a source of identity and the country of residence a source of right … . The result is a confusion between rights and identity, culture and politics, states and nations' (Kastoryano 2002: 160). Once more the question of durability enters: are such border-crossing political identities merely an issue for first-generation migrants? Bauböck (2003) addresses this by suggesting that 'even if transnationalism remains a *transient* phenomenon for each migration cohort, the emergence of new legal and political conceptions of membership signifies an important *structural* change for the polities involved' (emphasis in original).

With regard to the *'borders'* part of 'identities–borders–orders', Sassen suggests that states are 're-nationalizing' themselves in this area more than others. 'There is a growing consensus in the community of states to lift border controls for the flow of capital, information, and services and, more broadly, to further globalization', she notes. 'But when it comes to immigrants and refugees, whether in North America, Western Europe, or Japan, the national state claims all its old splendour in asserting its sovereign right to control its borders' (1996: 59). Almost regardless of global economic flows, inter-state pacts and other sides of globalization, nation-states firmly retain the right to admit or expel aliens, to maintain jurisdiction over what happens within their own territories, and through their border policies to control migration and membership. 'Territoriality', Fitzgerald (2000: 29) contends, 'continues to define the state even as its citizens cross state borders'.

Although challenging 'identities' and 'orders', migrant transnational practices do little to challenge state border controls (other than practices which sometimes seek to circumvent such controls). Indeed, it is usually the other way around: border policies often have a considerable impact on migrant transnational practices. Jacqueline Hagan (1994) shows how state policies are central to the formation of migrant communities, their survival strategies and transnational practices. She demonstrates how legal status – a powerful facet of border control – facilitates regular back and forth movement and exchanges, while lack of legal status seriously hinders such transnational practice. This is evident, too, following the recent beefing-up of border control measures in the United States (including, over the past decade, a tripling of its budget and a doubling of the size of the border patrol): these measures have meant that many undocumented Mexicans stay put in the USA rather than move back and forth through transnational circuits (Cornelius 2001).

With regard to the *'orders'* part of the triad, a broad range of policies surrounding migration and migrants is concerned with reproducing certain legal, social and political systems. In the realm of economic and cultural policy, for instance, 'migration has transformed the domestic political milieu ... the collective strength and pattern of alliances of political actors has changed; and migration has reshaped political interests and perceptions of these interests' (Held *et al.* 1999: 322). Perhaps foremost in this field, however, political sociologists and political scientists have been interested in the relationship between migration and citizenship. In much literature nationality and citizenship are treated as co-equivalent (although some scholars like Michael Jones-Correa [2001] argue that we should differentiate nationality as formal status of state membership, and citizenship as rights and duties within the nation-state). Notions of order, particularly within the identities–borders–orders framework, are put severely to the test by emerging migrant transnational practices around dual citizenship/nationality and 'homeland' political allegiances.

DUAL CITIZENSHIP/NATIONALITY

It has been suggested that dual citizenship/nationality represents one of 'the most fundamental questions about the relation between immigration and citizenship in the next century' (Pickus 1998: xxvii). Dual citizenship/nationality has a long history that is not always tied to the subject of immigration (see Koslowski 2001). Dual citizenship or dual nationality can be claimed through birth, marriage, claiming ancestral lineage or through naturalization.

Until recently there was a 'prevalent distaste' for dual nationality in states around the world; now, particularly post Cold War, that distaste is dissipating and we may be witnessing a long-term shift toward a more universal acceptance of dual nationality (Spiro 2002: 19–20). Long ago the League of Nations emphasized 'one nationality only', a platform reiterated in the early 1960s by the Council of Europe Convention on the Reduction of Multiple Nationality (Aleinikoff and Klusmeyer 2001). By 1997 the Council of Europe set forth its European Convention on Nationality emphasizing that both parents may transfer their respective nationalities to their children (Faist 2001).

There is now an upward trend in claims for dual citizenship/nationality, produced especially through migration. The loosening of rules concerning dual citizenship represents a global trend, particularly among migrant-sending countries (Hansen and Weil 2002). It is reported that at present some 89 countries – about half the world's countries – have some form of dual citizenship (Fritz 1998, Rogers 2001e). 'International and regional instruments', a United Nations report (UNPD 1998) points out, 'also seem to be reconciling principles of nationality with the trends towards multiple identities. This is evident by the reorientation of instruments regarding dual or multiple nationality'.

From an American perspective, Peter Schuck (1998: 153) writes that

> With current legal and illegal immigration approaching record levels, natu-
> ralization petitions quintupling in the last five years to almost two million
> annually, and legal changes in some of our largest source countries that
> encourage (and are often designed to encourage) naturalization in the
> United States, dual citizenship is bound to proliferate.

It is estimated that more than half a million children born in the United
States each year have at least one additional nationality (Aleinikoff and
Klusmeyer 2001). Among the one million people that naturalized in the
USA in 1996, nine out of ten main countries of origin allow some form of
dual nationality or citizenship (Fritz 1998). Similarly in 1996 seven of the
ten largest immigrant groups in New York City had the right to be dual
nationals (Foner 2000).

In other Western states, official attitudes on dual citizenship or dual
nationality vary considerably. The United Kingdom 'is perfectly indiffer-
ent' while France is tolerant and increasingly liberalizing (Hansen and
Weil 2002: 6–7). In Australia, the United States and much of Western
Europe the number of dual nationals is estimated to be several millions
and rising. Miriam Feldblum (1998) traces the increase to a variety of factors including not only increased migration and migrants' increasing
political claims, but gender equity reforms in nationality transmission and
retention, reforms in nationality criteria, and actual legislation to lift traditional bans on dual nationality. Irene Bloemraad (2004) details a rapid rise
in dual citizenship claims in Canada between 1981 and 1996, but also
notes differences among dual citizens surrounding characteristics such as
income, birthplace and province of residence. Even in countries like
Germany that traditionally do not tolerate dual citizenship, Thomas Faist
(2001) points out, about one-quarter to one-third of all naturalizations
from the 1970s to the 1990s resulted in multiple citizenship. Additionally,
every seventh German marriage is with a foreigner, leading to the off-
spring holding two nationalities under German law, and the millions of
Aussiedler (ethnic German repatriates) were not obliged to give up their
Russian or Kazakh citizenship (Thränhardt 2002). Indeed, Simon Green
(2005) points out how in Germany a high degree of political opposition
continues to exist alongside evidence of a similarly high degree of tolerance towards dual nationality in practice.

The transnational identities, border-crossings and mixed political
orders suggested by dual citizenship/nationality can be posed either as
contributing to, or hindering, the integration of newcomers (Faist 2001).

Such arguments are taken up by Randall Hansen and Patrick Weil (2002), who discuss five arguments against dual citizenship/nationality: (1) it can produce competing loyalties; (2) it creates a security threat; (3) it impedes immigrant integration; (4) it increases international instability; (5) it violates equality by giving dual nationals a wider range of rights and opportunities. Hansen and Weil engage these arguments by pointing out, among other things, that: (1) loyalty can indeed be multiple (e.g., the project of the European Union is based on this); (2) the security threat exists independently of dual citizenship/nationality; (3) far from impeding immigrant integration, dual citizenship/nationality furthers it (policies tolerant of dual citizenship/nationality are shown to increase naturalization rates); (4) the instability problem – exemplified in matters of military service, taxation and inheritance rules – is lessening through bilateral negotiations; and (5) equality issues are a concern, but the additional rights and opportunities offered by dual citizenship/nationality are often not much greater than those already extended by permanent resident status.

A kind of 'watering-down' of the meaning of citizenship and nationality is another concern for many as well. 'A second or even a third passport', writes Mark Fritz (1998: 1), 'has become not just a link to a homeland but also a glorified travel visa, a license to do business, a stake in a second economy, and escape hatch, even a status symbol'. This is seen by some as promoting a kind of 'citizenship of convenience'.

On the migrant-sending country side, dual citizenship has been difficult to push through many parliaments since domestic politicians see more disadvantage than advantage in allowing this (Østergaard-Nielsen 2003b). They often feel that emigrant or diaspora participation in domestic politics is distinctly not welcome – particularly absentee voting which might give too much domestic oppositional influence to people actually living outside the country.

In any case, as noted above, the incidence and impacts of dual citizenship/nationality are on the rise around the world, and migrant transnationalism plays a key role in this growth. In addition to shaping actual practices of migrants, such a trend is having important outcomes in government policy. As T. Alexander Aleinikoff and Douglas Klusmeyer (2001: 87) understand it, there is 'an emerging international consensus that the goal [of state policies] is no longer to reduce plural nationality as an end in itself, but to manage it as an inevitable feature of an increasingly interconnected and mobile world'.

The 'portability of national identity' (Sassen 1998) among migrants has combined with a tendency towards seeking membership in more than one place. While overlapping membership in different political communities obviously carries benefits of free movement between two societies, it needn't imply true political recognition and participation in each nation-state. In most cases only the rights of the country of residence are 'active' while rights pertaining to the other country remain 'dormant' (Bauböck 2002). Further, '[t]he migrant's act of taking on two nationalities', suggests Rey Koslowski (2001: 34), 'can be indicative of neither assimilation nor homeland political identification but rather of an ambivalent political identity, multiple political identities or even an apolitical identity'.

Among other issues currently raised in this field, one view holds that transnational ties among migrants weakens their integration in the immigration country (cf. Chapter 3), while another view suggests that democracy is actually enhanced by public recognition and representation of migrants' multiple identities within and outside the country of residence (Castles 1998, Vertovec 1999b). Relatedly, Irene Bloemraad's (2004) research points to the paradox that while multiple attachments can undermine some conventional aspects of the nation-state, dual citizenship might actually serve as a productive way to encourage immigrants' political and legal incorporation.

By way of another complex trend that is transforming the nation-state model, while dual citizenship – conceived as acquiring a pair of 'packages' of rights and obligations – is increasing on offer to mobile individuals, some countries are now differentially 'rationing' aspects of nationality and citizenship and 'qualifying' certain social and welfare rights (Feldblum 1998). Such measures cover issues such as voting and holding public office or public employment, inheritance, military service, ability to acquire private property, taxation, access to education, national insurance and pensions, and protection by labour laws.

Issues surrounding transnational migrants and citizenship – and the sometimes fierce political debates they have stimulated – underscore the need for more research and empirical data on the intersection of existing state policies, actual patterns of multiple membership, and long-term strategies of migrants and their families.

'HOMELAND' POLITICS

Another important realm in which multiple attachments are politically manifested is that summarized by the notion of 'homeland politics' – also sometimes described in terms of 'long-distance nationalism' (e.g. B.R. Anderson 1995), 'deterritorialized' nations (Basch *et al.* 1994) or 'the globalization of domestic politics' (Koslowski 2001). Once more harking back to the what's old/what's new question around transnationalism (Chapter 1), it is well documented that over 100 years ago many migrants maintained acute interest in the political plight of their place of origin (see e.g. Foner 2000). Now such interests – and particularly the ability to act upon them – have been heightened due to advances in communication, cheapness of transport and policy shifts such as the extension of dual citizenship/nationality.

Within and around transnational migrant communities, the politics of homeland can take a variety of forms (for instance, see Koopmans and Statham 2001, Guarnizo *et al.* 2003, Østergaard-Nielsen 2003a). Such forms include: exile groups organizing themselves for return, groups lobbying on behalf of a homeland, external offices of political parties, migrant hometown associations, and opposition groups campaigning or planning actions to effect political change in the homeland. Some migrant associations also manage to carry out dual programmes of action aimed at both sending and receiving countries (Østergaard-Nielsen 2001). Luis Guarnizo, Alejandro Portes and William Haller (2003: 1223) outline two major modes of transnational political participation:

> Transnational electoral participation includes membership in a political party in the country of origin, monetary contributions to these parties, and active involvement in political campaigns in the polity of origin. Transnational non-electoral politics includes membership in a hometown civic association, monetary contributions to civic projects in the community of origin, and regular membership in charity organizations sponsoring projects in the home country. Non-electoral activities are political because they influence local and regional governments by determining which public projects receive migrants' financial support. By so doing, they compel authorities to take immigrant wishes and priorities into account.

Still more 'homeland' political allegiances may involve additional dimensions, as well, in such highly diverse forms as:

* *diasporic politics.* These include the interests of long-established, subsequent generations stemming from migration (e.g. Irish Americans concerned with the situation in Northern Ireland) or religious/

ethnic communities who may have never even lived in a 'homeland' (e.g. relationships between some diasporic Jews and the state of Israel);

- *provisions for absentee voting.* Examples can be found among overseas nationals returning home en masse to vote in elections in Israel – sometimes with political parties paying for flights, high-profile unofficial polls among expatriate South Africans, and large-scale voting at overseas embassies as in Indonesian and Algerian elections (Rogers 1999b);

- *buying into regimes.* A prime illustration occurred in 1990 when Croatians abroad paid $4 million towards the election campaign of Fanjo Tudjman, and were rewarded with representation in parliament: 12 of 120 seats were allotted to diaspora Croats, more than to Croatia's own ethnic minorities (*The Economist* 2003a);

- *key roles in war and peace.* For years the financial backing of Tamil and Eritrean migrants (including an informal 2 per cent 'tax' levied among Eritreans worldwide) sustained the wars in Sri Lanka and along the border with Ethiopia; now these migrant diasporas are having a role in shaping the peace and facilitating post-conflict reconstruction (*The Economist* 2003a, Koser 2002). But for the first years following an initial conflict, a World Bank report warns, the risk of renewed conflict is much higher when large diasporas exist to financially fuel any new sparks (Collier and Hoeffler 2001);

- *mass protest and consciousness-raising.* A successful model of this followed the 1999 capture of Kurdish leader Abdullah Ocalan, when within a day organized mass demonstrations among Kurds took place around the world, bringing Kurdish issues to global attention (Rogers 1999a);

- *overseas support for insurgency and terrorism.* The potential role of migrant communities appears in backing guerrilla movements, such as among Tamils or Kurds, and terrorist actions, such as among Palestinian or Irish political movements. A RAND study identified 19 insurgency movements that received diaspora support between 1991 and 2000 (Byman *et al.* 2001; see also Hoffman 1998a).

The kind and degree of participation in 'homeland' politics differs with reference to a series of contextual factors, including the history of specific migration and settlement processes and political conditions in the country of origin. Through a substantial survey of various migrant groups in the USA, Guarnizo *et al.* (2003) demonstrated that Colombian immigrants are the least likely to take part in homeland politics, while Salvadorans and Dominicans are equally likely to do so. The broadest patterns of political transnationalism, Guarnizo *et al.* found, are 'a product of greater human capital, greater stability and experience in the receiving society, plus strong social connections and enduring moral ties with sending communities'.

At a deeper level, homeland political allegiance and engagement rests on the re-configuration of identities–borders–orders, such that people from a particular place regard themselves as legitimate members of the collective identity and social order of a place even though they are outside its borders. According to Fitzgerald (2000: 106) such a reconfiguration posits 'a model of citizenship that emphasizes rights over obligations, passive entitlements, and the assertion of an interest in the public space without a daily presence'. There is a tension, he goes on to say, between 'a reconceptualization of the polis as the transnational public space of the imagined community and the assertion that the polis should still be defined as a geographic space where citizens live together'. Hence governments of countries of emigration increasingly invoke national solidarity across state borders. This was exemplified by Vincente Fox's campaigning among Mexicans in California during 2000, in which he played upon the broader boundaries of an imagined nation and declared he would be the first President 'to govern for 118 million Mexicans', including 100 million in Mexico and 18 million living outside the country (Fitzgerald 2000, Rogers 2000). Similarly, following the Los Angeles riots of 1992, South Korean politicians evoked images of Korean-Americans as a 'colony' of the homeland (Shain 1999: 5), while in her 1990 inaugural address as Irish President, Mary Robinson proclaimed herself leader of the extended Irish family abroad. During election campaigns in Turkey and the Dominican Republic, candidates went abroad to encourage support through overseas 'nationals'. These visions of nationals abroad are akin to the notion of the 'deterritorialized nation-state', in which the boundaries of the nation-state are defined socially rather than geographically (Basch *et al.* 1994, Glick Schiller and Fouron 1998).

Pervasive rhetoric about extended nations abroad help explain the fact that overseas communities are increasingly engaging themselves in the economic, social and political life of their country of origin while sending states and other political actors are trying to channel this engagement to their own advantage. But although they use the same rhetoric, migrants and their sending states often have different expectations. Eva Østergaard-Nielsen (2003b: 5) explains that,

> While sending countries are quick to call for their expatriate population's economic and political contribution to development in the country of origin it is clear that most expatriates and their representative organizations expect this to be a two-way deal. Emigrants want their country of origin to support their struggle for equal rights and against discrimination on the labour market. More established migrant and diaspora groups demand more transparency and good governance in order to feel that their remittances and foreign direct investment is spent in the best possible way. And if migrants are expected to be good representatives and do some lobbying for their country of origin abroad, then they would often like some influence on the policies that they are expected to represent.

Ideas, activities and rhetoric find their way into government policies. There are a variety of reasons why specific countries develop certain kinds of policies toward expatriates (Levitt and de la Dehesa 2003). Policies regarding overseas nationals are usually intended to encourage a sense of membership (but not return) among national communities abroad (Østergaard-Nielsen 2003b). These include special ministries or government offices devoted to overseas nationals, special investment opportunities, special voting rights and, as we have seen, dual nationality/citizenship. Their effects, however, are broadly similar: 'Such policies', Peggy Levitt and Rafael de la Dehesa (2003: 588) believe, 'are reinventing the role of states outside of territorial boundaries and in this way reconfiguring traditional understandings of sovereignty, nation, and citizenship'.

Migrant transnational practices play a direct part in re-configuring identities–borders–orders. However, it is clear that at the same time many basic structures of the nation-state are intact, as it continues to exercise sovereignty over populations present on its territory. Ruud Koopmans and Paul Statham (2001) stress that the different ways migrants are enabled, or constrained, to make their homeland (and local) political claims in different countries demonstrate that the nation-state is alive and well and shaping transnational practices.

The spectrum of transnational political activity among migrant diasporas entails both nation-building and nation-wrecking. History provides many examples of nation-creation projects fashioned in exile (consider Garibaldi's, Lenin's, Gandhi's and Ho Chi Minh's periods abroad). Leaders of several 'stateless diasporas' struggle towards such projects today (among groups such as Kurds, Kashmiris and Sri Lankan Tamils). Diasporas play an increasingly significant part in processes of development and nation-building in poor countries and in ones which have undergone major transformation such as east European and former Soviet states. This is due to a number of factors including access to economic resources, greater ease in communication and travel, and the fact that many diasporas comprise expatriate professionals and entrepreneurs who have skills and experience to offer.

Today's attempts to bring migrant diasporas into nation-building processes often take the form of outreach policies developed by governments. Alan Gamlen (2006) provides a useful typology of such 'diaspora engagement policies' drawn from a sample of over 70 migrant-sending states. His typology is based around three broad areas: (1) capacity-building policies aimed at producing a state-centric 'transnational-national' society (including political rhetoric that symbolically includes expatriates in the national imaginary, the creation of ministries for overseas nationals, and supporting transnational media for consumption in the diaspora); (2) extending rights to the diaspora (such as dual citizenship, voting rights, parliamentary representation and special consular services); and (3) extracting obligations from the diaspora, based on the presumption that emigrants owe loyalty to their nation-state of origin (from urging participation in transnational lobbies, through creating 'brain circulation' programmes to bring expatriate expertise back to the homeland, to extracting taxes from the diaspora). Gamlen concludes that whatever the type, diaspora engagement policies are not directly correlated with any one kind of state (in political, geographical or economic terms) nor with any particular model of citizenship (based on primarily ethnic or civic categories).

> Through these various initiatives, governments are seeking to preserve the loyalty of the expatriates and to increase and channel their remittances, investments, and charitable contributions. The significance of these official initiatives may be seen in the fact that almost every sending country government has undertaken them: from Mexico to Turkey; from Colombia to Eritrea; and from the Dominican Republic to the Philippines.
>
> (Portes *et al.* 2007: 253)

However, it appears in many cases that migrants' own modes of transnational political or nation-building (or at least local community-building) practices usually developed first, with 'governments jumping onto the bandwagon only when their importance and economic potential became evident' (ibid.). This is certainly what has happened with regard to perhaps the foremost means of diasporic nation-building: individual remittances followed by hometown associations and transnational charitable initiatives (see Chapter 5).

Another mode of diasporic nation-building, or at least maintenance, comes through disaster relief. There are many examples of substantial aid flowing from diasporas following catastrophes such as Hurricane Mitch in Central America in 1998 and the earthquakes in Turkey in 1999 and in Gujarat in 2001. Diaspora groups relevant to areas throughout the Indian Ocean responded generously to the 2004 tsunami. Yet even where such humanitarian responses arise, corrosive diaspora politics may be present. According to reports, this occurred with diaspora aid to Gujarat which actually served to sustain anti-Muslim pogroms, while there are claims that following the tsunami various Tamil organizations conducted massive fraud to raise money for weapons and materials used by the Liberation Tigers of Tamil Eelam.

This brings us to the fact that there are diasporas also involved in nation-wrecking. Violence and war in a homeland usually stimulates reactions throughout a diaspora. Diasporic groups have had major roles to play in fomenting and supporting conflict in places as diverse as the former Yugoslavia, Ethiopia, Nagorno-Karabakh, Kashmir, Israel and Palestine. Financial support may flow from various parts of a diaspora to insurrectionist groups or a particular government's efforts to eradicate them (when this is an interethnic conflict, two or more diasporas might be pitted against each other as was evident in the breakup of Bosnia).

In all their forms, homeland political allegiances, mobilizations and engagements rest on the re-configuration of identities. In this way people from a particular place regard themselves as legitimate members of the collective identity and socio-political order of a place even though they reside outside its borders. Because they are facing both ends of a migration flow (however contemporary or historical), diasporic identities and activities tend to have different implications for homelands and host countries.

For host countries, the dual political loyalties suggested by diasporas raise fears of mobilized fifth columns, 'enemies within' and terrorist sleeper cells. Such suspicions feed into racism and other forms of discrimination. For 'homelands', national regimes certainly want money, may appreciate lobbying, but may resent too much political entanglement. That is why some offer limited forms of dual nationality without extending too much by way of voting and parliamentary representation.

With regard to all these dimensions of 'homeland politics', however, diversity within diasporas must be stressed. In any case of lobbying, charitable donation or conflict support, we can rarely speak of 'the diaspora' acting as one. Most diasporas – whether based on ethno-linguistic or national criteria – include opposing factions and dissenting voices. These, however, are often muffled by better organized, networked and financed actors (who are often the ones pushing nationalist or ethnic particularist agendas). Political orientations are certainly not of one kind, either; indeed, Mary Kaldor (1996) points to the presence not only of left-leaning cosmopolitans and anti-nationalists, but also of hard-core, reactionary ethno-nationalists within numerous diasporas (see also Ignatieff 1993, B.R. Anderson 1995, Rajagopal 1997).

Diasporas powerfully embody broader trends in the changing nature of nation-states. Today there is no longer a singular norm equating national/ethnic identification, political community and place of residence. Instead we are witnessing an increasing overlap of political identities and practices displayed between and within diasporic homelands and host societies. Such trends will continue to be enhanced, too, as 'digital diasporas' of various kinds offer new possibilities for transnational political engagement through recruiting expertise, soliciting and disseminating information, and mobilizing support for political campaigns (Brinkerhoff 2004).

The discussion in this chapter has endorsed the view, expressed by Held *et al.* (1999: 9), that 'the power of national governments is not necessarily diminished by globalization but on the contrary is being reconstituted and restructured in response to the growing complexity of processes of governance in a more interconnected world'. Alongside other globalization processes and manifestations, political features of migrant transnationalism – particularly surrounding dual citizenship/ nationality and 'homeland' allegiances – are not necessarily challenging the existence of the nation-state model, but they are certainly contributing to a fundamental reconfiguration of the related conceptual nexus of 'identities–borders–orders'.

5

ECONOMIC TRANSFORMATIONS

In 1907 immigrants in America sent $275 million (about $6 billion in today's currency) through 2,625 money agents in grocers, bakers and other shops (*The Economist* 2007a). Recent estimates of global remittances sent by migrants exceed $300 billion (IFAD 2007). Clearly there are and have always been significant economic aspects of migration and transnationalism; this is not surprising since economic considerations are often the prime reasons why migrants move in the first place. Yet economic aspects of transnationalism take many forms and have myriad consequences (economic ones to be sure, but also social and political ones). This chapter considers several of these forms and consequences.

TRADE AND ENTREPRENEURSHIP

In his insightful overview of the topic, Luis Guarnizo (2003) emphasizes that economic aspects of migrant transnationalism involve both multiple economic activities and a range of economic 'multiplier effects' generated by migrants' relations with their homelands. Such variety of activity and effect may often be seen within a single group, too, as shown by Patricia Landolt (2001) when she describes the range of variation of individual and household-level transnational economic activity among Salvadorans – despite their common origins and common post-migration contexts.

Some relevant transnational activities directly involve migrants, such as transnational ethnic entrepreneurship (Portes *et al.* 2002) or the facilitation of international trade (Light *et al.* 2002). Others only indirectly involve migrants, especially spin-off industries catering for migrant transnational practices. Indeed, as Guarnizo (2003) discerns, some of the biggest growth sectors within the telephone, air transportation, and financial industries are international long-distance calling, ethnic tourism and the private remittance of money – all industries directly focused on migrants as clientele. Further, the last decade has seen the rapid development of industries or enterprises (such as supermarkets or breweries) based in migrant-sending countries but marketing to customers in diaspora. In Ecuador, for instance, hundreds of new business services have been established catering to emigrants, including travel agencies, cybercafes and companies specializing in shipping abroad traditional Ecuadorian foods and medicinal herbs (Rogers 2001c).

Patricia Landolt, Lilian Autler and Sonia Baires (1999) distinguish four types of transnational migrant enterprises: circuit firms which transfer goods and remittances, cultural enterprises importing goods from countries of migrant origin, ethnic enterprises or small retail firms catering to immigrant communities, and return migrant microenterprises established in homelands by returned migrants and continuing to rely on contacts in the receiving country (cf. Itzigsohn *et al.* 1999, Portes *et al.* 2002). Another form is identified by David Kyle (1999, 2000), who describes the back and forth movement of a 'trade diaspora' of Peruvians who sell locally produced goods abroad. A specifically gendered example of such a trade diaspora is to be found among Cape Verdean women traders and Cape Verdean communities abroad (Marques *et al.* 2001).

Based on an extensive survey across groups, Alejandro Portes, Luis Guarnizo and William Haller (2002) found that transnational entrepreneurs represent a large portion, often the majority, of self-employed persons in an immigrant community. They demonstrate that transnational entrepreneurs are generally better educated, higher salaried and have more solid legal standing, if not citizenship, then many of their immigrant counterparts.

Still other economic facets of migrant transnationalism involve homeland government schemes aimed at emigrants, addressed in Chapter 4. These include policies, initiatives and structures designed to attract migrants' foreign currency, such as expatriate bonds, high-interest foreign currency accounts and tax exemptions for saving and investment.

Economically, however, by far the most transformative processes and phenomena of migrant transnationalism have concerned remittances – the money migrants send to their families and communities of origin. The following sections consider several significant dimensions of remittances and their transformative effects and potentials.

REMITTANCES

'Remittances have become the most visible evidence and measuring stick for the ties connecting migrants with their societies of origin', writes Guarnizo (2003: 666). There are a great many (and an ever-rapidly increasing number of) studies probing the volume of remittances, their determinants and impacts (especially their 'productive' uses) in migrant-sending contexts, and their channels of transference. Remittances are sent by all types of migrant workers: male and female, legal and undocumented, long-term and temporary, manual and highly skilled. Money is transferred through banks, agencies of various kinds, directly on-line, through professional couriers or through social networks.

Remittances tend to follow three spending phases, namely (1) family maintenance and housing improvement, (2) 'conspicuous' consumption and (3) 'productive' activities (Nyberg-Sørensen et al. 2002; cf. Massey et al. 1999). Remitted funds often do stretch into phase 3. Overall it has been suggested that migration and remittances function as a rational strategy for risk diversification (Stark 1991). Yet, despite their rationale, what are some of the transformative effects of migrant remittances?

Drawing upon research in El Salvador, Landolt (2001: 234) gives a rich description of some of the ways remittances transform families and communities:

> Households that receive remittances demonstrate tangible improvement in their standard of living. Remittance dollars grant access to education and health, and may permit a family to buy agricultural land or make improvements on an existing property. Remittances, combined with knowledge of wages and conditions in Salvadoran settlement cities, may also alter the labourer's relationship to the local economy. Weighing the value of their labour in transnational terms, workers have more leverage to reject the miserably low wages offered by Salvadoran employers. Entire communities are transformed, as enterprises, land holdings, and basic survival increasingly revolve around the remittance transfer. In turn, locals inserted in the circuits of Salvadoran economic transnationalism prosper relative to

> marginal, non-transnational locations, which remain mired in poverty. As
> they subsidize households and alleviate the worst forms of poverty, remit-
> tances finally have the unintended consequence of perpetuating a bankrupt
> economic system.

As Landolt suggests, remittances have broad effects, including the stimu-
lation of change within a variety of socio-cultural institutions (such as
local status hierarchies, gender relations, marriage patterns and consumer
habits). However, it is the economic impacts of remittances that receive
most attention.

In numerous settings around the world, remittances have been shown
to be directly invested in small businesses such as manufacturing and
crafts companies, market halls, bakeries and transport agencies (Taylor
1999, van Doorn 2001). However, various studies show differing pro-
portions of remittances spent on consumer goods versus 'productive'
investments. Among the reported negative impacts of migrant remittances are the following (Vertovec 2000a). Remittances tend to: displace
local jobs and incomes; induce consumption spending (often on foreign
imports); inflate local prices of land, housing, and food; create disparity
and envy between recipients and non-recipients; and create a culture of
economic dependency.

However, J. Edward Taylor (1999), among others, has criticized much
conventional research on remittances. He points out that most economic
surveys assume a naïve model of remittance expenditure; instead, there is
a need to consider whole-household and community economy. Taylor
(ibid.: 64) emphasizes that 'remittances may reshape migrant-sending
economies through indirect channels that are missed by traditional
research approaches'. This view corroborates research demonstrating the
multiplier effect of 'migradollars'. Durand and his associates (1996: 425)
argue that work focusing solely on the productive uses of remittances has
'ignored the indirect effects that consumer spending has on economic
production and income'. Their research on multiplier effects suggests
that, at that time, the $2 billion in remittances that entered the Mexican
economy was responsible for a $6.5 billion increase in production in agri-
culture, manufacturing, services and commerce. 'In short,' says Taylor
(1999: 72), 'an important channel through which remittances stimulate
productive investments may, paradoxically, be through migrant-
households' consumption spending'. Supporting this view and confirm-
ing the data of Durand *et al.*, one study in Bangladesh estimated that

remittances of $610 million created additional demand for $351 million in Bangladeshi goods and services and generated at least 577,000 jobs (Arnold 1992).

It must be stressed that a large proportion of migrants send money to families for mere subsistence (Suro *et al.* 2002). Also, schooling and other costs of education are often not factored into studies on the 'productive' use of remittances. 'In any case,' says Peter Stalker (2000: 81), 'it can be argued that many forms of consumption, particularly on housing, better food, education, and health care, are a good form of investment that will lead to higher productivity'.

Drawing on fieldwork in Jamaica, Heather Horst and Daniel Miller (2006: 144ff) identify three basic categories of remittances: those received for specific purposes, such as paying school fees; those received on an occasional basis, such as around Christmas or birthdays (although these might still be regarded as a means to meet day-to-day expenses); and those received in regular monthly payments (usually in support of spouses and children).

In order not to paint a misleading picture, it should be emphasized that migrants do indeed often channel remittances directly into investment, and that in this field we are not just talking about countries of the South. Throughout Central and Eastern Europe, for instance, thriving remittance systems are in place among migrants. Polish workers in Germany, for instance, send home as much as 80 per cent of their earnings (Vickerman 2002). Recent research suggests that throughout Central and Eastern Europe, moreover, migrants' money goes more toward investment – especially for establishing small businesses – than it does towards consumption (Piracha and Vickerman 2002).

The sheer scale of contemporary global remittances itself represents a type of transformation. Figures from the International Monetary Fund's annual Balance of Payments data show a massive increase in the amount of formal remittances worldwide, from less than $2 billion in 1970 to at least $105 billion in 1999 (van Doorn 2001). Over 60 per cent of this amount has gone to developing countries, and over the last decade remittances have become a much larger source of income for developing countries than official development assistance (Gammeltoft 2002).

Taking advantage of improved ways of recording financial transfers, the International Fund for Agricultural Development (IFAD), an agency of the UN, has more recently estimated the total flow of global remittances in 2006 to be over $300 billion. This sum has been sent by some

150 migrants worldwide in more than 1.5 billion separate financial transactions. Typically sent in amounts of $100 or $200 at a time, the IFAD suggests such funds sent directly to households reach approximately 10 per cent of the world's population (IFAD 2007).

Beyond official figures, unofficial remittance transfers may amount to further billions of dollars (*The Economist* 2003b). As much as 46 per cent of Mexican remittances may be hand-carried to recipients (Lowell and de la Garza 2000). In many African countries it is estimated that perhaps only about 50 per cent of remittances go through official channels (Mohan 2002: 134). One survey in Japan found that 70 per cent of Thai and Filipino workers sent money home by illegal means, while in 1998 Japanese police found underground banks sending up to 176 billion yen ($1.48 billion) in illegal transfers to China, Thailand, South Korea, Iran, Taiwan, Myanmar and Nepal (Rogers 1999c). In Pakistan formal remittances (currently over $1 billion) are thought to represent only a fifth or sixth of all remittances (Rogers 2001d).

One particularly important unofficial system for transnational money transfer is the centuries-old institution of *hawala*, practiced in many Islamic societies (see El Qorchi *et al.* 2003, Ballard 2003b). Although it might take various forms, the basis of *hawala* is a network of brokers, or *hawaladars*. A single *hawaladar* will receive a sum from a client in one location and subsequently contact a partner *hawaladar* in another location with an instruction to pay out to the client's contact the equivalent sum (perhaps minus a commission). Finally, based almost wholly on honour, the two *hawaladars* will settle the debt with each other at a future time. Unknown – but certainly very substantial – amounts of money flow around the world via *hawala*. Following 9/11, American authorities have tried to limit the system as it was thought to support criminal and terrorist finances.

Whether through official or unofficial means, remittances mean a lot to the countries – to say nothing of the families and communities – that receive them. In 2000 remittances from abroad comprised more than 10 per cent of the gross domestic product (GDP) of countries such as El Salvador, Jamaica, Haiti, Ecuador, Eritrea, Jordan, and Yemen (UNPD 2002). They account for as much as one-quarter of the national income of Nicaragua. Remittances have exceeded the total value of exports in El Salvador, and constitute more than half the value of exports in the Dominican Republic and Nicaragua (Orozco 2001). The Inter-American Development Bank calculates that across Latin America the annual growth of remittances is 7–10 per cent: the 2001 figure of more than £23 billion in remittances for this region may be worth more than $70 billion by 2012 (Rogers 2002). Remittances are so important to the current and future economy of many nations that they are now used as a valuation instrument to upgrade the credit-worthiness of impoverished countries to secure large-scale international loans (Guarnizo 2003).

Still, most experts on remittances argue that recipient groups and countries are not getting their full worth. Most formal financial transfer institutions charge a fee of 6 to 15 per cent and additional costs can make the total deduction over 20 per cent (Lowell and de la Garza 2000). Of Latin America's $23 billion in remittances in 2001, it is reckoned some $3 billion was lost in transfer fees (Rogers 2002). Government investigations, campaigns by non-government organizations (NGOs) and class action lawsuits have all focused on the often exorbitant fees charged by international transfer agencies like Western Union and MoneyGram. The high and uncertain costs of transfers are known to be the most serious concern voiced by remitters (Suro *et al.* 2002).

It is widely believed that the value of remittances would be much higher if the cost of transferring money was lower. A study of over 70 remittance companies demonstrates that improved and increased competition in the financial transfer sector would drive down the level of fees (Orozco 2002). Within Latin America, it is estimated that reducing the transfer costs to 5 per cent would free up more than $1 billion a year for some of the poorest, migrant background households in the USA (Suro *et al.* 2002). Some agencies are considering moves toward a flat fee rather than a percentage. There are currently a number of moves within government (such as the Wire Transfer Fairness and Disclosure Act of 1999), among NGOs and in financial institutions themselves to create more transparency in pricing and greater consumer awareness. While the Inter-American Development Bank and other international agencies have continued to hold conferences and promote money-saving policies in this field, President Bush and other Western Hemisphere leaders discussed lowering the price of migrant remittances during their summit of 2004, in 2006 the UN Secretary-General called for the reduction of transfer costs and the enhanced use of remittances for development purposes, and in 2007 the Global Campaign Against High Cost of Remittances was launched in the United States. Organized by immigrant communities including Mexicans, Salvadorans, Somalis, Kenyans and Filipinos, the Campaign calls for the adoption of

'Transnational Community Benefits Agreements' (TCBA) that would lower remittance fees, establish fairer exchange rates, and provide for community reinvestment.

New technologies might represent one important mechanism for reducing fees and other complications, too. In a detailed study of the spread and uses of mobile phones in Jamaica, Heather Horst and Daniel Miller (2006) demonstrate how communication technologies are becoming integral to the growth of remittance economies (see also Miller *et al.* 2005). Elsewhere, in 2007 Kenya's biggest mobile phone operator (Safaricom, part owned by Vodaphone) rolled out a new system called M-PESA, which is expected to revolutionize money transfers in a country where more than 80 per cent of people are excluded from the formal financial sector (Rice 2007). M-PESA entails transferring money between mobile phones using virtual accounts and widespread agents for cashing, with rates far below commercial banks.

> It is simply an extra line on your mobile phone menu that says: 'Send Money'. You go to an office, transfer funds onto your phone account, and then send them to your friends, or family, or anybody else with a mobile. Then, they go to an office, show the code on the mobile and some ID, and collect the cash.
>
> (Mason 2007)

In time M-PESA will allow people to make direct purchases, borrow and repay money. It is expected that the international remittance market will come to play a major part in this kind of system, and it is being watched closely by the multibillion dollar transfer industry.

Subsequently, Vodaphone and Citigroup announced a new mobile-based international money transfer service building upon M-PESA. Customers in the UK will first use the service to send money to Kenya on a trial basis; following this, the companies plan to focus on Eastern European and Asian remittance markets such as Poland and India. As the companies' press release describes it,

> Uniquely, the product being developed will allow the remitter and the beneficiary to choose from a range of options as to how the money is sent and received. The sender can initiate the transfer using either a mobile phone or a secure Internet website to give instructions on where to send the funds. The funds will be able to be received in a bank or through the receiver's mobile phone in the form of a voucher and secure PIN that will enable the

receiver to redeem the cash at a wide range of outlets, typically the airtime distribution points operated by the in-country mobile network service provider. For these latter services, the beneficiary does not need to have a bank account, will have a wide range of locations to collect the funds and only has to be in the possession of a mobile phone that can receive an SMS on any mobile network.

More money, effectively transferred, should have considerable consequences for those who get it. Given that recipients of remittances are largely in underdeveloped contexts, how can remittances contribute to broader economic development?

... and development

It is widely recognized that remittances by themselves are not a panacea for impoverishment. Indeed,

> remittances flowing to emigration areas often wind up producing what John Kenneth Galbraith called 'private affluence and public squalor', or new homes reachable only over dirt roads. What is clearly needed is some way of harnessing some fraction of the remittances in order to develop the infrastructure that can help a region develop economically.
>
> (Widgren and Martin 2002: 223)

Some advisers have suggested that migrant-sending countries could earmark, perhaps through an import tariff, a portion of remittances for a specific development fund. There have been failed attempts, however, to create such funds in the Philippines, Pakistan, Thailand and Bangladesh (Puri and Ritzema 1999). It is likely most migrants themselves are, or would be, sceptical of such schemes: this is due not only to anxieties over possible corruption, but to past experiences and frustrations with the ineffective, preferential or nonexistent development programmes of national governments and international agencies.

Susan Martin (2001: 5) asks, '[T]o what effect can the multiplier effect of remittances be increased by initiatives to encourage local purchase of locally produced goods'? Perhaps a more laissez-faire policy climate will suffice, such that migrants and their families can find the right ways to develop their communities themselves, albeit perhaps with some NGO advice, appropriate banking schemes and government support (but not control). Schemes and initiatives of these kinds are described below.

The multiplier effect involves a tricky equation, however. It is never clear as to what counts as cost, and what as benefit, and what as ultimately productive spending of remittances. For instance, remittance investment in housing is said to generate more multiplier effects than any other industry (Taylor 1999). But in Ecuador, for example, where some 95 per cent of remittances are spent on new housing, this expenditure fuelled substantial inflation in land prices and construction costs that had a negative impact on most of the local population (Rogers 2001c). In Egypt remittances are often used to purchase gold, which has a high cultural status value. This would appear to be a fairly non-productive use without multiplier effects. Yet in Egypt and many other settings, gold is locally regarded as a kind of insurance – something that will retain financial value in times of uncertainty and high inflation, which can be advantageously cashed in at a later date (Fouad Ibrahim, personal communication).

It should be borne in mind that 'development' should include not only matters of economic growth, but social (including gender, civil and democratic), health, environmental and technological issues. In many places one of the most common and extensive uses of remittance money is toward healthcare expenses (DeSipio 2000). Some NGOs are developing schemes to use remittances creatively to provide regular transnational health care coverage. A different kind of multiplier or 'protective effect' concerns the general development of health profiles among remittance-receiving families. Research by Reanne Frank and Robert Hummer (2002) points to a direct correlation indicating that infants in migrant-sending families are less likely to suffer infant death or to be of low birth weight – a key determinant in health outcomes later in life. Remittances offset the effects of poverty by raising standards of living, improving nutrition and facilitating access to medical care. It is conjectured that financial remittances are also likely to flow alongside what Levitt (2001b) calls social remittances (values and behaviours) – in this case health information and practices. Frank and Hummer (2002: 761) conclude that more attention should be given to 'how transnational activity affects the relationship between health and migration and in what ways'.

To more fully appreciate the impact of remittances on development, it must also be recognized that the implications of migration and remittances for development vary according to level of analysis, from individual to community, nation or state (Skeldon 1997). A kind of level or institutional structure linking these other levels can be found by way of migrant associations.

... and hometown associations

Hometown associations represent but one of a growing range of migrant transnational organizations and structures devoted to philanthropy and homeland development (see for instance Portes *et al.* 2007). There is a long history of migrant associations sending money for collective benefit in the home town or village. Nancy Foner (2000: 171–2) illustrates this by pointing to how, between 1914 and 1924, New York's Jewish *landsman-shaftn* or hometown associations sent millions of dollars to their war-ravaged home communities in Europe. Yet now 'we are seeing a very specific type of home-town association, one directly concerned with socio-economic development in its communities of origin and increasingly engaging both governmental and civic entities in sending and receiving countries in these projects' (Sassen 2002: 226).

There has been a marked growth in the number and function of migrant hometown associations (HTAs) throughout the 1990s (see for instance Lowell and de la Garza 2000, Orozco 2000a, 2001, Alarcón 2001). A concomitant change in HTA structures and roles has also been observed (Goldring 1998, Mahler 1998, Alarcón 2001, Levitt 2001a, S.F. Martin 2001). Their significance should not be underestimated. One study in Los Angeles found that 'HTAs are clearly the most numerous and ubiquitous form of voluntary organization among first generation immigrants' (Zabin and Rabadan 1998: 1). Furthermore, HTAs represent the clearest form of institutionalization of transnational ties (Orozco 2001).

Manuel Orozco (2000a) contends that HTAs exhibit at least four features. They conduct a range of activities, from charitable aid to investment; their structures vary; their decisions depend on factors such as resource base, organizational structure and relationship with hometown; and they tend to have a small economic base. HTA activities embrace charitable work such as donating clothes, goods for religious festivals and construction materials for repairing the town church. They raise money for improving infrastructure such as sewage treatment plants and health-care facilities. They support educational institutions, such as providing scholarships and library books. Yet another kind of HTA activity involves managing collective capital investment for income-generating projects in sending contexts that are often co-managed by locals and migrants (Orozco 2000b, World Bank 2001). HTAs also play a significant role in organizing disaster relief following catastrophes such as Hurricane Mitch in Central America in 1998 and the earthquakes in Turkey in 1999 and Gujarat in 2001 (Rogers 2001b).

HTAs are not of a single kind, nor are they the only mode of migrant transnationalism involved in collective remittance sending. Caroline Ndofor-Tah identifies a range of diasporic organizations involved in African development, including hometown associations, ethnic associations, alumni associations, religious associations, professional associations, investment groups, political groups and supplementary schools (in Mohan and Zack-Williams 2002). Their activities include community-to-community transfers, identity-building, lobbying in current homeland on issues related to the original homeland, trade and investment with homeland, and payment of taxes in the homeland. Whatever the form of collective remitting, Alejandro Portes and Patricia Landolt (2000: 543) conclude,

> Life conditions in municipalities that receive grassroots transnational aid confirm the relevance of this collective remittance strategy. Towns with a hometown association have paved roads, electricity, and fresher painted public buildings. The quality of life in transnational towns is simply better.

'Consider the Salvadoran "United Community of Chinameca": their first largesse was $5,000 to build a school, and then they built a septic tank worth $10,000. Later they constructed a Red Cross clinic at a cost of $43,000, and bought an ambulance worth $32,000' (Lowell and de la Garza 2000: 2). Hagan (1994) likewise describes how a hometown group in Houston, calling themselves *Amigos de San Pedro*, organized and paid for medical supplies and a health clinic in San Pedro, Guatemala. They also established organization linkages and exchange programmes with American health workers. Another noteworthy case is the University of Hargeisa, established in 1998 in Somaliland (Mohan 2002). This was made possible by transnational networking of Somalis in Australia, Italy, Sweden, Kuwait, Canada, the USA and Britain. While local businesses in Somaliland took responsibility for rehabilitating a dilapidated, government-owned school building, Somalis in Sweden provided 750 chairs and tables and Somalis in Kuwait provided computers. The Somaliland Forum, an Internet-based diasporic network, raises money, maintains email groups and forms taskforces to support the University.

Such forms of migrant transnational organization are so importantly engaged in local development that, R.C. Smith (1998: 227–8) believes, they are generating 'parallel power structures' and 'forcing the state to engage them in new ways, either in kind or degree, but engage the state they must'. Some state and local governments match the funds raised by HTAs in order to magnify their impact (Martin 2001). Since 1993, one of the most noted programmes of this type has been the 'two for one' initiative of the *Programa para las Comunidades Mexicanas en el Extranjero* (PCME, Program for Mexican Communities Abroad; see Goldring 1998, 2001, R.C. Smith 1998, Mahler 2000). The programme operates through a network of 42 consulates and 23 institutes or Mexican cultural centres in the USA (Orozco 2001). The idea of 'two for one' is that for every dollar raised by a hometown association abroad, the state (e.g. of Zacatecas) and the federal government each put in a dollar for a community project. In 1995 in Zacatecas alone the 'two for one' programme added to the HTAs' $600,000 to provide $1.8 million towards 56 projects in 34 Mexican towns (Mahler 1998).

'Two for one' was subsequently extended to a 'three for one' programme, in which each migradollar is matched with one dollar from the federal government, one from the state government and one from the municipal government. Between 1999 and 2001, migrants invested $2.7 million in such programmes (World Bank 2001). Despite some limitations, these initiatives in Mexico 'have produced a deep impact in the local communities and have been recognized as new and effective forms of public–private collaboration' (ibid.: 6). The ultimate objective, according to World Bank analysts, would be

> to develop a self-sustainable private system for the development of projects and local programs financed totally or partially with remittances and savings from the Mexican community abroad. Available funds of international cooperation could be used for supporting some of the initiatives.
>
> (ibid.: 7)

HTAs are not the only players in these kinds of schemes. Financial services firms such as Raza Express have joined in, contributing $0.75 to the collective funds for each $300 sent through their company. In this way Raza Express has contributed more than $50,000, alongside $500,000 from the government of Jalisco, in schemes creating 15,000 jobs (Orozco 2001).

The collective remittance work of HTAs for development is not entirely rosy, however. Disagreements on how to use the funds raised by HTAs are endemic. For example, the association from Jalpa, a town of 13,500 in the state of Zacatecas, raised $2 million, but got into a serious dispute over how to spend the money in Jalpa (*Migration News*, December 2002). Sarah Mahler (1998) and Luin Goldring (2001) both emphasize that while HTAs enjoy a veneer of altruism and democratic structure, they often significantly exclude women, reinforce existing power relations within a community, sometimes promote projects which are not the most needed but which generate the most symbolic power, and may be open to cooption and exploitation by government.

The relationship between HTAs and the state of origin are not unproblematic, either. HTAs might be 'left doing the lion's share of the government's work' in development while the government itself steps back from this responsibility (Levitt 2001a: 209). Mahler (2000) predicts that in Central America the region will see an ever-increasing amount of government activity concerning emigrants abroad, particularly regarding their remittances. 'While such efforts are comprehensible,' she says (ibid.: 32), 'they are drawing increasing criticism because they place responsibility for Central America's economic stability disproportionately on the shoulders of migrants'. Moreover, the more governments attempt to control and channel remittances, the more migrants are pushed toward remitting via unofficial means (Meyers 1998).

In proportion to total remittances sent through families, collective remittances channelled through HTAs and other migrant transnational frameworks are small – although likely to increase (Orozco 2001). Despite this fact, and that of the sometimes problematic nature of such organizations and their relationship to the state, the forms of institutionalization they represent have much valuable potential for effectively directing remittances to highly needed and effective forms of local development. Other, newer forms of institutionalization in the shape of microfinance present important possibilities as well.

... and micro-finance

Taylor (1999: 74) usefully proposes that

> Migration is likely to have a larger effect on development where local institutions exist to gather savings by migrant households and make them

available to local producers – that is, where migrants do not have to play the simultaneous roles of workers, savers, investors, and producers.

National governments have sought to establish economic schemes, such as special investment funds or savings accounts, to channel remittances and encourage business development. These have met with very mixed results (Puri and Ritzema 1999).

Micro-finance institutions (MFIs) offer prospects for channelling migrant remittances in ways similar to those suggested by Taylor. The idea of MFIs began in the 1970s but took off among development agencies and researchers throughout the 1990s. More recently there has occurred what Marguerite Robinson (2001) describes as 'a paradigm shift' in micro-finance development strategies, from government- or donor-subsidized credit delivery systems to self-sufficient institutions providing finance on very local levels. MFIs have the potential to meet a massive global demand for local banking services that many governments and donor agencies increasingly recognize as a priority (ibid.; see also www.microfinancegateway.org).

A core function of MFIs is to provide small, low-interest loans (micro-credit, e.g. from $10 to $3,000) and savings services to poor families – and often specifically to women, who ordinarily do not have access to formal financial institutions. Such loans are to help people engage in productive activities (involving, for instance, small farms, petty trading, craft enterprises or local business). MFIs offer credit, savings and insurance in often remote rural areas. They may also give financial and business advice and training. Many MFIs are non-profit NGOs, credit unions or cooperatives; there are also new commercial MFIs. Currently augmented by new information technologies, MFIs are growing in number, extent and function throughout the developing world.

One critical problem facing 'the micro-finance revolution' is scarcity of capital (M. Robinson 2001). Therefore channelled remittances – especially pooled funds represented by HTAs – can go a long way toward supporting the establishment and work of MFIs. In contrast to rural credit programmes which earlier absorbed large sums of money over several decades, many relevant agencies – such as the International Labour Organization, the World Bank and the Inter-American Development Bank – are increasingly interested in the potential interface between remittances and MFIs. The Multilateral Investment Fund of the Inter-American Development Bank promotes and funds initiatives that will allow emigrants to invest their money in development projects in places of origin. In 2001 the Fund extended a grant of $1.1 million to support projects in Mexico facilitating the linkage of remittance transfers, local financial services and productive investments by migrants and their families. A further six such projects have been developed in 2002.

At one workshop on these issues convened by the International Labour Organization (ILO 2000: 15), it was agreed that micro-finance institutions

> appear particularly well suited to capture and transform remittances for several reasons: (i) they deal with small-scale transactions where personal relations were important, (ii) they extensively involve groups and associations of intermediaries and (iii) they integrate the formal and the informal sector practices.

The ILO workshop group also advocated a number of additional factors that should contribute to the successful linkage of MFIs and remittances, including the provision of a large number of local contact points, a wide range of financial services products at the local level, and the widening of partnerships between micro-finance institutions and other organizations. The ILO group also believed that governments should at best mainly observe, but also act to create a positive regulatory framework and ideally provide matching funds to stimulate the use of MFIs for routing remittances for local community development.

Shivani Puri and Tineke Ritzema (1999: 25) suggest in a report to the ILO that,

> rather than focusing on 'migrant-specific' investment programmes, labour exporting countries might wish to induce micro-finance institutions to capture remittances. The basic idea would be to design policies to transfer funds of the migrant workers through to entrepreneurs. Savings and credit schemes and investment instruments specifically designed to suit migrant workers' risk profiles could be important vehicles.

Puri and Ritzema emphasize that labour-exporting countries would benefit from policies and programmes that enable micro-finance institutions that are trusted at the village level to play a key role in directing remittances, thus ensuring that families have access to safe and secure savings and credit schemes as well as business skill development programmes.

One of the best ways to achieve remittance-MFI benefits may be through credit unions, who would use any transfer fees to reinvest in community development (Martin 2001). Especially in comparison to banks and financial transfer agencies, credit unions are shown to offer some of the best practices in remitting opportunities to migrants (Orozco 2002). In fact, the World Council of Credit Unions has established the International Remittance Network, or IRNet (Grace 2001). Set up originally in cooperation with the Mexican government, this should enable credit union members to use IRNet's money-transfer services to 41 countries at one-third to one-half the commercial cost (Rogers 2001a). Indeed, IRNet charges less than $7 for most transactions. The use of credit unions can also provide needed access to savings, loans and insurance services, as well as broadly to 'increase the culture of banking' in both migrant-sending and -receiving countries (Grace 2001: 4). This may represent a particularly significant transformation, as research shows that many if not 'most remittance senders and receivers do not currently have bank accounts of any sort and probably never have had' (Suro *et al.* 2002: 17).

Another set of proposals seeks largely to cut out the financial middleman altogether. In 2002 the Bank of America began a low-cost service that allows people to use tellers, phone calls or the Internet to send money to relatives in Mexico, who in turn can get cash from any of the 20,000 automated-teller machines throughout the country (Wessel 2002). Naturally, this idea is only good for those with realistic access to such machines. A further idea is that of creating 'telecenters-cum-microbanks' in an array of village localities (S. Robinson 2001). In this way, it is proposed that a collectively managed and secure system of digital remittance pooling through Internet satellite facilities could considerably lower the transfer cost (from currently sometimes 20 per cent down to perhaps 5 per cent) while providing rural areas with microcredit and banking services. These centres might be appendices to established credit unions or local savings and loan institutions. 'On the back side of each village microbank is a telecenter – a public, low-cost access point for Internet and IP services, including telephony' (ibid.: 4). These could have a role in local institutions and training programmes, especially as auxiliaries to schools, continuous education colleges, and health clinics.

Bangladesh's Grameen Bank is often regarded as an exemplary MFI (cf. M. Robinson 2001, Jain and Moore 2003) – Grameen Bank and its founder, Muhammad Yunas, shared the Nobel Peace Prize in 2006. Grameen Bank provides services for 2.4 million borrowers – 95 per cent of whom are women – through 1,176 outlets. In recent years the bank has branched out into a variety of enterprises, including telecommunications (and the 'village phone' programme mentioned earlier). The combined facilities for micro-banking, overseas transfers and international telephony have great development potential, as concluded by one report for the Canadian International Development Agency:

> The Grameen Bank's long-term focus on providing electronic communication facilities between its head office, zonal offices and branch offices, together with the telecommunication infrastructure of GrameenPhone, are important steps in enabling it to provide safe electronic banking services that could assist with channelling remittances from overseas workers to their relatives in villages.
>
> (Richardson *et al.* 2000: 28)

MFIs are certainly not a solution to all economic problems in developing countries, and they are not without their problems and failures (cf. Jain and Moore 2003). Nevertheless MFIs and the innovations in technology surrounding them have much transformative potential steering remittances – perhaps particularly collective ones – toward optimal development outcomes.

Drawing on a variety of studies for the Inter-American Development Bank, Orozco (2001: 36) observes that '[t]he links established through remittances suggest radical changes are remaking the look of countries' economies'. Migrant-sending countries themselves certainly recognize this. Consequently, many have introduced policies to maximize their benefits; in this way, '[c]ooperation to increase remittances, reduce the cost of transferring money, and matching that share of remittances that are invested could open a new era in cooperative economic development' (Widgren and Martin 2002: 223).

The local and national economies of developing countries are changing for a variety of concurrent reasons, from the growing power of multilateral economic regimes and shifting international aid policies, through changing commodity markets and emerging patterns of global tourism, to expanding sources and impacts of foreign direct investment. This section has focused on ways in which patterns of migrant transnationalism – particularly surrounding remittances – are contributing to the re-institutionalizing of local and national structures of development. Throughout many periods of migration hometown associations have sent money back to villages for the repair of schools and churches. Now the sheer scale, kind and degree of institutionalization (increasingly involving HTAs and the sending state), along with the use of advanced telecommunications and new methods of financial transfer, have meant that remittances can transform the nature and pace of local development in migrant-sending areas by, among other things, constructing infrastructures, providing equipment and offering finance for enterprise.

Some observers have wondered whether the flow of remittances has peaked (see *The Economist* 2008). In 2007, for instance, remittances to Mexico dropped by 6 per cent while in Brazil they dropped by 4 per cent; in Turkey remittances dropped from a peak of $5.3 billion in 1998 to $951 million in 2005. Some experts blame tougher immigration controls at the border, meaning migrants are less likely to circulate transnationally (and therefore to invest assets in their home country) and more likely to settle in the country of immigration. Other experts suggest that earlier estimates were exaggerations, and that now authorities are much better at counting remittance flows so that the new figures are not actually reductions but truer data (*The Economist* 2007b).

Such issues underline several significant questions that continue to concern the place of remittances in national development. These include how long remittances will continue to flow, and whether high levels of international migration are needed to sustain remittance levels and thereby national social and economic development. Most remittances worldwide continue to be sent by individuals, and these may indeed tail off over time. Although this source of remittances will diminish, HTA or other forms of institutionalized collective remittance-sending – perhaps increasingly utilizing micro-finance institutions – may be better poised to persist and provide the broadest benefits directly to migrant-sending communities.

Remittance questions lead to a further, currently hot question: instead of having a system in which migrants' money flows one way from migrant-receiving to migrant-sending contexts, what about a system of transnationalism in which the workers themselves move systematically back and forth?

CIRCULAR MIGRATION

Circular migration appears to be all the rage in international policy circles. A variety of policy-makers within national and international institutions are advocating measures to facilitate the movement of migrants to and fro between their homelands and foreign places of work. Their main idea is that circular migration systems could be managed in ways that bring proverbial 'win–win–win' results (i.e. benefits for receiving countries through meeting labour market shortages, for sending countries through guaranteeing remittances for development, and for migrants themselves through offering employment and control over the use of their wages). Circular migration is also being advocated as a potential solution (at least in part) to a number of challenges surrounding contemporary migration. What are policy-makers suggesting, why now, and what should we bear in mind if circular migration is indeed to be the way forward in global policy?

Much of the interest in circular migration stems from the way that migration itself is now widely understood. These days many academics and policy-makers alike comprehend migration largely through a paradigm that emphasizes the importance of border-crossing social networks – that is, transnationalism. As we have discussed throughout this book, migration scholars have increasingly studied migrant transnationalism over the past 15 years or more; yet recently policy-makers too have come to recognize the ways that transnational ties condition migration processes. This shift largely came through a rather sudden realization that remittances have become a major global economic resource.

Subsequently there has been widespread interest in the roles that national, bi- or multi-national and international policies can play in fostering and managing various dimensions of migrant transnationalism. Alongside national governments, several international agencies, intergovernmental forums and government departments are now drafting policies surrounding the relationship between migration and development (especially concerning the transfer and use of remittances), the activities of migrant hometown associations (mostly regarding support for specific development projects), and ways to 'tap' diasporas for various purposes (mainly through philanthropy, entrepreneurship or political lobbying). Similarly, policy-makers have acknowledged transnational connections in their efforts to create policies to reverse the impact of 'brain drain' by facilitating 'brain circulation' of professionals through temporary return visits or through 'virtual return' over telecommunication systems.

Circular migration patterns themselves are based on, and create further, transnational networks. The current policy turn – or better, re-turn (see below) – to temporary and circular migration policies stems in large part from the relatively recent recognition of the significance of migrant transnational practices. Indeed, most of the policy documents cited below preface their remarks on circular migration with statements acknowledging the prevalence, ubiquity and significance of transnational practices among migrants today.

A look at several recent documents produced by international and national agencies shows not only the prominence of circular migration as a preferred, forward-looking mode of migration management, but also the diversity of issues which circular migration policies might also address.

The Global Commission on International Migration (GCIM), established by the then UN Secretary General Kofi Annan, published its Report after two years of extensive consultations (GCIM 2005). As part of its comprehensive overview, the GCIM noted how 'the old paradigm of permanent migrant settlement is progressively giving way to temporary and circular migration. ... The Commission underlined the need to grasp the developmental opportunities that this important shift in migration patterns provides for countries of origin' (ibid.: 31). In order to make the most of this shift, the GCIM recommended that 'countries of destination can promote circular migration by providing mechanisms and channels that enable migrants to move relatively easily between their country of origin and destination' (ibid.). In keeping with its terms of reference, the GCIM did not offer much more on this topic by way of suggesting specific measures or potential impacts.

In 'World Migration 2005', the International Organization for Migration (IOM) also proposed that more circular migration could bring benefits, especially to developing countries (IOM 2005). The IOM advocated that migrant-receiving countries should open up more avenues for regular, repeat temporary labour migration and give incentives to migrants by offering future return to the same job. It also suggested that making residence or dual citizenship available to certain migrants and establishing more flexible visa regimes would act as encouragements to productive, free exchange between countries.

The World Bank's Europe and Central Asia Region section has produced a major study on international labour migration in Eastern Europe and the former Soviet Union (World Bank 2006). Here, interest in circular migration goes beyond economic development of migrant-sending contexts. This report suggested that managed circular migration might increase broad opportunities for trade and investment linkages, reduce 'brain drain' by facilitating the international transfer of skills, and reduce negative social and familial consequences associated with illegal migration. It is also noteworthy that, in advocating circular migration, the World Bank was not suggesting that such systems will necessarily provide superior economic benefits; rather, it pragmatically proposed that circular migration might be a more palatable idea in places where public opinion is strongly resistant to migration of the unskilled.

In 2005 the European Commission addressed circular migration in two documents. The first, the 'Communication on Migration and Development' (EC 2005a), proposed that circular migration policies could play a key role in fostering the transfer of skills to the developing world (ibid.: 25). This paper also advocated that:

> policies to maximise the developmental impact of temporary migration ... should focus on encouraging circular migration, by giving a priority for further temporary employment to workers who have already worked under such schemes and have returned at the end of their contract, and also by offering appropriate rewards to participating migrants.
>
> (ibid.: 7)

This document reiterated general calls elsewhere, but added a degree of specificity by suggesting such employment priority measures could be EU policy.

The second document, the Commission's 'Policy Plan on Legal Migration' (EC 2005b), outlined at least three possible measures that could enable viable, managed circular migration systems: the provision of long-term multi-entry visas for returning migrants; an understanding that former migrants be given priority for obtaining new residence permits for further temporary employment under a simplified procedure; and the creation of an EU database of third-country nationals who left the EU at the expiration of their temporary residence or work permit. Again, a broad interest in circular migration and its benefits were taken a step further by way of proposing specific policy instruments.

A final policy document to consider comes from the United Kingdom. Following a lengthy review process, the House of Commons International Development Committee published its Report entitled 'Migration and Development: How to make migration work for poverty reduction' (House of Commons 2004). 'The UK Government,' it says, 'should explore the potential development benefits which might be gained from more circular migration, and – alongside its developing country partners – should examine the different ways in which such circular migration might be encouraged' (ibid.: 48). Interestingly, the Committee approaches circular migration from a rather different vantage point when it recommended that in sectors such as health, policies could be created so as 'to help migrants to return home temporarily by offering leave of absence from employment and other forms of assistance' (ibid.: 88). Here circular migration is envisioned as taking place from the receiving country to the sending country and back, rather than the other way around. The Committee's advice also went beyond that of other agencies by suggesting that circular migration schemes could act as an incentive for sending countries to assume more responsibility for countering illegal migration.

To recap, many policy-focused agencies are promoting the creation of managed circular migration systems. Perceived potential benefits include: (a) with reference to the interests of migrant sending states, encouraging circulation of human capital and ensuring flow of remittances for development; and (b) with reference to the interests of migrant receiving states, plugging sectoral labour shortages, ensuring that temporary migrants leave, and mitigating illegal migration. We might also add: (c) with reference to employers' interests, recruiting from a known and reliable pool of workers, retaining trained and experienced people, and keeping wages low.

What about the migrants themselves? What does circular migration hold for them? It is important to underscore the fact that circular migration represents an age-old pattern of mobility, whether rural–urban or cross-border (see e.g. Elkan 1967, Chapman 1979, Cordell *et al.* 1996). Such patterns have varyingly been called repeat, rotating, multiple, seasonal, cyclical, shuttling, or circuit-based modes of migration. Most research on circular migration patterns has examined what we might call 'unregulated' systems – that is, migration flows that have been established by migrants themselves between homelands and places of work, as opposed to formal or regulated systems by which employers and states collaborate to recruit, transport and employ workers from abroad. Based on such research (including D.S. Massey 1987, D.S. Massey and Espinosa 1997, Duany 2002, and Constant and Zimmerman 2004), the following traits seem evident.

In today's world a considerable proportion of migrants are not 'first movers'; many have made multiple trips within their home country and abroad (from across a near border to indeed across the world) in order to work. Moreover, frequency matters: studies indicate that there is an increasing probability of making repeat moves the more an individual has already moved. This finding underscores what, in migration theory, is known as the self-perpetuating nature of migration. With each move, migrants learn more about migration, where and how to find jobs and housing, and so on. Such knowledge, sets of social connections and experience is also referred to as 'migration-specific capital': the more you have of this, the less risk you face moving, the lower the costs and the better the chances of success – all factors encouraging circular migration.

Further, after a few moves, it seems that a migrant's legal status is not relevant to the likelihood of repeat movement. Once people learn how to cross borders (or have established reliable facilitators to help them cross), they are less concerned with whether they go legally or not. The exception comes with rising human capital: as people gain skills and experience that may allow them to progress in terms of socio-economic mobility, they become more concerned with being legal. The likelihood of circular migration also depends on social traits. Repeat movements are likeliest among young, unmarried men; this likelihood falls with marriage, and increases again with children. However, when migrants have children in school (particularly in receiving contexts), they are less likely to engage in circular migration. Dual citizens are more likely to circulate – not surprisingly, since they generally can do this with little hassle at the border.

Of special note with regard to the development agenda behind much emerging policy, circular migrants tend to remit more money to their home localities. This finding makes sense given that circular migrants plan to return in the near future in order to make use of these posted earnings themselves. And does circular migration increase or diminish opportunities for socio-economic mobility? Here social scientists come up with contrary analyses. Some researchers suggest that the experience and money obtained abroad does give migrants scope to get better jobs (either in the homeland or receiving context); others say that circular migrants tend to remain stuck in low levels of employment, such as seasonal agricultural labourers. This might particularly be the case in regulated circular migration systems, which see people returning year after year to the same job rather than trying to negotiate their way into better jobs and localities like unregulated circular migrants might do.

Examining one well-known, regulated system of circular migration, Tanya Basok's (2003) study of the Canadian Mexican Seasonal Workers Programme importantly shows contrasting dimensions of such schemes.

Basok demonstrates that the Programme provides undoubtedly positive development benefits in migrants' homelands. The circular migrants on this scheme invest their earnings in land, business, children's education, housing and medical treatment. More widely, their remittances stimulate local economic growth around their villages and towns in Mexico. While working in Canada, they might be doing the same low-level work; back in Mexico, they might be building a business. However, Basok points out (ibid.: 20),

> in order to maintain the lifestyle which these migrants and their households enjoy, migrant workers need to continue participating in the Canadian guest worker programme for many years and this dependency forces them to accept various forms of abuse by Canadian growers.

Contemporary calls for the policy-systematization of circular migration may well address many of the various issues raised in the documents discussed above. For migrants themselves, the rolling out of more circular migration schemes may indeed bring considerable benefits. However, as with other kinds of temporary migration policies (cf. P.L. Martin 2003, 2005, Ruhs 2005), there are a number of concerns to bear in mind when designing circular migration policies. These include questions such as:

- Will migrant workers get 'locked-in' to modes of dependency and exploitative relationships with employers?
- Will circular migrants' work permits be non-portable (i.e. restricted to specific employers or sectors), thereby increasing chances of exploitation and lessening chances of socio-economic mobility?
- Will policy-regulated circular migration systems become closed labour markets, with limited opportunities for access among new would-be migrants?
- Since any temporary migration scheme will only function if migrants indeed return after their statutory period of employment, will enforcement mechanisms become more draconian?
- Since circular or other temporary migrants will be required to leave after short stays, will this preclude any kind of 'integration' strategies for them (including language training or information about living in the society of reception)? Consequently, will lack of integration strategies make migrants more vulnerable, socially excluded and geographically segregated?

- Again, since they will have to leave after a time, will there be no chances for circular migrants to naturalize (and, in doing, gain dual citizenship which would help them 'circulate' more easily)?
- Even given creation of ideal circular migration policies and systems, will it not remain cheaper and less bureaucratically burdensome for employers simply to continue hiring undocumented migrants? Or will tough employer sanctions be put in place to mitigate against this at the same time as circular migration schemes are rolled out?

A final question arises when considering the current popularity of circular migration in policy circles. Haven't such schemes, such as the American *bracero* programme and the German *Gastarbeiter* system, all been tried – and dropped – a long time ago? This question is directly addressed by Stephen Castles (2006), who answers both 'yes' and 'no'. He details how, while they do indeed share important features in common, current approaches are significantly different from the well known pre-1974 temporary migration policies.

Why are many policy-makers specifically calling for circular migration now? There are surely numerous reasons (again see Castles 2006) but at least four can be drawn from the documents considered above:

1 Recognition of the prevalence and importance of transnational practices among migrants has spurred new thinking, especially about remittances and the developmental potential of organized migrant labour schemes.

2 The 'win–win–win' mantra is being taken seriously, again especially around migration and development. Circular migration appears to be a readily available option to provide immediate three-way benefits.

3 Circular and other temporary forms of migration are considered by policy-makers to be more amenable to public opinion, which has clearly and increasingly hardened against migration in most parts of the developed world.

4 Many policy-makers believe they now have the technical know-how (such as 'e-borders', Advance Passenger Information Systems, and large shared databases) that would potentially enable them to keep track of numerous eligible migrants as they come and go between homelands and foreign places of work. It remains to be seen whether these lines of reasoning will prove sufficient to roll out new international guidelines and schemes.

For sending countries, receiving countries and migrants themselves, mutual gains may indeed be had if circular migration policies become manifest. Moreover, as recent policy documents suggest, circular migration policies might positively contribute to tackling challenges around economic development, labour shortages, public opinion and illegal migration. Yet when considering anything – particularly an approach to global policy – that claims to be a kind of magic bullet, caution should certainly be taken. The 'wins' of the win–win–win scenario may not be as mutual as imagined.

Nevertheless, it is interesting to observe how national and international policy-makers have come to recognize and are attempting to harness migrant transnationalism – particularly its multiple economic dimensions.

6

RELIGIOUS
TRANSFORMATIONS

Just as in the domains described in previous chapters, migrant transnational practices involve, or have marked impacts upon, religious phenomena. This includes patterns of organization, personal and group identities, intergroup relations, modes of practice and even elements of faith. However, many profound patterns of change or structural transformation affecting religion among migrants also occur prior to the effects of transnationalism. Therefore, in order to attempt a better understanding of processes of change and variable stimuli prompting or conditioning such processes, it is worthwhile to distil different dynamics or levels of such religious change.

The following chapter surveys a range of literature in order: (a) to outline some of the understandings of 'diaspora' that have developed since the 1990s, (b) to argue that current 'diaspora' concepts often suffer from conflation with 'migration', 'minority' and 'transnationalism', and that each of these areas of study involve distinct – albeit related – dynamics of religious transformation, and (c) to indicate some patterns of religious change in connection with each of these concepts.

MEANINGS OF DIASPORA

Although I have invoked the notion of diaspora intermittently throughout this book, a more focused discussion of the term is warranted in this chapter because I want to distinguish – here, with regard to religious matters – certain features and processes from those we might associate with migration, minority status and transnational practices.

Since the 1990s – parallel to the boom in transnationalism studies – there has been a proliferation of literature and a mushrooming of interest, among members of ethnic minority groups as well as among academics, surrounding the notion of 'diaspora'. Historians and social scientists describe myriad facets of diaspora, while an ever-increasing number of self-conscious communities call themselves diasporas. 'Where once were dispersions,' Kachig Tölölyan (1996: 3) observes, 'there now is diaspora'. Indeed, as James Clifford (1994: 306) writes,

> For better or worse, diaspora discourse is being widely appropriated. It is loose in the world, for reasons having to do with decolonisation, increased immigration, global communication and transport – a whole range of phenomena that encourage multi-locale attachments, dwelling, and travelling within and across nations.

Or, in other words, 'diaspora' has become 'one of the buzzwords of the postmodern age' (P. Cohen 1999: 3; cf. K. Mitchell 1997a).

Most recent works on the concept of diaspora naturally commence with a few statements on etymology (for example, Tölölyan 1996, R. Cohen 1997, Baumann 2000). The word 'diaspora' derives from the Greek *diaspeirō* 'to distribute'; it is a compound of *speirō*, 'to sow, to scatter' like seed, and *dia-* 'from one end to the other'. The term has of course become associated with the Jewish historical experience, and hence is associated with being a dispersed people sharing a common religious and cultural heritage.

However, the Hebrew verb *galah* and noun *galut* – each expressing deportation and exile – perhaps convey the experience more accurately from the Jewish perspective. '[I]t is this close relationship between exile and consciousness of exile that is the singular feature of Jewish history; it is that which, over the centuries of migrations and vicissitudes, kept Jewish national consciousness alive' (Marienstras 1989: 120). *Galut* broadly designates the period from the destruction of the second Temple in 70 AD until the creation of the state of Israel. Hence a distinction is made by a number of scholars between *diaspora* – implying free movement, and especially pertaining to ancient Jews living among Greeks (Modrzejewski 1993) – and *galut*, implying involuntary movement due to a conquest of the territory that was/is considered home (Marienstras 1989).

Nevertheless, the overall Jewish history of displacement has embodied the long-standing, conventional meaning of diaspora. Martin Baumann (1995) indicates that there have been at least three inherent, and rather different, referential points with respect to what we refer to as the Jewish (or any other group's) historical experience 'in the diaspora'. That is, when we say something has taken place 'in the diaspora' we must clarify whether we refer to (a) the *process* of becoming scattered, (b) the *community* living in foreign parts, or (c) the *place* or geographic *space* in which the dispersed groups live. The kind of conceptual muddle that may arise from the failure to distinguish these dimensions continues to plague the many more recently emergent meanings of the notion of diaspora.

Academics have, in the term diaspora, found a useful concept through which to reorganize their research interests. This cuts across disciplines. The term has proliferated in conferences and publications within Anthropology, Sociology, Cultural Studies and Political Science. In 1999, by way of further example, the American Historical Association (AHA) held its annual conference on the theme 'Diasporas and Migrations in History'. The Chairman of the organizing committee, John O. Voll, said he received literally hundreds of session proposals and was surprised by their diversity: 'Everywhere we looked, in almost every sub-field, people wanted to talk about diasporas,' he said (in Winkler 1999). However, not all of his colleagues welcomed the trendy topic: at the opening plenary of the 1999 AHA meeting, Colin A. Palmer opined that, '[d]iaspora is a problem that invites a great deal of methodological fuzziness, ahistorical claims, and even romantic condescension' (in Winkler 1999).

Another account of the growing popularity of the term comes from Kachig Tölölyan, the editor of the academic journal entitled *Diaspora*. Tölölyan (1996: 3) has witnessed the fact that '[t]he rapidity of material and discursive change in the past three decades has increased both the number of global diasporas and the range and diversity of the new semantic domain that the term 'diaspora' inhabits'. Once, as it were, there were three 'classic diasporas' studied by social scientists – the Jewish, Greek and Armenian. By 1998 (only seven years after its launch), Tölölyan's journal had covered no less than 36 communities who had been identified by academics as, or who have called themselves, 'diasporas' (Kachig

Tölölyan, personal communication). These number pale in comparison to other examples of the discursive expansion of 'diaspora' in the public sphere. At the time of writing this chapter, a simple Google search of the Internet turned up no less than 10,600,000 hits for the term 'diaspora'. Irish, 'African', Chinese, Filipino, Indian, Arab, Tamil, Ukrainian, Iranian, Slovak – even Baganda, Anasazi, and Tongan – diasporas appear prominently with their own web pages along with numerous ones devoted to the 'classic' Jewish, Greek and Armenian diasporas. Erica McClure (2000) found 650 websites for the little known Assyrian (Iraqi Christian) diaspora alone.

Why has there been such a shift of discursive category, particularly as a self-definition among dispersed groups? After all, drawing on the Jewish model, diaspora has arguably been a notion associated with suffering, loss, and victimization. Do contemporary, globally scattered communities opt to characterize themselves in this way?

One reason for the term's appeal to a range of groups lies in its relevance to addressing, in a summary fashion, a core dilemma faced by any dispersed or transplanted people: how to survive as a group. Here, J.D. Cohen Shaye and Ernst S. Frerichs (1993: i) underscore the nature of diaspora in the ancient world and signal its continued pertinence to the present:

> The contemporary common usage of the word 'diaspora' which links the word to the experience of the Jewish people in their exile to Babylon and their dispersion throughout the Mediterranean world, is too exclusive an application. Viewed as a mass migration or movement or flight from one location or locations, diaspora could be viewed as an event in the history of several peoples of antiquity. Clearly the fact of dispersion and its many consequences have been an experience of many people, ancient and modern. Major issues for investigation include the question of whether, and how, those 'dispersed' peoples maintain a sense of self-identity and a measure of communal cohesion. The central question for diaspora peoples is adaptation: how to adapt to the environment without surrendering group identity. These questions faced by the diaspora communities of antiquity are still apparent in modern times.

Further, the groups who now describe themselves as diasporas have wholly reappropriated and redefined the term as a new tool in cultural politics (P. Cohen 1999). Diaspora discourse has been adopted to move collective identity claims and community self-ascriptions beyond multiculturalism and beyond its related 'impasse' involving 'the notions of "racial and ethnic minorities" created with their emphasis on inter-group processes and their static notions of culture and difference' (Anthias 1998: 576). Diaspora has arisen as part of the postmodern project of resisting the nation-state, which is perceived as hegemonic, discriminatory and culturally homogenizing. The alternative agenda – now often associated with the notion of diaspora – advocates the recognition of hybridity, multiple identities and affiliations with people, causes and traditions outside the nation-state of residence. 'Diasporic identity has become an occasion for the celebration of multiplicity and mobility – and a figure of our discontent with our being in a world apparently still dominated by nation-states' (Tölölyan 1996: 28).

Overall, during the past few years the term diaspora has become a loose reference confusing categories such as immigrants, guest-workers, ethnic and 'racial' minorities, refugees, expatriates and travellers. In fact, 'the word diaspora is used today to describe any community that has emigrated whose numbers make it visible in the host community' (Marienstras 1989: 125). Among academics and 'community leaders' alike, the over-use and under-theorization of the notion of diaspora threatens the term's descriptive usefulness (Safran 1991, R. Cohen 1995, Vertovec 1999a).

In his seminal volume *Global Diasporas* (1997), Robin Cohen seeks to clarify and typologize the relationship between the, as it were, original conceptualizations of the term as it applied to Jews and the contemporary extensions of the term often made to and by other groups who are dispersed worldwide. He undertakes his project with the view that '[a]ll scholars of diaspora recognize that the Jewish tradition is at the heart of any definition of the concept. Yet if it is necessary to take full account of this tradition, it is also necessary to transcend it' (1997: 21). He accepts that there will be 'inevitable dilutions, changes and expansions of the meaning of the term diaspora as it come to be more widely applied' (1997: 22). To be sure, Jewish scholars themselves have intensively begun to re-think the category of diaspora with reference to the historical and modern development of Judaism (see, for instance, Boyarin and Boyarin 1993, Webber 1997, Tromp 1998). But drawing on a number of other key writers on the topic such as Kachig Tölölyan, Gabriel Sheffer and William Safran, Cohen suggests a set of features considered to be common among groups we might categorize together as sharing a diasporic existence. These are listed in Box 6.1.

Box 6.1 Common features of a diaspora

1. Dispersal from an original homeland, often traumatically, to two or more foreign regions;
2. Alternatively, the expansion from a homeland in search of work, in pursuit of trade or to further colonial ambitions;
3. A collective memory and myth about the homeland, including its location, history and achievements;
4. An idealization of the putative ancestral home and a collective commitment to its maintenance, restoration, safety and prosperity, even to its creation;
5. The development of a return movement that gains collective approbation;
6. A strong ethnic group consciousness sustained over a long time and based on a sense of distinctiveness, a common history and the belief in a common fate;
7. A troubled relationship with host societies, suggesting a lack of acceptance at the least or the possibility that another calamity might befall the group;
8. A sense of empathy and solidarity with co-ethnic members in other countries of settlement; and
9. The possibility of a distinctive creative, enriching life in host countries with a tolerance for pluralism.

Source: Cohen 1997: 26, after Safran 1991

In addition to these core traits outlined by Cohen, it has been said that diasporic groups are characterized by a 'triadic relationship' (Sheffer 1986, Safran 1991) between (1) a collectively self-identified ethnic group in one particular setting, (2) the group's co-ethnics in other parts of the world, and (3) the homeland states or local contexts whence they or their forebears came.

While attempts to theorize and typologize diaspora are certainly beginning to clarify a number of significant dimensions and developments surrounding today's globally dispersed populations, it is clear that their religious elements (or sometimes, cores) have received relatively far less attention. Most writings on diaspora today have, in fact, 'marginalized the factor of religion and relegated it to second place in favour of ethnicity and nationality' (Baumann 1998: 95).

Why study religion and diaspora? As a response to this question, Ninian Smart (1999) offers three basic reasons why it is important to study the connection between religion and diaspora (or, we might further suggest, why it is important to study the religious aspects of diasporic experience). First, the study of diasporas and their modes of adaptation can give us insights into general patterns of religious transformation. Second, diasporas may themselves affect the development of religion in the homeland: the wealth, education and exposure to foreign influences transferred from diaspora may have significant effects on organization, practice and even belief. Finally, because of the great incidence of diasporas in the modern world, 'multiethnicity is now commonplace' (Smart 1999: 421). These three facets are addressed in more detail under various headings below.

In appreciating the transformative potentials of religion in diaspora, we must first recognize that this is nothing new. Jonathan Z. Smith (1978) notes that almost every religion in Late Antiquity occurred in both a homeland and in diasporic centres (see, for instance, van der Toorn 1998, Dirven 1998). In homelands during this period, religions developed inextricably with local loyalties and ambitions, included as part of resistance to foreign domination.

> Each native tradition also had diasporic centers which exhibited marked change during the Late Antique period. There was a noticeable lessening of concern on the part of those in the diaspora from the destiny and fortunes of the native land and a relative severing of the archaic ties between religion and the land. Certain cult centers remained sites of pilgrimage or sentimental attachment, but the old beliefs in national deities and the inextricable relationship of the deity to particular places was weakened.
>
> (J.Z. Smith 1978: xii)

In probing the meanings of religion, diaspora and change, we must also consider the implications of what we might call religious travel. James Clifford (1992) has written of 'traveling cultures', suggesting how the meanings and relationships of dwelling-and-travelling displace conventional notions of culture and place (as well as challenge the ability of conventional methods of ethnography for representing cultures on the move). Since ancient times, religious travel has included pilgrimage, proselytization and the movement of students and scholars as well as exiles and migrants. Dale F. Eickelman and James Piscatori (1990a, b) have underlined the importance of such travel on the development of Islam. They consider travel foremost as a journey of the mind, including an imaginary connection with many sacred centres that has a significant impact on notions of religious belonging over distance, collective identity with those elsewhere, and ritual practice that is both universal and localized. Obviously these ideas have relevance for the understanding of diasporic dynamics.

In thinking about travelling religion, however, Ninian Smart raises a caveat through the example of Hinduism. He asks us to consider:

> themes such as caste, yoga, *bhakti* [devotion], pilgrimage, temple rituals, austerity (*tapasya*), wandering holy men, instruction in the scriptural traditions, regional variation, pundits, a strong sense of purity and impurity, household rituals, veneration of the cow, the practice of astrology, belief in reincarnation, the importance of acquiring merit, etc. These themes, which are woven together into the complicated fabric of Hinduism in India, do not all travel equally easily to new environments.
>
> (Smart 1999: 424)

Regarding categories and definitions, R. Cohen (1997) questions whether religions can or should be described as 'diasporas' alongside the dispersed ethnic groups which conventionally comprise the term. For Cohen, religions generally do not constitute diasporas in and of themselves. He describes religions at best as posing phenomena 'cognate' to diasporas. This is largely because religions often span more than one ethnic group and, in the case of faiths that have come to be widely spread around the globe, religions normally do not seek to return to, or to recreate, a homeland. From Cohen's perspective, while religions do not constitute diasporas in themselves, they 'can provide additional cement to bind a diasporic consciousness' (ibid: 189) .

Judaism and Sikhism are the obvious exceptions, as Cohen recognizes. Dispersed members of these two traditions do represent diasporas since they are considered to comprise discrete ethnic groups, albeit especially marked by their religion, among whom many do indeed hold strong views about their conceived homelands. To these two, we should add groups like Ismailis, Alevis, Bahais and Rastafarians whose respective religious distinctiveness usually tends to set them apart as ethnic groups. I have argued elsewhere (Vertovec 2000b), too, that it is possible to talk of a 'Hindu diaspora' especially because, no matter where in the world they live, most Hindus tend to sacralize India and therefore have a special kind of relationship to a spiritual homeland.

Other scholars are quicker to work with notions of 'diaspora religion' (such as Smart 1999). John Hinnells (1997a: 686) defines diaspora religion as 'the religion of any people who have a sense of living away from the land of the religion, or away from "the old country"'; he even extends the term to cover situations in which a religion represents 'a minority phenomenon' (ibid.). Gerrie ter Haar (1998) connects religion and diaspora through the assumption that migration means diaspora, migrants practice religion, and therefore diaspora implicates religion.

However, this is where conceptual waters begin to get muddy. Firstly, we begin to obfuscate the relationships of religion and diaspora, not to mention diaspora itself, if we regard it as involving any kind of migration or dispersal. It broadens the term far too much to talk – as many scholars do – about the 'Muslim diaspora', 'Catholic diaspora', 'Methodist diaspora' and so forth. These are of course world traditions that span many ethnic groups and nationalities that have been spread by many other means than migration and displacement. Hinnells (1997a) himself flags up one problem with his own definition: are Muslims in Pakistan part of a diaspora religion because Islam is derived from Arab origins and broadly centred on Mecca?

Secondly, to co-equate migration and subsequent minority status with diaspora also unnecessarily lumps together related yet arguably distinct conditions. '[O]ne does not announce the formation of the diaspora the moment the representatives of a people first get off the boat at Ellis Island (or wherever)' Robin Cohen quips (1997: 24). The same holds for patterns of 'transnationalism', a concept that also tends to be wrongly used interchangeably with diaspora. Migration and minority status, diaspora and transnationalism are intuitively linked, of course (Vertovec and Cohen 1999b). But linked does not mean synonymous. Each of these abstract categories can be seen to comprise specific processes of socio-religious transformation.

Here, I argue that religious and other socio-cultural dynamics develop distinctively within the realms of (a) migration and minority status (of course a dual category that, given space to discuss, needs much unpacking as well), (b) diaspora, and (c) transnationalism. I consider migration to involve the transference and reconstitution of cultural patterns and social relations in a new setting, one that usually involves the migrants as minorities becoming set apart by 'race', language, cultural traditions and religion. I refer to diaspora here especially as an imagined connection between a post-migration (including refugee) population and a place of origin and with people of similar origins now living elsewhere in the world. (By 'imagined', I do not mean such connections might not be actual. Rather, by this I emphasize the often strong sentiments, narratives, memories and mental pictures according to which members of diasporas organize themselves and undertake their cultural practices. This recalls Richard Marienstras's definition of a diaspora as a group based on 'a degree of national, or cultural, or linguistic awareness' of 'a relationship, territorially discontinuous, with a group settled "elsewhere"' (1989: 120).) By transnationalism I refer to the actual, ongoing exchanges of information, money and resources – as well as regular travel and communication – that members of a diaspora may undertake with others in the homeland or elsewhere within the globalized ethnic community. Diasporas arise from some form of migration, but not all migration involves diasporic consciousness; all transnational communities comprise diasporas, but not all diasporas develop transnationalism.

These categories, their associated patterns and processes are discussed below. The list of themes or types of transformation briefly summarized under each heading is not meant to be exhaustive but suggestive, having been sieved from a variety of cases.

RELIGION, MIGRATION AND MINORITY STATUS

In many of the classic studies on immigrant incorporation processes, researchers have pointed to the continued salience of religion among immigrants (Herberg 1955, Glazer and Moynihan 1963, Gordon 1964). Although remaining important, the social organization and practice of religion is usually modified nevertheless by a variety of factors involved in movement and resettlement in a new context. Dimensions of change, and some of the factors impacting upon them, include the following.

Organization and mobilization

Upon settling in a new environment, immigrants often soon set about collectively organizing themselves for purposes of religious worship. The formation of associations is one prominent kind of socio-religious organization, established to raise and distribute funds and coordinate activities (Rex *et al.* 1987). Sometimes immigrant associations seek to draw upon a remembered past in an attempt to replicate as nearly as possible an old ethnic-religious community in a new setting. Pre-migration social and cultural factors play important roles in the creation of immigrant religious institutions (Clarke *et al.* 1990), as do residential patterns in the new setting (Ebaugh *et al.* 2000).

The establishment and maintenance of religious institutions among immigrants not unusually involves a high degree of conflict and contestation. John Bodnar (1985: 166–7) states that in the nineteenth century, for instance,

> no institution in immigrant America exhibited more discord and division than the Church. ... Usually the Church and other religious organizations were the only immigrant institutions to contain an entrenched, premodern cadre of leaders ... [who] labored feverishly to centralize authority, revitalize faith, and maintain the loyalty of their flocks in a rapidly changing world.

Processes surrounding associations and other institutions also reflect the size and development of the immigrant population itself. Aspects of this are described with reference to successive stages of community 'fusion' and 'fission' reflecting the size and distribution of migrants drawn from distinct caste/social status, regional and linguistic backgrounds (Dahya 1974, Bhardwaj and Rao 1990, R.B. Williams 1992).

David Bowen (1987) has described such organizational phases among Gujarati Hindus in Bradford, England. These are characterized by: (1) the establishment of homogeneity among new immigrants looking for some kind of commonality through religious lowest common denominators, (2) the emergence of specific devotional congregations based upon demographic factors (such as neighbourhood) and devotional orientations (especially adherence to certain parochial traditions of a homeland), (3) the formation of caste associations as families were reunited and numbers of Gujaratis grew, and (4) the re-establishment of a kind of homogeneity by way of umbrella organizations created to interface with local government (cf. Vertovec 1994a).

The politics of recognition

Another important set of activities that immigrant associations engage concerns campaigns for legal tolerance or cultural rights surrounding specific practices, freedom from discrimination, and access to public resources offered to other groups (Vertovec and Peach 1997, Vertovec 1999b, 2001b). Such needs arise not only due to immigrant but to minority status. Some areas and examples of such engagement are (Vertovec 1997): modes of practice such as religious slaughter of animals and, for Muslims, the provision of *halal* food in public institutions; aspects of education (from ensuring modesty of dress among female pupils through approaches to religious education to questions surrounding sex education, as well as the entire issue of separate religiously-based schools); law (especially family law governing matters including marriage, divorce and inheritance) and legal protection against religious discrimination or incitement to religious hatred; and access to public resources and social services (state funding for community activities, the recognition of special community needs in health and housing).

Women's position and roles

Following migration the position of women in families and in the wider immigrant community often undergoes considerable transformation (see Chapter 3; also Willis and Yeoh 2000). This is particularly the case if women take up post-migration employment in contrast to their pre-migration status. In many cases more significant and decisive functions of women arise in religious community associations and affairs: women often take the lead in the organization and management of collective religious activities. What remains central, or indeed may be enhanced, following migration is the key role women play in reproducing religious practice – particularly by way of undertaking domestic religious practice (for example among Hindus, see McDonald 1987, Logan 1988, Rayaprol 1997).

Generations

Issues of religious and cultural reproduction naturally raise questions concerning the maintenance, modification or discarding of religious practices among the subsequent generations born and raised in post-migration settings. Everyday religious and cultural practices, religious nurture at home and religious education at school, and participation at formal places of worship all shape the identities and activities of the so-called second and third generations (Larson 1989, Jackson and Nesbitt 1993). Some conditioning factors affecting identity and activity among second- and third-generation youth which set them apart from their immigrant parents include (Vertovec and Rogers 1998): education in Western schools and the inculcation of discursive practices belonging to secular and civil society; youth dissatisfaction with conservative community leaders and religious teachers who do not understand the position of post-migrant youth; growth of 'vernacular' religious traditions across Europe; compartmentalization of religion (see below); and immersion in American/European popular youth culture.

Ethnic and religious pluralism

The situation of being migrants from another place and, thereby, of being minority 'others' often stimulates a mode of religious change through heightened self-awareness. As Barbara Metcalf (1996: 7) puts it, '[t]he sense of contrast – contrast with a past or contrast with the rest of society – is at the heart of a self-consciousness that shapes religious style'. The process has been observed by Kim Knott (1986: 46), who notes that

> Many Hindus in Leeds are only too aware that their religion is one amongst others. Not only are there indigenous faiths, generally grouped together by Hindus as 'Christian', but there are also other South Asian faiths. ... In this country Hinduism is just one minority faith amongst others. An awareness of religious pluralism has affected the way Hindus think about themselves and their faith.

And in Penny Logan's (1988: 124) research on culture and religion among Gujaratis in Britain,

> many adults reported that they had become more aware of their religion in Britain, as a result of belonging to a minority group in a predominantly irreligious society. They could no longer take their religion and their children's assumption of it for granted.

We should not assume that religious pluralism only refers to the co-presence of different faiths. Migrants – like travellers – often come across, for the first time, members and practices of distinct traditions within their own religion. As Eickelman and Piscatori (1990a: xv) point out,

> the encounter with the Muslim 'Other' has been at least as important for self-definition as the confrontation with the European 'Other'. ... The ironic

counterpart to travel broadening one's consciousness of the spiritual unity of the umma is that travel may define frontiers between Muslims and thus narrow their horizons.

The self-consciousness of migrant minorities due to a condition of pluralism relates to, and may in certain ways overlap with, the identity dynamics associated with the condition of diaspora.

RELIGION AND DIASPORA

As Shaye and Frerichs (1993) emphasized above, matters of cultural and religious adaptation-yet-continuity are foremost on the agendas of most diasporic groups. '[W]hat we have to grasp is a diasporic duality of continuity and change', suggests Martin Sökefeld (2000: 23), while we remain cognizant that '[t]he rhetoric of continuity obscures that [sic] actors constantly re-constitute and re-invent (or refuse to re-constitute) in diverse manners what is imagined as simply continuing'. (We must appreciate, too, that parallel forms of change may well be happening in the homeland as well, stimulated either from the diaspora or by non-diasporic factors altogether.) The 'diasporic duality of continuity and change' is evident in a number of socio-religious domains.

Identity and community

'[R]eligious identities,' writes R. Stephen Warner (1998: 3), 'often (but not always) mean more to [individuals] away from home, in their diaspora, than they did before, and those identities undergo more or less modification as the years pass'. One reason this occurs, he suggests, is because '[t]he religious institutions they build, adapt, remodel and adopt become worlds unto themselves, 'congregations', where new relations among the members of the community – among men and women, parents and children, recent arrivals and those settled – are forged' (ibid.). One example of this is to be found among Cubans in the United States who make pilgrimages to a purpose-built shrine in Miami. There, 'through transtemporal and translocative symbols at the shrine, the diaspora imaginatively constructs its collective identity and transports itself to the Cuba of memory and desire' (Tweed 1997: 10).

However, identities are not fixed, and tend to change in order to define and position groups and individuals in light of surrounding contexts

(Chapter 3). Moreover, diasporic identification involves complexities and permutations: some people continue to regard their land of birth as 'home', while others come to identify primarily with their land of settlement. Others may feel at home in neither place. And – perhaps in most cases – there may also be multiple, co-existing identities.

Ritual practice

Complexities and permutations also often characterize processes of modifying or 'streamlining' religious practices in diaspora (Hinnells 1997b). By way of illustration, in some places outside India basic Hindu ritual procedures have become truncated (as in Malaysia; Hutheesing 1983), refashioned (in Britain; Michaelson 1987), or eclectically performed (in East Africa; Bharati 1976); in others, much of the style or corpus of rites has been virtually 'invented' in conjunction with social change in the community (evident in Trinidad; Vertovec 1992), and in still other places, basic rites have been mutually 'negotiated' so as to provide a kind of socio-religious bridge between migrants from regionally distinct traditions (in England, Knott 1986; in Scotland, M. Nye 1995; and in the USA, Lessinger 1995). In most places, many rites have been popularized in order to appeal to young, diaspora-born Hindus, to the chagrin of conservative elders: in Malaysia, for instance, Hindu leaders have complained that the inclusion of India-produced music has wrought the 'disco-ization' of Hindu ritual (Willford 1998)!

'Re-spatialization'

Jonathan Z. Smith described how, in the ancient world of the Mediterranean and Near East,

> For the native religionist, homeplace, the place to which one belongs, was *the* central religious category. One's self-definition, one's reality, was the place into which one had been born – understood as both geographical and social place. To the new immigrant in the diaspora, nostalgia for homeplace and cultic substitutes for the old, sacred center were central religious values. ... Diasporic religion, in contrast to native, locative religion, was utopian in the strictest sense of the word, a religion of 'nowhere', of transcendence.
>
> (1978: xiv, emphasis in original)

Barbara Metcalf seems to recapitulate Smith through her interest in religious/diasporic 'spaces' that are non-locative. '[I]t is ritual and sanctioned practice that is prior and that creates "Muslim space"', she proposes (1996: 3), 'which thus does not require any juridically claimed territory or formally consecrated or architecturally specific space'. She extends the spatial metaphor through reference to the 'social space' of networks and identities created in new contexts away from homelands, the 'cultural space' that emerges as Muslims interact, and 'physical space' of residence and community buildings founded in new settings. Together, these spaces comprise the 'imagined maps of diaspora Muslims' (ibid.: 18).

Pnina Werbner (1996) echoes Metcalf's 'imagined maps' by suggesting that Muslims in diaspora connect via a 'global sacred geography'. This is created anew through the ritual sacralization of space in diasporic settings – a process Werbner describes among Pakistani Sufis in Britain, which inherently conjoins sites both at home in Pakistan and in Manchester, UK. Similarly for Senegalese Sufis (Mourides) in diaspora, their holy city of Touba is metaphorically 'recreated in the routine activities of the migrants and through recurrent parallels of the migrants' lives with that of the founder of the order, Cheikh Amadu Bamba' (Carter 1997: 55).

Diasporic transformation also involves a changing sense of religious time as well as space. As Werner Schiffauer (1988: 150) recalls, among Turkish Muslims in Germany:

> The specifically peasant experience of an oscillation of one's social world between states of religious community and society is no longer present. During sacred times, society no longer changes into a religious community but, rather, one leaves the society and enters the religious community – if possible, we must add, since the opposition between secular and sacred times is now determined by the more fundamental notions of the working day and leisure.

Religion/culture

The reconfigured distinctions of sacred and secular space and time that occur in diaspora are matched by the sharpening of distinctions between religion and culture. To illustrate, David Pocock (1976) observed that in one branch (the Bochasanwasi Shri Akshar Purushottam Sanstha) of the Hindu Swaminarayan movement a tendency has emerged to consider certain aspects of Gujarati culture (including family structure, language, diet, marriage networks, and the position of women) as quasi-religious phenomena – that is, as behavioural and ideological facets contributing to the fulfilment of *dharma*. The subsequent problem Pocock discerned for the Sanstha is that of 'dis-embedding a set of beliefs and practices – a "religion" from a "culture" which would then be defined as "secular"' (1976: 362). This is a critical yet common dilemma for Hindus throughout the diaspora (and, some observe, in India itself). It entails moves toward a self-conscious 'rationalization of the distinction religion/ culture' (ibid.: 357) despite the everywhere-asserted dictum that 'Hinduism is a way of life'.

Processes of self-consciously distinguishing elements of religion/ culture are bound to have differing results in various domains (in temples, in religious or cultural associations, in homes, in the workplace). In each case among Hindus in diaspora, such processes inherently involve both some kind of adaptation to religiously and culturally plural environments and the generation or heightening of distinct 'ethnic' sentiments.

Martin Sökefeld (2000: 10) considers relevant developments among Alevis in diaspora:

> One could speak of an Alevi revival in Germany (and in Turkey) since 1989, but this revival was not a simple renewal of Alevism as it had been practiced until a few decades ago in Turkey. Instead, it implicated a serious transformation of Alevism and its rituals which can be glossed over as 'folklorization': Although originally 'religious' rituals were practiced, Alevism was re-constituted mainly as a secular culture.
>
> (Sökefeld 2000: 10)

The secularization of Alevism occurred, not least, due to the role of hard-core, anti-religious Marxists within the Alevi community in Germany. A further process of 'desacralization' has occurred, Sökefeld notes, through the core Alevi collective ritual (*cem*) being turned into a public ritual solely to affirm identity based on symbolic cultural difference (from other Turks and Sunni Muslims)

In a similar way, both Madawi Al-Rasheed (1998) and Erica McClure (2000) detail ways in which members of the Assyrian diaspora sharply contend whether religion or ethnicity (or language) forms the basis of community identity.

Many young South Asian Muslim women interviewed by Kim Knott and Sadja Khokher (1993) are also conceptually establishing a firm distinction between 'religion' and 'culture' – a distinction between what, for their parents (particularly prior to migration), were largely indistinguishable realms. Further, they are rejecting their parents' conformity to ethnic traditions that the parents consider as emblematic of religiosity (such as manner of dress) while wholly embracing a Muslim identity in and of itself. Among these young women, Knott and Khokher explain, there is a 'self-conscious exploration of the religion which was not relevant to the first generation' (1993: 596).

RELIGION AND TRANSNATIONALISM

As Susanne Hoeber Rudolph (1997: 1) reminds us, 'Religious communities are among the oldest of the transnationals: Sufi orders, Catholic missionaries, and Buddhist monks carried work and praxis across vast spaces before those places became nation-states or even states.' These kinds of long-distance connections had a profound and long-lasting impact on the development of global traditions. Further, the transference and transformation of religion accompanied some of the modern period's earliest yet perhaps most powerful forms of globalization and transnationalism, too – namely mercantilism, conquest and colonial domination. Today,

> Modern forms of travel and communication have accelerated religious transnationalism – the flow of ideologies, access to information on organizational forms and tactics, and the transformation of formerly elite movements to mass movements – rendering obsolete earlier notions of frontier as defined primarily by geographical boundaries.
>
> (Eickelman 1997: 27)

New technologies, such as computer-mediated communication, are now having a considerable impact on transnational religious organization and activity (see e.g. Castells 1997, Eickelman and Anderson 1999, Miller and Slater 2000).

Contemporary patterns and processes of migrant transnationalism also give rise to significant forms of religious transformation. Given the boom in transnational migration studies, however, there is surprisingly much less research concerning religious links maintained between post-migration communities and their origins (cf. Levitt 1998). The following section nevertheless draws on a number of helpful studies that demonstrate key domains of transformation surrounding the religious life of transnationally linked migrants.

Networks

As underlined in Chapters 2 and 3, migrant transnationalism is inherently composed of social networks. These may become institutionalized to various degrees and for various purposes. Networks with religious functions – such as pastoral care, ritual activity, moral safeguarding, or official representation in public settings – also develop from and through social networks. These, too, entail varying degrees of institutionalization. Rudolph (1997) contrasts two prominent patterns of contemporary global socio-religious organization. One she describes by way of many long-standing forms of organization or 'hierarchy' (marked by bureaucracy, concentration of decision making and coordination of action); these she contrasts to largely emergent forms of 'self-organization' (characterized by 'grassroots' activity, local or folk religious traditions, decentralization and spontaneity). While in many religious traditions it was forms of bureaucracy or hierarchy that long functioned transnationally (e.g. the Catholic Church), now – mostly on the back of migrant transnational connections – those forms of 'self-organization' have come to play increasingly significant global roles within world religions. Consequently and at the same time, this growing significance often creates new tensions between hierarchy-sustained religious authorities and popular, believer-backed religious activity.

Transnational networks can function to enhance individual religiosity as well. This is exhibited by Haitian Catholic and Protestant preachers who maintain congregational ties in Haiti and to immigrants in the United States (Basch *et al.* 1993), and by Trinidadian Catholic priests who serve pastoral roles for members of the diaspora via the Internet (Miller and Slater 2000).

And of course, there are many cases in which the bureaucratic, the transnational 'grassroots', and individual forms of religion are deeply entangled. For instance, Bruno Riccio (1999) describes how Sufi brotherhoods (especially the Mouride) play key organizational roles (including the facilitation of trading networks) in sustaining religious identity and practice through the diasporic experience of Senegalese in Italy (see also Ebin 1996, Carter 1997). The transnational brotherhood provides members with continuous feedback in order to maintain morality. 'In other words', Riccio (1999: 132) writes, it is the fact that the Mouride movement is embedded in a transnational social field that makes it so successful in controlling potentially deviant behaviour. Within this field Mouride transnational formations are kept alive by oral conversation, the selling of cassettes, where besides prayers and Kasaids [sacred poems] one finds information about *ndiguel* (orders, decrees) from the Kalif or from the Touba establishment.

Riccio also depicts the movement of Marabouts, living saints or spiritual leaders who visit diasporic communities and provide followers with blessings and advice. The visits 'reaffirm the link and the identification between the sacred place (Touba [whence the founder of the movement comes]), the Saint … and the diasporic community of Mourides' (Riccio 1999: 133).

An altogether different kind of example demonstrating new modes of transnational religious networks is represented by the 'milk miracle' of September 1995. As reported by many news agencies, religious images or *murtis* in Hindu temples around Britain (London, Leicester, Birmingham and Leeds) and around the world (including New York, Delhi, Hong Kong and Bangkok) were observed to 'drink' substantial quantities of milk. News of such a 'miracle' in one temple location was rapidly conveyed to another, where milk was subsequently offered: if 'drank' by the *murti*, the news was immediately relayed elsewhere. Practically in the course of a day, news of similar incidents spread around the world. A South Asian religious diaspora, now connected through advanced global telecommunications, had wrought 'the age of the instant miracle' (*The Guardian*, 23 September 1995). Hindus the world over were devotionally inspired. However, according to Chetan Bhatt (1997), the event was created (or at least manipulated) by the Hindu religious-nationalist organizations Vishwa Hindu Parishad and Rashtriya Swayamsevak Sangh who mobilized their international networks to generate the appearance of the miracle globally.

Migration and minority status, diaspora and transnationalism each relate to different, but overlapping, grounds upon which religious transformations take place. The social scientific task of comprehending and analysing these trends calls for a high degree of clarity as to which of these realms we are addressing at any time. Fuzziness and conflation of categories will cause us to chase our theoretical tails.

With special reference to South Asian religions, for instance, potentially useful methodological frameworks for comparative study of the factors conditioning change among religious communities through migration, diaspora and transnationalism have been suggested by authors such as Jayawardena (1968, 1980), Clarke *et al.* (1990), Knott (1991), Ballard (1994), Hinnells (1997b) and Vertovec (2000b). They emphasize the need to take into mutual account pre-migration factors (including economic patterns, social structure and status relations), modes of migration, atmospheres and frameworks of reception and settlement, and trajectories of adaptation.

Enquiry into patterns of religious change surrounding this set of categories – migration and minority status, diaspora and transnationalism – will shine significant light on yet broader processes affecting religion in the world today. The final list of themes and short examples below suggest some of these.

Awareness of global religious identities

Smart (1999) points to the fact that, due in large part to migration, diasporas and transnationalism, there are now world organizations for every major religious tradition and subtradition located in most parts of the world. 'Such a consciousness of belonging to a world community has grown considerably in very recent times', Smart writes (1999: 423). 'Consequently, the divergences between diaspora and home communities are diminishing.' Even for relatively remote groups, transnational narratives 'construct and negotiate the relationships between multiple identities' by tying individuals and communities into larger common constituencies (J. Robbins 1998: 123). Dale F. Eickelman and Jon Anderson (1999) emphasize how such a new sense of collective awareness and connection among Muslims in various parts of the globe has especially been forged through new communication technologies.

Daniel Miller and Don Slater (2000) discovered a perceived need among many local Hindus in an out-of-the-way place like Trinidad – in a community largely cut off from India for generations – to connect with a wider, indeed global, form of Hinduism:

> The Internet allows for an expansion of communication, but in this case it is used to repair a discrepancy, thereby helping communities and people come closer to a realization of who they already feel they 'really' are. The mechanics involved require a sense of geography that defies the usual separation of the local and the global. In these cases the increasingly global use

of the Internet across the Diaspora is a function of the re-establishment of local communications that had become sundered.

(Miller and Slater 2000: 178)

Universalization versus localization

Ira Lapidus (2001) describes how there has always been inherent tension between Islamic universals and the experience of specific traditions being rooted in particular cultural contexts. Much of Islamic history has seen an 'oscillation' between the two. Similar tensions are found in every world religion, and processes surrounding migration, diaspora and transnationalism continue to exercise or exacerbate them.

This is apparent in Camilla Gibb's (1998) study of Muslim immigrants from the Ethiopian city of Harar. In Harar there exists a centuries-old Islam of syncretic saints' cults. Yet in diaspora (in this case, Canada) there has arisen an Islam constructed to appeal to a multinational congregation. 'As a result,' Gibb concludes (1998: 260),

> what appears to be happening is a homogenization or essentialization of Islamic practices, where culturally specific aspects of Islam that are not shared with other Muslim populations are likely to disappear, since they are not reinforced by Muslims from other groups in this context.

Indeed, Harari children in Canada are not taught about their heritage, and they are indeed turning against any religious practices directed toward saints' cults.

Among the Bangladeshis with whom Katy Gardner worked, too, 'Migrants to Britain and the Middle East have moved from an Islam based around localised cultures and moulded to the culture and geography of the homelands, to an international Islam of Muslims from many different countries and cultures' (1993b: 225). On an individual level, Miller and Slater (2000: 179) met a young Trinidadian Muslim woman who was using the Internet 'to try to sort out in her own mind which aspects of her practice were orthodox and which were local'.

Perhaps at the same time we are seeing a shift to global forms of religion, however, new processes of localization are taking place. In this way Raymond Williams (1988) and Diana Eck (1996) both describe the emergence of an 'American Hinduism' alongside a purported process bringing about the 'Americanization' of Muslims (Haddad and Esposito 2000).

What is essential in a religious tradition?

As we have already seen above, the conscious disaggregation of 'religion' from 'culture' is sometimes prompted among people in diaspora. Raymond Williams (1984: 191) comments,

> The critical assumption here is that there are some aspects associated with past religious practice that are fundamental and essential to the continuation of the religion and others that are cultural accoutrements that are not so fundamental. Thus, the process of searching for an adaptive strategy becomes the attempt to distinguish what is essential in the religion and what is not.

Jacques Waardenburg (1988) points to the growing trend (especially among young people) for discarding national or regional traditions and focusing upon the Qur'an and Sunna in order to distinguish what is truly Islamic – that is, normative – from what is secondary. The felt need to make this distinction is often what prompts young people in diaspora situations to join so-called 'fundamentalist' movements (Schiffauer 1999).

Politico-religious activity

Religious-cum-political groups and networks that are dispersed across the borders of nation-states – or indeed, scattered globally – have in recent times developed their agendas in arguably new and distinct ways. The rise and development of al-Qaeda is but one powerful example. The adoption of diverse modes of communication (including electronic and computer-mediated forms), the changing nature and manipulation of resources (channelling people, funds and information to and from a number of localities), and the maintenance of various kinds of relationships in relation to encompassing social and political contexts (including ties with people in the homeland/settlement land and elsewhere in the world) are among the factors characterizing many politico-religious movements as diasporic or transnational.

Politico-religious movements in diaspora comprise many possible types. A movement's aim may be to change a particular country's current regime or its entire political system. A diasporic group may be concerned with affecting the religion and politics of a nation-state of origin, it may be seeking to create its own autonomous region or nation-state, or it may be dedicated to the cause of 'exporting' a politico-religious ideology from one place of origin to another setting. The composition of a worldwide politico-religious group may be multi-ethnic or made up of people with a single ethnic identity. Other diasporic or transnational dimensions of politico-religious groups are represented in the following examples.

Religious nationalism in India is represented by the Vishwa Hindu Parishad (VHP), the Bharatiya Janata Party (BJP) and the Rashtriya Swayamsevak Sangh (RSS). Such revivalist Hinduism, observes Chetan Bhatt (1997: 155), 'has relied extensively on its followers in the US, Britain, Canada and Europe to generate global support and funds for its political ventures in India' (see also Rajagopal 1997, Mukta and Bhatt 2000). Yet religion often provides an ally or source for secular nationalists too, as witnessed among Armenians (Pattie 1997). Thomas A. Tweed (1997) similarly describes how a Cuban-Catholic shrine in Miami functions as a place specifically to express a very particular (anti-Castro) diasporic nationalism.

Transnational religious terrorism is now high on the agenda of many security-conscious institutions (Hoffman 1998b). The network-without-centre manner of organization now facilitated by new technologies is ideal for groups involved in extreme forms of politico-religious activity (Eickelman and Piscatori 1990b, Castells 1997). In this way Eickelman (1997) describes links between Islamicist groups, as well as the nature of relationships within the groups themselves, as decentred, multiple, fluid and subject to severance at short notice.

Peter Mandaville (1999: 23) finds that it is usually amongst diasporic Muslims of the Western world that we find the Internet being appropriated for political purposes.

> A more sober examination of the situation, however, reveals that very few of the Muslim groups who have a presence on the Internet are involved in this sort of activity. Moreover, there are also those who argue that the Internet has actually had a moderating effect on Islamist discourse. Sa'ad al-Faqih [a reform movement leader], for example, believes that Internet chat rooms and discussion forums devoted to the debate of Islam and politics serve to encourage greater tolerance. He believes that in these new arenas one sees a greater convergence in the centre of the Islamist political spectrum and a weakening of its extremes.

Such a view is reinforced by Rima Berns McGown's work with Somali refugees in Canada and England. She suggests:

> The Islamists' influence is obvious in the very way that the practice of Islam has evolved for diaspora Somalis. The old religious symbolism – the local Sufi shaykh, the dhikr, the token Qur'anic memorization – has given way to a sense of Islam as a vital force in understanding how to live in this new world, a force that might require more blatant identification (via, for instance, a beard or the hijab) or personal study (a parallel with the Jewish yeshiva might be made here). While diaspora Somalis may accept or reject one or other Islamist group's interpretation of doctrine or prescription for action, they share the sense of the religion's vitality that is the Islamists' driving force.

> (1999: 229)

Re-orienting devotion

Jonathan Z. Smith's (1978: xiv) account of religion of Late Antiquity posits that

> Rather than a god who dwelt in his temple or would regularly manifest himself in a cult house, the diaspora evolved complicated techniques for achieving visions, epiphanies or heavenly journeys. That is to say, they evolved modes of access to the deity which transcended any particular place.

Such modes represented fundamental shifts in belief or religious orientation.

Other core shifts have been observed in connection with migration or displacement. In a study of letters written by nineteenth-century immigrants to the United States, Jay P. Dolan (1998) found it difficult to determine the religious affiliation of the letter writers. In one stirring fact, Dolan observed a complete absence of Jesus, as well as of the Virgin Mary and individual saints. Instead, the immigrants' general religious orientation was toward God as a constant companion and guide, seemingly meant to mitigate another constant theme of this-worldly suffering. The afterlife was commonly thought of as a place of joy and reunion. Dolan (1998: 153) concludes, 'This understanding of the afterlife as a place of reunion mirrored the social experience of the immigrants and the sense of separation inherent in the immigrant experience.'

In a slightly different look at how migrant and diasporic experience affects religious orientations, Bhikhu Parekh (1994) accounts for the centrality of one sacred text, the Ramayana, among numerous overseas

Hindu communities. He does so by highlighting several themes, images and messages conveyed by the text, relating the ways these resonate with and appeal to the diasporic condition. This includes reference to the Ramayana's themes of exile, suffering, struggle and eventual return, which resonated especially with the indentured migrant labourers who ventured overseas.

A reorienting of devotion is also evident in the rise of orthodox, universal forms already mentioned in a number of places above. Overall, Smart (1999: 425) reckons '[t]he diasporas of the Global Period [of the last 25 years] have become somewhat more orthodox in tone'. Katy Gardner's work on the social and economic dynamics linking the Sylhet district of Bangladesh with the East End of London (1993a, b, 1995) demonstrates ways in which transnational migration processes and practices lead to increased religious fervour, puritanism and orthodoxy based on scripturalism. As a driving force of such change, Gardner found the richest transmigrants to be most interested in enforcing orthodoxy – mainly for purposes of demonstrating status and acquiring social capital.

Compartmentalization

In assessing developments affecting religions and diasporas, Hinnells (1997b) stresses the impact of contemporary Western notions of religion on transplanted non-Western faiths. Such notions include secularization, liberal notions of interfaith dialogue, and a broad tendency to treat religion as just another 'compartment' of life. Hence it may come as no surprise that for many Hindus in Britain, Hinduism now

> has the status of a 'compartment', or one of a number of aspects of life. ... Some are beginning to think of Hinduism as many people do Christianity, something to be remembered during large festivals and at births, marriages and deaths.
>
> (Knott 1986: 46)

This kind of religious shift should not be limited to non-Western traditions, however. As Susan Pattie (1997: 214) discovered, '[f]or Armenians today, especially those in London, the sphere of religion is becoming increasingly isolated and definable as a distinct category of experience'. Peggy Levitt (1998) relatedly suggests that Dominicans in diaspora have developed a more formal and utilitarian relationship to their church than their counterparts in the Dominican Republic.

The problem with the past

Pattie (1997: 231) describes the 'double bind' characterizing the situation of the Armenian Apostolic Church among Armenians in diaspora:

> On the one hand, its role as a national institution, imbued with visual, linguistic, and musical traditions, forges deep psychological links with the past. Looking at their diaspora situation, Armenians in Cyprus and London place great value on this continuing, seemingly unchanging aspect of the Church. Yet at the same time the old presentation is not always understood and, worse, not even experienced, as attendance and participation dwindle with each new generation.

In the Armenian example, it would seem the past is of lessening interest to newer generations. On the other hand, '[n]ow that modern communication and travel technology brings dispersed peoples together more than ever, the usual assumption that attachment to the homeland will decline significantly after the first generation, and even more after the second, seems less self-evident' (Tweed 1997: 140). But of course – like with notions of presumed diasporic 'continuity' discussed above – the idea of 'attachment' to a homeland and a past signals what will most likely be a highly transformed mode and meaning of relationship.

Trajectories

A final theme of change involves the possible trajectories of collective identities and of local/regional or sectarian traditions in contexts of diaspora and transnationalism.

Possibilities for trajectories of identity are represented by Jacques Waardenburg's (1988) proposed set of 'options' for Muslims in Europe (cf. Vertovec and Peach 1997, Vertovec and Rogers 1998). These can be summarized as (1) the secular option – discarding Muslim identity altogether; (2) the cooperative option – playing on Muslim identity in the process of pursuing common goals with other groups; (3) the cultural option – maintaining particular social and cultural practices without much religious sentiment; (4) the religious option – emphasizing wholly scriptural modes of religious affiliation at the expense of cultural aspects (an option described by some as 'fundamentalist'); (5) the ethnic-religious option – perpetuating a specific national or regional form of Islam (e.g. Moroccan); (6) the behavioural option – expressing Islamic tenets through moral or ritual behaviour only; and (7) the ideological option – identifying with or opposing the 'official' Islam of a particular home country.

The possible trajectories of specific sub-traditions, I have suggested (Vertovec 2000b), come down to the following: (1) remaining intact, as represented by processes of community 'fission' described earlier; (2) homogenizing parochial forms through lowest common denominators of belief and practice (as developed within Hinduism in the Caribbean; van der Veer and Vertovec 1991, Vertovec 1992, 1994b); (3) promoting a kind of ecumenism, in which a number of forms co-exist under a kind of umbrella organization (R.B. Williams 1988); (4) universal-izing a specific form (such as the Hinduism of the VHP) by claiming it to be all-encompassing; and (5) cosmopolitanism, whereby the possibility of multiple, successive forms is celebrated (cf. Williams 1998).

The possible trajectories of identity and tradition in diaspora – like most of the themes of transformation suggested throughout this chapter – are not mutually exclusive. They are taking place simultaneously world-wide, and often within the same diaspora.

By isolating, as discrete categories, conditions surrounding migration and minority status, diaspora and transnationalism, we can gain more concise insights into processes and patterns of religious change. These tell us as much about a specific group's experience as they do about general characteristics of religious transformation.

7

CONCLUSION

INTERCONNECTED MIGRANTS IN AN INTERCONNECTED WORLD

Although not the most rigorous mode of social scientific investigation, observing what happens around sport can be a good way to gauge certain views, understandings and trends in society. A nice example, when they won the 1998 World Cup and ever since, is the French national football team. Comprising players from (or sons of immigrants from) Guadeloupe, Algeria, Senegal, the Congo, French Guiana and elsewhere, the team has been widely considered as an exemplar of contemporary, culturally diverse French society (see for instance J.W. Anderson 2006). During the 2008 European Championships, players on many national football teams were born elsewhere – making the phenomenon now a rather matter-of-fact occurrence reflecting 'a continent shaped by migration' and hailed as 'European cosmopolitanism on display' (Hawley 2008a). Transformative examples of transnationalism were on display, too. For example, many Germans empathized with Lukas Podolski, a Polish-born player on the German team who scored two goals to beat Poland: afterwards, Podolski spoke of his 'torn heart' and reluctance to celebrate victory over a country to which he still feels closely connected. German-Turks also struggled with such a 'Podolski feeling' when Turkey faced Germany in the semi-finals (Zaimoglu 2008). Prior to the match, in Turkish neighbourhoods like Kreuzberg in Berlin,

> alongside the Turkish flag in many of the windows and on many of the cars, a German one is also flying. ... many loyalties in Kreuzberg and other Turkish communities across Germany are genuinely split. Now, it seems almost as though Kreuzberg at least would like to use this game to put to rest integration concerns. "This game is the best of both worlds!" yells vegetable seller Riza Isler, who was born in Turkey but who has lived in Germany most of his life. "No matter who wins, I will have a team to support in the finals!"
>
> (Hawley 2008b)

Perhaps most notably, even populist tabloid newspapers in Germany tended to respect the divided sympathies of Podolski and the German-Turks.

This development marks a departure from earlier attitudes toward divided sentiments, national sport and attitudes toward migrants and ethnic minorities. In 1990 the senior Conservative Party politician Norman Tebbitt famously proposed the 'cricket test'. The loyalty and belonging of immigrants and their descendants could be judged, Tebbitt suggested, according to which side they cheer for during international cricket matches (e.g. the West Indies versus England or Pakistan versus England). Sixteen years later, British writer Darcus Howe (2006) observed how, as opposed to when he migrated from Trinidad a generation ago, migrants today benefit from the revolution in communication, placing them

> in immediate contact with the countries from which we came. A phone card costs £3, and for that price we can speak to the West Indies, Ghana, Pakistan and India for 50 minutes. The internet binds us in a way that was not possible in the past. No longer can we be shaken by allegations condemning our loyalties to those sporting teams which originate from our past.

Therefore, Howe concluded, 'Tebbitt's test did not survive the passage of time and is now truly dead'.

Across Britain there is now, arguably, greater acknowledgement – tolerance? – of minorities' transnational connections as exemplified through sports. In fact – and most clearly overturning the 'cricket test' perspective – multiple sporting loyalty was portrayed as a significant British strength within the successful London bid to host the 2012 Olympics: the campaign's official website proclaimed that '[i]n 2012, our multicultural diversity will mean every competing nation in the Games will find local supporters as enthusiastic as back home' (www. london2012.org).

Such observations do not amount to profound social analysis, but they do provide a window onto everyday manifestations of change. Of course these instances do not suggest the end of racism or xenophobia, either, but point at least to a growing and ever-more routinized recognition of people's multiple attachments. They seem to demonstrate that migration-driven diversity and ongoing transnational ties are, for a broad span of the non-migrant population, now coming to be regarded as unsurprising or nothing special, commonplace and unquestioned – in many contexts, expected. They are contemporary facts gradually more known and accepted by many, though still – to be sure – raising deep concerns for some (not least nationalists and politicians on the right). Growing multi-dimensional diversity, increasing social complexity and migrant transnationalism are being broadly acknowledged as ordinary, or at least unavoidable, facets of contemporary, globalized society. This ordinariness attests to a considerable transformation, as described in Chapter 1: that is, a set of incremental, mutually conditioning changes leading to something far-reaching on both macro and micro scales.

It has particularly been increased mobility, combined with the various forms of globalization-as-interconnectedness, that has led to the significant societal transformations described in this book. Such transformations are just as consequential in the developing 'South' as in the developed 'North', in 'the West' and in 'the East'. As Peter Koehn and James Rosenau (2002: 132) put it, 'the mobility upheaval has brought about the worldwide distribution of transnationally proficient migrants'. Politicians and policy-makers have certainly realized the global growth of migration and the enhanced abilities of migrants to maintain transnational connections (see IOM 2005). In his 2006 Report to the General Assembly, UN Secretary-General Kofi Annan emphasized the importance of recognizing how migrants can 'maintain transnational lives' (UN 2006: 5). He pointed out that,

> No longer do those who emigrate separate themselves as thoroughly as they once did from the families and communities they leave behind. ...

> Owing to the communications and transportation revolution, today's inter-
> national migrants are, more than ever before, a dynamic human link
> between cultures, economies and societies. Penny-a-minute phone cards
> keep migrants in close touch with family and friends at home, and just a few
> seconds are needed for the global financial system to transmit their earn-
> ings to remote corners of the developing world, where they buy food, cloth-
> ing, shelter, pay for education or health care, and can relieve debt. The
> Internet and satellite technology allow a constant exchange of news and
> information between migrants and their home countries. Affordable air-
> fares permit more frequent trips home, easing the way for a more fluid back-
> and-forth pattern of mobility.
>
> (ibid.: 6, 7)

Annan's comments underscore the growing recognition of the ways in which patterns of contemporary international migration, impacts on migrant origin and destination contexts, and experiences of migrants themselves are inherently interwoven with other processes of increasing global interconnectedness.

The Report of the Global Commission on International Migration, which Kofi Annan established in 2003, was entitled *Migration in an Interconnected World* (GCIM 2005). The Commission made a strong call to comprehend current migration dynamics against the backdrop of processes of globalization through which societies and economies are increasingly integrated and interdependent, particularly through new technologies enabling the rapid transfer of information, capital, goods and services. It stressed how migration and its emergent practices of transnationalism are both fostered by and contribute to such processes. Such an understanding of migrant transnationalism has in fact come to the fore not only in social scientific approaches to migration but also among a range of national and international policymakers, as discussed in Chapter 5.

Not only has transnationalism wrought transformations in practices, public understanding and policy development, but the nature of migra-
tion itself has been transformed in many if not most contexts. This has been particularly through processes in which migrants make use of information and communication technologies (ICTs). Drawing on the work of Manuel Castells (1996, 1997, 1998) concerning ICTs, information flows and the networked society, Adela Ros and her colleagues (2007: 6) underline the point that '[c]ontemporary international migration is embedded in the dynamics of the information society, following

common patterns and interconnected dynamics. Without the existence of the information society, contemporary migration patterns would look totally different.' Further, they suggest that

> current international migration is the inevitable result of the interconnection processes generated by the communication and information flows. Information and communication networks are stimulating and bringing about changes in the trends and meanings of the movement of people around the world. Without the intensity of the interconnections it is difficult to imagine migratory movements like the current ones, in terms of both the countries of origin and host countries.

> (ibid.: 7–8)

Throughout this book such uses and their effects have been highlighted, particularly the role of cheap phone calls and their fundamental part in maintaining social networks (especially families). ICTs are also instrumental within other key migrant transnational formations too, such as political parties and movements, homeland outreach programmes and policies, diasporic marketing and business practices, remittance activities and hometown associations. Here, clearly, an interconnected world has enabled migrants themselves to better connect for a variety of purposes. Subsequently, such gradual manifestations produce knock-on effects, usually entailing further changes within or across social, cultural, economic, political and religious domains.

Overall, the connection between migrant transnational practices and modes of transformation suggested in this book reflect the progression of changes suggested by Alejandro Portes (2001a: 191):

> Once migrant colonies become well established abroad, a flow of *transnational* economic and informational resources starts, ranging from occasional remittances to the emergence of a class of full-time transnational entrepreneurs. The cumulative effects of these dynamics come to the attention of national governments who reorient their *international* activities through embassies, consulates, and missions to recapture the loyalty of their expatriates and guide their investments and political mobilizations. The increased volume of demand created by migrant remittances and investments in their home countries support, in turn, the further expansion of the market for multinationals and encourage local firms to go abroad themselves, establishing branches in areas of immigrant concentration. [emphasis in original]

Each set of changes entails small-scale and everyday practices of individuals and groups. Incrementally and cumulatively, these practices may generate far-reaching modes of transformation affecting migrants, their families and communities in places of origin, wider populations surrounding transnational networks, and entire societies permeated by migrant transnationalism.

Many forms of migrant transnationalism and their related modes of transformation are likely to widen, intensify and accelerate. The governments of migrant-sending and -receiving states will continue to address a range of migrant transnational practices with greater attention and policy intervention. Technological changes (especially the building and extension of ICT infrastructures in developing countries) will make it ever easier and cheaper to communicate and exchange resources, including remittances, across borders and at long-distance. Hometown associations and other such diasporic organizations have become institutionalized to a degree that they will likely be sustained, and probably enhanced, at least over the next several years. Individuals within post-migration second and subsequent generations will probably not maintain the everyday orientations and practices of their migrant forebears, but such parental orientations and practices are apt to have an enduring impression on the next generation's identities, interests and socio-cultural activities.

As is evident in the massive literature on globalization, an array of global transformations are currently underway due to a confluence of contemporary social, political, economic and technological processes. Migrant transnational practices are stimulated and fostered by many of these globalization processes. In turn, such transnational migrant practices accumulate to augment and perhaps amplify such transformational processes themselves.

In Chapter 1 it was pointed out that, just like globalization, transnationalism's constituent processes and outcomes are multiple and messy. This variegation will no doubt persist, even intensify. Transnational practices are enabled, limited and coloured by all kinds of disparities in power and resources. Across various groups and even within the same diaspora, there are haves and have-nots, the transnationally well-connected and less-connected. Often disconnection is due to illiteracy or poverty; simply the lack of a mobile phone can represent a major form of transnational exclusion (Ros *et al.* 2007). Uneven trends are likely to continue to characterize migrant transnationalism as migration and 'integration' patterns themselves develop, as technological changes take place, as government policies arise and take effect, and as world events occur and send ripples through public perceptions and political economies. The variables are too many to predict future transnational trends, except to say that their everyday, normative nature will continue to manifest and become institutionalized.

One profound unknowable will be whether some, or many, nation-states will be sites for anti-globalization/anti-transnationalism backlash. Alongside debates around economic protectionism, this is already witnessed in limited ways through calls to tighten borders, limit citizenship, unravel multiculturalism and enforce migrants' assimilation. As suggested above, broad patterns of transformation entailing the gradual acknowledgement of increasing diversity, complexity and multiple attachments are already underway, and perhaps the forms of backlash are but last gasps of a bygone model of the nation-state. 'Events' – not least including major terrorist activity or worldwide economic crisis – might take place so as to turn limited instances of backlash into dominant approaches to world and country. Yet without such rash incidents, the direction of transformation seems to point toward maintained growth in mobility, socio-cultural diversification and global interconnectedness.

Migration and transnational practices certainly bring many kinds of diversity to migrant-receiving societies; in turn, they carry 'social remittances' and other reverse-cultural flows – of ideas, values and tastes, practices and material culture – back to the migrants' societies of origin. Since most transnational connections are actually translocal, or linking specific sites with specific sites – in the short run this often means a transnational maintenance of local cultural forms. However, as migrants adapt to their new settings and take up new habits, preferences, and orientations, as they inevitably do, we may witness the continued emergence or indeed domination of syncretic, 'lowest common denominator' cultural forms and values spanning communities 'at home' and 'abroad' (as already exist, for instance, between the USA and Dominican Republic, France and the Congo, England and Pakistan). Such forms may threaten global cultural diversity not by cultural homogenization – as many have feared with reference to globalization – but through a kind of cultural siphoning through which only those forms and values viable on both ends of the transnational connection remain.

Although such siphoning may be one further mode of transformation stimulated by transnationalism, it will almost certainly represent just one possible trajectory. At the end of Chapter 6, five possible trajectories for specific religious traditions and groups were outlined: namely, remaining intact, homogenization, ecumenism, universalism and cosmopolitanism. These will likely also parallel the possible options or processes surrounding the cultural practices and identities of migrant transnational communities. It is noted in Chapter 3 that cosmopolitanism, represented by individuals' multiple cultural competences, seems to provide one of the most advantageous outcomes in terms of migrants' ability to position themselves in 'home' and 'host' contexts and 'participate effectively in activities that cut across two or more national boundaries' (Koehn and Rosenau 2002: 114).

A more cosmopolitan future is one possible outcome of the current global transformations described in this book. At present this seems a future toward which numerous processes of global interconnection – spearheaded, in many ways, by migrant transnational practices – are moving. However (as Chou En-Lai famously said of whether the French Revolution had had transformative effects), it is certainly 'too early to tell'.

BIBLIOGRAPHY

Al-Ali, N. (2002) 'Gender relations, transnational ties and rituals among Bosnian refugees', *Global Networks* 2(3): 242–62

Al-Ali, N. and K. Koser (eds) (2002) *New Approaches to Migration? Transnational Communities and the Transformation of Home*, London: Routledge

Al-Ali, N., R. Black and K. Koser (2001) 'Refugees and transnationalism: The experience of Bosnians and Eritreans in Europe', *Journal of Ethnic and Migration Studies* 27(4): 615–34

Al-Rasheed, M. (1998) *Iraqi Assyrian Christians in London: The Construction of Ethnicity*, Lewiston, NY: Edwin Mellen Press

Alarcón, R. (2001) 'The Development of Home Town Associations in the United States and the Use of Social Remittances in Mexico', Washington DC: Inter-American Dialogue, Final Report

Alba, R. and V. Nee (2003) *Remaking the American Mainstream: Assimilation and Contemporary Immigration*, Cambridge, MA: Harvard University Press

Albert, M., D. Jacobson and Y. Lapid (eds) (2001) *Identities, Borders, Orders: Rethinking International Relations Theory*, Minneapolis: University of Minnesota Press

Albrow, M. (1997) *The Global Age: State and Science beyond Modernity*, Cambridge: Polity Press

Aleinikoff, T.A. and D. Klusmeyer (2001) 'Plural nationality: Facing the future in a migratory world', in *Citizenship Today*, T.A. Aleinikoff and D. Klusmeyer (eds), Washington, DC: Carnegie Endowment for International Peace, pp. 63–88

Alger, C. (1997) 'Transnational social movements, world politics and global governance', in *Transnational Social Movements and Global Politics*, J. Smith, C. Chatfield and R. Pagnucco (eds), Syracuse, NY: Syracuse University Press, pp. 260–75

Alicea, M. (1997) '"A chambered nautilus": The contradictory nature of Puerto Rican women's role in the social construction of a transnational community', *Gender and Society* 11(5): 597–626

Ålund, A. (1991) 'Modern youth and transethnic identities', *European Journal of Intercultural Studies* 2(2): 49–62

Amin, A. and P. Cohendet (1999) 'Learning and adaptation in decentralised business networks', *Environment and Planning D: Society and Space* 17: 87–104

Amit-Talai, V. (1995) 'Conclusion: The "multi" cultural of youth', in *Youth Cultures*, V. Amit-Talai and H. Wulff (eds), London: Routledge, pp. 223–33

Anderson, B. (2000) *Doing the Dirty Work? The Global Politics of Domestic Labour*, London: Zed Books

—— (2001) 'Different roots in common ground: Transnationalism and migrant domestic workers in London', *Journal of Ethnic and Migration Studies* 27: 673–84

Anderson, B.R. (1995) 'Ice empire and ice hockey: Two *fin de siécle* dreams', *New Left Review* 214: 146–50

Anderson, J.W. (2006) 'A multi-hued national team thrills racially uneasy France', *Washington Post*, 7 July

Ang, I., J.E. Brand, G. Noble and D. Wilding (2002) *Living Diversity: Australia's Multicultural Future*, Artamon, Sydney: Special Broadcasting Service Corporation

Anthias, F. (1998) 'Evaluating "diaspora": Beyond ethnicity?', *Sociology* 32(3): 557–80

Appadurai, A. (1990) 'Disjuncture and difference in the global cultural economy', *Public Culture* 2: 1–24

—— (1995) 'The production of locality', in *Counterworks*, R. Fardon (ed.), London: Routledge, pp. 204–25

—— (1996) *Modernity at Large: Cultural Dimensions of Globalization*, Minneapolis: University of Minnesota Press

Appadurai, A. and C. Breckenridge (1989) 'On moving targets', *Public Culture* 2: i–iv

Arnold, F. (1992) 'The contribution of remittances to economic and social development', in *International Migration Systems*, M.M. Kritz, L.L. Lim and H. Zlotnik (eds), Oxford: Clarendon, pp. 205–20

Back, L. (1996) *New Ethnicities and Urban Culture: Racisms and Multiculture in Young Lives*, London: UCL Press

Ballard, R. (1994) 'Introduction: The emergence of *Desh Pardesh*', in *Desh Pardesh: The South Asian Presence in Britain*, R. Ballard (ed.), London: C. Hurst, pp. 1–34

—— (2003a) 'The South Asian Presence in Britain and its transnational connections', in *Culture and Economy in the Indian Diaspora*, B. Parekh, G. Singh and S. Vertovec (eds), London: Routledge, pp. 197–222

—— (2003b) 'Hawala transformed: Remittance-driven transnational networks in the post-imperial economic order', paper presented at World Bank/DFID conference on 'Migrant Remittances', London

Bamyeh, M.A. (1993) 'Transnationalism', *Current Sociology* 41(3): 1–95

Barnes, J.A. (1954) 'Class and committees in a Norwegian island parish', *Human Relations* 7: 39–58

Barnett, G.A. (2001) 'A longitudinal analysis of the international telecommunication network, 1978–1996', *American Behavioral Scientist* 44: 1638–55

Basok, T. (2003) 'Mexican seasonal migration to Canada and development: A community-based comparison', *International Migration* 41(2): 3–26

Basch, L., N. Glick Schiller and C. Szanton-Blanc (1993) *Nations Unbound: Transnational Projects, Postcolonial Predicaments, and Deterritorialized Nation-States*, New York: Routledge

Bauböck, R. (1994) *Transnational Citizenship: Membership and Rights in International Migration*, Aldershot, UK: Edward Elgar

—— (2002) 'Political community beyond the sovereign state: Supranational federalism and transnational minorities', in *Conceiving Cosmopolitanism: Theory, Context and Practice*, S. Vertovec and R. Cohen (eds), Oxford: Oxford University Press, pp. 110–36

—— (2003) 'Towards a political theory of migrant transnationalism', *International Migration Review* 37(3): 700–23

Baumann, M. (1995) 'Conceptualizing diaspora: The preservation of religious identity in foreign parts, exemplified by Hindu communities outside India', *Temenos* 31: 19–35

—— (1998) 'Sustaining "Little Indias": Hindu diasporas in Europe', in *Strangers and Sojourners*, G. ter Haar (ed.), Leuven: Peeters, pp. 95–132

—— (2000) 'Diaspora: Genealogies of semantics and transcultural comparison', *Numen* 47: 313–37

Beck, U. (1998) 'The cosmopolitan manifesto', *New Statesman*, 20 March, pp. 28–30

—— (2002) 'The cosmopolitan perspective: Sociology in the Second Age of modernity', in *Conceiving Cosmopolitanism*, S. Vertovec and R. Cohen (eds), Oxford: Oxford University Press, pp. 61–85

Bell, D. and B.M. Kennedy (eds) (2000) *The Cybercultures Reader*, London: Routledge

Benítez J.L. (2006) 'Transnational dimensions of the digital divide among Salvadoran immigrants in the Washington DC metropolitan area', *Global Networks* 6(2): 181–99

Berns McGown, R. (1999) *Muslims in the Diaspora: The Somali Communities of London and Toronto*, Toronto: University of Toronto Press

Bhabha, H. (1994) *The Location of Culture*, New York: Routledge

Bharati, A. (1976) 'Ritualistic tolerance and ideological rigour: The paradigm of the expatriate Hindus in East Africa', *Contributions to Indian Sociology* 10: 317–339

Bhardwaj, S.M. and N.M. Rao (1990) 'Asian Indians in the United States: A geographic appraisal', in *South Asians Overseas*, C. Clarke, C. Peach and S. Vertovec (eds), Cambridge: Cambridge University Press, pp. 197–217

Bhatt, C. (1997) *Liberation and Purity: Race, New Religious Movements and the Ethics of Postmodernity*, London: UCL Press

Bloemraad, I. (2004) 'Who claims dual citizenship? The limits of postnationalism, the possibilities of transnationalism, and the persistence of traditional citizenship', *International Migration Review* 38(2): 389–426

Bodnar, J. (1985) *The Transplanted: History of Immigrants in Urban America*, Bloomington, IN: Indiana University Press

Bosco, F.J. (2001) 'Place, space, networks and the sustainability of collective action', *Global Networks* 1(4): 307–329

Bott, E. (1957) *Family and Social Network: Roles, Norms, and External Relationships in Ordinary Urban Families*, London: Tavistock

Bourdieu, P. (1977) *Outline of a Theory of Practice*, Cambridge: Cambridge University Press

—— (1980) 'Le capital social: Notes provisoires', *Actes de la recherche en sciences socials* 31: 3–6

—— (1990) *The Logic of Practice*, Stanford: Stanford University Press

Bourne, R.S. (1916) 'Transnational America', *The Atlantic Monthly* July: 86–97

Bowen, D.G. (1987) 'The evolution of Gujarati Hindu organizations in Bradford', in *Hinduism in Great Britain*, R. Burghart (ed.), London: Tavistock, pp. 15–31

Boyarin, D. and J. Boyarin (1993) 'Diaspora: Generation and the ground of Jewish identity', *Critical Inquiry* 19(4): 693–725

Boyd, M. (1989) 'Family and personal networks in international migration: Recent developments and new agendas', *International Migration Review* 23(3): 638–70

Brettell, C.B. (2000) 'Theorizing migration in anthropology: The social construction of networks, identities, communities and globalscapes', in *Migration Theory*, C.B. Brettell and J.F. Hollifield (eds), London: Routledge, pp. 97–135

Bridge, G. (1995) 'Gentrification, class and community: A social network approach', in *The Urban Context*, A. Rogers and S. Vertovec (eds), Oxford: Berg, pp. 259–86

Brinkerhoff, J. (2004) 'Digital diasporas and international development: Afghan-Americans and the reconstruction of Afghanistan', *Public Administration and Development* 24: 397–413

Brown, L. (2003) 'Ethnic power', *Intele-CardNews*, January [www.intelecard.com]

Brubaker, R. (2001) 'The return of assimilation? Changing perspectives on immigration and its sequels in France, Germany, and the United States', *Ethnic and Racial Studies* 24(4): 531–48

Bryceson, D. and U. Vuorela (eds) (2002) *The Transnational Family: New European Frontiers and Global Networks*, Oxford: Berg

Burt, R.S. (1980) 'Models of network structure', *American Journal of Sociology* 85: 79–141

—— (1992) 'The social structure of competition', in *Networks and Organizations*, N. Nohria and R.G. Eccles (eds), Boston: Harvard Business School Press, pp. 57–91

Byman, D.L., P. Chalk, B. Hoffman, W. Rosenau and D. Brannan (2001) *Trends in Outside Support for Insurgent Movements*, Santa Monica, CA: Rand

Caglar, A. (1994) German Turks in Berlin: Migration and Their Quest for Social Mobility, Ph. D. Thesis, Anthropology, McGill University, Montreal

—— (2001) 'Constraining metaphors and the transnationalisation of spaces in Berlin', *Journal of Ethnic and Migration Studies* 27(4): 601–13

—— (2002) 'Media corporatism and cosmopolitanism' in *Conceiving Cosmopolitanism*, S. Vertovec and R. Cohen (eds), Oxford: Oxford University Press, pp. 180–90

Cairncross, F. (1997) *The Death of Distance*, London: Orion

Cano, G. (2005) 'The Mexico-North Report on Transnationalism', paper at the 63rd– Annual Conference of the Midwest Political Science Association, Chicago

Carnoy, M. and M. Castells (2001) 'Globalization, the knowledge society, and the network state: Poulantzas at the millennium', *Global Networks* 1(1): 1–18

Carter, D.M. (1997) *States of Grace: Senegalese in Italy and the New European Immigration*, Minneapolis: University of Minnesota Press

Castells, M. (1996) *The Rise of the Network Society*, Oxford: Blackwell

—— (1997) *The Power of Identity*, Oxford: Blackwell

—— (1998) *End of Millennium*, Oxford: Blackwell

Castles, S. (1998) 'New Migrations, ethnicity and nationalism in Southeast and East Asia', Oxford: ESRC Transnational Communities Programme Working Paper WPTC-98-09

—— (2001) 'Studying social transformation', *International Political Science Review* 22(1): 13–32

—— (2002) 'Migration and community formation under conditions of globalization', *International Migration Review* 36(4): 1143–68

—— (2003) 'Towards a sociology of forced migration and social transformation', *Sociology* 37(1): 13–34

—— (2006) 'Back to the future? Can Europe meet its labour needs through temporary migration?', Oxford: International Migration Institute Working Paper No. 1

Castles, S., M. Korac, E. Vasta and S. Vertovec (2003) *Integration: Mapping the Field*, London: Home Office Online Report 28/03

Chapman, M. (1979) 'The cross-cultural study of circulation', *Current Anthropology* 20(1): 111–114

Charsley, K. (2007) 'Risk, trust, gender and transnational cousin marriage among British Pakistanis', *Ethnic and Racial Studies* 30(6): 1117–31

Chow, R. (1993) *Writing Diaspora: Tactics of Intervention in Contemporary Cultural Studies*, Bloomington, IN: Indiana University Press

Clarke, C., C. Peach and S. Vertovec (1990) 'Introduction: Themes in the study of the South Asian diaspora', in *South Asians Overseas*, C. Clarke, C. Peach and S. Vertovec (eds), Cambridge: Cambridge University Press, pp. 1–29

Clifford, J. (1992) 'Traveling cultures', in *Cultural Studies*, L. Grossberg, C. Nelson and P. Treichler (eds), New York: Routledge, pp. 96–116

—— (1994) 'Diasporas', *Cultural Anthropology* 9: 302–38

Cohen, J. and I. Sirkeci (2005) 'A comparative study of Turkish and Mexican transnational migration outcomes: Facilitating or restricting immigrant integration?', in *Crossing Over*, H. Henke (ed.), Lanham, MD: Lexington, pp. 147–62

Cohen, P. (1999) 'Rethinking the Diasporama', *Patterns of Prejudice* 33(1): 3–22

Cohen, R. (1995) 'Rethinking "Babylon": iconoclastic conceptions of the diasporic experience', *New Community* 21, pp. 5–18

—— (1996) 'Diasporas and the nation-state: from victims to challengers', *International Affairs* 72, pp. 507–20

—— (1997) *Global Diasporas: An Introduction*, London: University College London Press

—— (1998) 'Transnational social movements', Oxford: ESRC Transnational Communities Programme Working Paper WPTC-98-10

Cohen, R. and P. Kennedy (2000) *Global Sociology*, Houndmills, UK: Macmillan

Cohen, R. and S.M. Rai (2000) 'Global social movements: Towards a cosmopolitan politics', in *Global Social Movements*, R. Cohen and S.M. Rai (eds), London: Athlone, pp. 1–17

Coleman, J.S. (1988) 'Social capital and the creation of human capital', *American Journal of Sociology* 94: 95–121

Collier, P. and A. Hoeffler (2001) 'Greed and grievance in civil war', Washington, DC: The World Bank, *Policy Research* Working Paper 2355

Constant, A. and K.F. Zimmerman (2004) 'Circular movements and time away from the host country', London: Centre for Economic Policy Research Discussion Paper 4228

Cordell, D.D., J.W. Gregory and V. Piché (1996) *Hoe and Wage: A Social History of a Circular Migration System in West Africa*, Boulder, CO: Westview Press

Cornelius, W.A. (2001) 'Death at the border: Efficacy and unintended consequences of US immigration control policy', *Population and Development Review* 27(4): 661–85

de la Cruz, V. (2002) 'Selling southward', *Intele-CardNews*, August [www.intelecard.com]

Dahya, B. (1974) 'The nature of Pakistani ethnicity in industrial cities in Britain', in *Urban Ethnicity*, A. Cohen (ed.), London: Tavistock, pp. 77–118

DeMars, W.E. (2005) *NGOs and Transnational Networks: Wild Cards in World Politics*, London: Pluto Press

DeSipio, L. (2000) 'Sending Money Home... For Now: Remittances and Immigrant Adaptation in the United States', Washington, DC: Inter-American Dialogue and the Tomás Rivera Policy Institute, Working Paper

Dicken, P. (1992) *Global Shift: The Internationalization of Economic Activity*, London: Paul Chapman, 2nd ed.

Dicken, P., P.F. Kelly, K. Olds and H. W-C. Yeung (2001) 'Chains and networks, territories and scales: Towards a relational framework for analysing the global economy', *Global Networks* 1(2): 89–112

Dirven, L. (1998) 'The Palmyrene diaspora in East and West: A Syrian community in the diaspora in the Roman period', in *Strangers and Sojourners*, G. ter Haar (ed.), Leuven, Belgium: Peeters, pp. 59–75

Dolan, J.P. (1998) 'The immigrants and their gods: A new perspective in American religious history', in *Religion in American History*, J. Butler and H.S. Stout (eds), New York: Oxford University Press, pp. 146–56

Duany, J. (2002) 'Mobile livelihoods: The sociocultural practices of circular migrants between Puerto Rico and the United States', *International Migration Review* 36(2): 355–88

Durand, J., E.A. Parrado and D.S. Massey (1996) 'Migradollars and development: A reconsideration of the Mexican case', *International Migration Review* 30(2): 423–44

Dutton, W.H. (1999) *Society on the Line: Information Politics in the Digital Age*, Oxford: Oxford University Press

Ebaugh, H.R., J. O'Brien and J. Saltzman Chafetz (2000) 'The social ecology of residential patterns and memberships in immigrant churches', *Journal for the Scientific Study of Religion* 39(1): 107–116

Ebin, V. (1996) 'Making room versus creating space: The construction of spatial categories by itinerant Mouride traders', in *Making Muslim Space in North America and Europe*, B. Metcalf (ed.), Berkeley, CA: University of California Press, pp. 92–109

EC/Commission of the European Communities (2005a) 'Migration and development: Some concrete orientations', Brussels: Communication from the Commission to the Council, the European Parliament, the European Economic and Social Committee and the Committee of the Regions, COM(2005) 390 Final

—— (2005b) 'Policy Plan on Legal Migration', Brussels: Communication from the Commission, COM(2005) 669 Final

Eck, D.L. (1996) 'American Hindus: The Ganges and the Mississippi', paper presented at Conference on 'The Comparative Study of the South Asian Diaspora Religious Experience in Britain, Canada and the USA', School of Oriental and African Studies, London

Economist, The (2003a) 'Special Report on Diasporas: A World of Exiles', 4 January

—— (2003b) 'Our kinda ciudad', 11 January, p. 39

—— (2007a) 'Special Report on Migration: Open Up', 5 January

—— (2007b) 'Counting the cash', 6 October, p. 102

—— (2008) 'Slowing the money trail', 7 April, pp. 52–3

Eickelman, D.F. (1997) 'Trans-state Islam and security', in *Transnational Religion and Fading States*, S. Hoeber Rudolph and J. Piscatori (eds), Boulder, CO: Westview Press, pp. 27–46

Eickelman, D.F. and J.W. Anderson (eds) (1999) *New Media in the Muslim World: The Emerging Public Sphere*, Bloomington, IN: Indiana University Press

Eickelman, D.F. and J. Piscatori (1990a) 'Preface', in *Muslim Travelers*, D.F. Eickelman and J. Piscatori (eds), London: Routledge, pp. xii–xxii

—— (1990b) 'Social theory in the study of Muslim societies', in *Muslim Travelers*, D.F. Eickelman and J. Piscatori (eds), London: Routledge, pp. 3–25

El Qorchi, M., S.M. Maimbo and J.F. Wilson (2003) *Informal Funds Transfer Systems: An Analysis of the Informal Hawala System*, Washington, DC: International Monetary Fund and World Bank

Elkan, W. (1967) 'Circular migration and the growth of towns in East Africa', *International Labour Review* 96(6): 581–89

Elkins, D.J. (1999) 'Think locally, act globally: Reflections on virtual neighbourhoods', *The Public* 6(1): 37–54

Emirbayer, M. and J. Goodwin (1994) 'Network analysis, culture, and the problem of agency', *American Journal of Sociology* 99: 1411–54

Escobar, A. (1994) 'Welcome to Cyberia: Notes on the anthropology of cyberculture', Current Anthropology 35(3): 56–76

Faist, T. (2000) The Volume and Dynamics of International Migration and Transnational Social Spaces, Oxford: Oxford University Press

—— (2001) 'Dual Citizenship as overlapping membership', Malmö: School of International Migration and Ethnic Relations, Willy Brandt Series of Working Papers 3/01

Faist, T. and E. Özveren (eds) (2004) Transnational Social Spaces: Agents, Networks and Institutions, Aldershot, UK: Ashgate

Favell, A. (2001) 'Migration, mobility and globalony: Metaphors and rhetoric in the sociology of globalisation', Global Networks 1: 389–398

FCC/Federal Communications Commission (2002) Trends in Telephone Service, Washington, DC: Federal Communications Commission, Report

Feldblum, M. (1998) 'Rationing citizenship: New trends in policymaking', paper presented at Comparative Citizenship Conference, Carnegie Endowment for International Peace, Washington, DC

Fitzgerald, D. (2000) Negotiating Extra-Territorial Citizenship: Mexican Migration and the Transnational Politics of Community, La Jolla, CA: Center for Comparative Immigration Studies, Monograph Series No. 2

—— (2002) 'Locating the national and local in "transnationalism"', paper at the UCLA Second Annual Interdisciplinary Conference on Race, Ethnicity and Immigration, Los Angeles

Flecker, J. and R. Simsa (2001) 'Co-ordination and control in transnational business and non-profit organizations', in New Transnational Social Spaces, L. Pries (ed.), London: Routledge, pp. 164–84

Foner, N. (1997) 'What's new about transnationalism? New York immigrants today and at the turn of the century', Diaspora 6(3): 355–75

—— (2000) From Ellis Island to JFK: New York's Two Great Waves of Immigration, New Haven, CN: Yale University Press

Fouron, G. and N. Glick Schiller (2001) 'All in the family: Gender, transnational migration, and the nation state', Identities 7(4): 539–82

Frank, R. and R.A. Hummer (2002) 'The other side of the paradox: The risk of low birth weight among infants of migrant and nonmigrant households within Mexico', International Migration Review 36(3): 746–65

Fritz, M. (1998) 'Pledging multiple allegiances', Los Angeles Times, 6 April

Gamlen, A. (2006) 'Diaspora Engagement Policies: What are they, and what kinds of states use them?', Oxford: ESRC Centre on Migration, Policy and Society (COMPAS) Working Paper No. WP-06-32

Gammeltoft, P. (2002) 'Remittances and other financial flows to developing countries', International Migration 40(5): 181–211

Gardner, K. (1993a) 'Desh-Bidesh: Sylheti images of home and away', *Man* 28(1): 1–15

—— (1993b) 'Mullahs, migrants, miracles: Travel and transformation in Sylhet', *Contributions to Indian Sociology* 27(2): 213–35

—— (1995) *Global Migrants, Local Lives: Travel and Transformation in Rural Bangladesh*, Oxford: Clarendon Press

—— (2002) 'Death of a migrant: Transnational death rituals and gender among British Sylhetis', *Global Networks* 2(3): 191–204

Gardner, K. and R. Grillo (2002) 'Transnational households and ritual: An overview', *Global Networks* 2(3): 179–90

GCIM/Global Commission on International Migration (2005) *Migration in an Interconnected World: New Directions for Action*, Geneva: Global Commission on International Migration

Georges, E. (1990) *The Making of a Transnational Community: Migration, Development and Cultural Change in the Dominican Republic*, New York: Columbia University Press

Gibb, C. (1998) 'Religious identification in transnational contexts: Becoming Muslim in Ethiopia and Canada', *Diaspora* 7(2): 247–69

Gill, H. (2004) Dominican *vodù* and Migrant Strategy: Transnational Networks of Religion, Work and Music, DPhil. thesis, University of Oxford

Gillespie, M. (1995) *Television, Ethnicity and Cultural Change*, London: Routledge

Gilroy, P. (1987) *There ain't no Black in the Union Jack*, London: Hutchinson

—— (1993) *The Black Atlantic: Modernity and Double Consciousness*, London: Verso

Glazer, N. and D.P. Moynihan (1963) *Beyond the Melting Pot: The Negroes, Puerto Ricans, Jews, Italians and Irish of New York City*, Cambridge, MA: MIT Press

Glick Schiller, N. (1999) 'Transmigrants and nation-states: Something old and something new in the U.S. immigrant experience', in *The Handbook of International Migration*, C. Hirschman, J. Dewind and P. Kasinitz (eds), New York: Russell Sage Foundation, pp. 94–119

Glick Schiller, N. and G. Fouron (1998) 'Transnational lives and national identities: The identity politics of Haitian immigrants', in *Transnationalism from Below*, M.P. Smith and L.E. Guarnizo (eds), New Brunswick, NJ: Transaction Publishers, pp. 130–61

Glick Schiller, N. and P. Levitt (2006) 'Haven't we heard this somewhere before? A substantive view of transnational migration studies by way of a reply to Waldinger and Fitzgerald', Princeton, NJ: Center for Migration and Development Working Paper 06–01

Glick Schiller, N., L. Basch and C. Blanc-Szanton (eds) (1992a) *Towards a* transnational perspective on migration: Race, class, ethnicity and national-ism reconsidered, New York: New York Academy of Sciences

—— (1992b) 'Transnationalism: a new analytic framework for understand-ing migration', in Toward a Transnational Perspective on Migration, N. Glick Schiller, L. Basch and C. Blanc-Szanton (eds), New York: New York Academy of Sciences, pp. 1–24

Golbert, R. (2001) 'Transnational orientations from home: Constructions of Israel and transnational space among Ukrainian Jewish youth', Journal of Ethnic and Migration Studies 27(4): 713–31

Goldring, L. (1998) 'The power of status in transnational social fields', in Transnationalism from Below, M.P. Smith and L.E. Guarnizo (eds), New Brunswick, NJ: Transaction Publishers, pp. 165–95

—— (2001) 'The gender and geography of citizenship in Mexico–U.S. transnational spaces', Identities 7(4): 501–37

Gordon, M.M. (1964) Assimilation in American Life: The Role of Race, Religion and National Origins, New York: Oxford University Press

Goulbourne, H. (1999) 'The transnational character of Caribbean kinship in Britain', in Changing Britain, S. McRae (ed.), Oxford: Oxford University Press, pp. 176–97

Grace, D. (2001) 'The development potential of remittances and the credit union difference', paper at the Regional Conference Remittances as a Development Tool, Washington, DC: Multilateral Investment Fund, Inter-American Development Bank

Granovetter, M.S. (1973) 'The strength of weak ties', American Journal of Sociology 78: 1360–80

—— (1985) 'Economic action and social structure: The problem of embed-dedness', American Journal of Sociology 91: 481–510

—— (1992) 'Problems of explanation in economic sociology', in Networks and Organizations, N. Nohria and R.G. Eccles (eds), Boston, MA: Harvard Business School Press, pp. 25–56

Grant, K., P. Levine and F. Trentmann (eds) (2007) Beyond Sovereignty: Britain, Empire and Transnationalism, c. 1880–1950, Basingstoke, UK: Palgrave Macmillan

Grasmuck, S. and P. Pessar (1991) Between Two Islands: Dominican International Migration, Berkeley, CA: University of California Press

Green, S. (2005) 'Between ideology and pragmatism: The politics of dual nationality in Germany', International Migration Review, 39(4): 921–52

Guarnizo, L.E. (1997) 'The emergence of a transnational social formation and the mirage of return migration among Dominican transmigrants', Identities 4(2): 281–322

—— (2003) 'The economics of transnational living', International Migration Review 37(3): 666–99

Guarnizo, L.E. and M.P. Smith (1998) 'The locations of transnationalism', in *Transnationalism from Below*, M.P. Smith and L.E. Guarnizo (eds), New Brunswick, NJ: Transaction Publishers, pp. 3–34

Guarnizo, L.E., A. Portes and W. Haller (2003) 'Assimilation and transnationalism: Determinants of transnational political action among contemporary migrants', *American Journal of Sociology* 108(6): 1211–48

Guarnizo, L.E., A. Ignacio Sánchez and E.M. Roach (1999) 'Mistrust, fragmented solidarity and transnational migration: Colombians in New York City and Los Angeles', *Ethnic and Racial Studies* 22(2): 367–96

Guillén, M.F. (2001) 'Is globalization civilizing, destructive or feeble? A critique of five key debates in the Social Science literature', *Annual Review of Sociology* 27: 235–60

Gupta, A. and J. Ferguson (1992) 'Beyond "culture": space, identity, and the politics of difference', *Cultural Anthropology* 7: 6–23

Haddad, Y.Y. and J.L. Esposito (eds) (2000) *Muslims on the Americanization Path*, New York: Oxford University Press

Hagan, J.M. (1994) *Deciding to be Legal: A Maya Community in Houston*, Philadelphia, PA: Temple University Press

Hall, Stuart (1990) 'Cultural identity and diaspora', in *Identity: Community, Culture, Difference*, J. Rutherford (ed.), London: Lawrence and Wishart, pp. 222–37

—— (1991) 'Old and new identities, old and new ethnicities', in *Culture, Globalization and the World-System*, A.D. King (ed.), Houndmills, UK: Macmillan, pp. 41–68

—— (2002) 'Political belonging in a world of multiple identities', in *Conceiving Cosmopolitanism*, S. Vertovec and R. Cohen (eds), Oxford: Oxford University Press, pp. 25–31

Hannerz, U. (1980) *Exploring the City: Inquiries Toward an Urban Anthropology*, New York: Columbia University Press

—— (1987) 'The world in creolisation', *Africa* 57: 546–559

—— (1990) 'Cosmopolitans and locals in world culture', in *Global Culture*, M. Featherstone (ed.), London: Sage: pp. 237–51

—— (1992a) 'The global ecumeme as a network of networks', in *Conceptualizing Society*, A. Kuper (ed.), London: Routledge, pp. 34–56

—— (1992b) *Cultural Complexity: Studies in the Social Organization of Meaning*, New York: Columbia University Press

—— (1996) *Transnational Connections: Culture, People, Places*, London: Routledge

Hansen, R. and P. Weil (2002) 'Introduction: Dual citizenship in a changed world: Immigration, gender and social rights', in *Dual Nationality, Social Rights and Federal Citizenship in the U.S. and Europe*, R. Hansen and P. Weil (eds), Oxford: Berghahn, pp. 1–15

Harney, N.D. and L. Baldassar (2007) 'Tracking transnationalism: Migrancy and its futures', *Journal of Ethnic and Migration Studies* 33(2): 189–98

Hawley, C. (2008a) 'Importing goals at Euro 2008', *Spiegel* online, 6 June, <www.spiegel.de/international>

—— (2008b) 'Germany–Turkey clash shines spotlight on integration', *Spiegel* online, 25 June, <www.spiegel.de/international>

Hebdige, D. (1987) *Cut 'n' Mix: Culture, Identity and Caribbean Music*, London: Routledge

Hegedus, Z. (1989) 'Social movements and social change in self-creative society: New civil initiatives in the international arena', *International Sociology* 4(1): 19–36

Heisler, M.O. (2001) 'Now and then, here and there: Migration and the transformation of identities, borders, and orders', in *Identities, Borders, Orders*, M. Albert, D. Jacobson and Y. Lapid (eds), Minneapolis: University of Minnesota Press, pp. 225–47

Held, D., A. McGrew, D. Goldblatt and J. Perraton (1999) *Global Transformations: Politics, Economics and Culture*, Cambridge: Polity Press

Herberg, W. (1955) *Protestant–Catholic–Jew*, New York: Doubleday

Herrera Lima, F. (2001) 'Transnational families: Institutions of transnational social space', in *New Transnational Social Spaces*, L. Pries (ed.), London: Routledge, pp. 77–93

Hinnells, J.R. (1997a) 'The study of diaspora religion', in *A New Handbook of Living Religions*, J.R. Hinnells (ed.), Oxford: Blackwell, pp. 682–90

—— (1997b) 'Comparative reflections on South Asian religion in international migration', in *A New Handbook of Living Religions*, J.R. Hinnells (ed.), Oxford: Blackwell, pp. 819–47

Hochschild, A.R. (2000) 'Global Care Chains and Emotional Surplus Value', in *On the Edge: Globalization and the New Millennium*, A. Giddens and W. Hutton (eds), London: Sage, pp. 130–146

Hoffman, B. (1998a) *Inside Terrorism*, New York: Columbia University Press

—— (1998b) 'Old madness, new methods: revival of religious terrorism begs for broader U.S. policy', *Rand Review* 22(2): 12–17

Hondagneu-Sotelo, P. (1994) *Gendered Transitions: Mexican Experiences of Immigration*, Berkeley, CA: University of California Press

Hondagneu-Sotelo, P. and E. Avila (1997) '"I'm here, but I'm there": The meanings of Latina transnational motherhood', *Gender and Society* 11(5): 548–71

Horst, H.A. (2006) 'The blessings and burdens of communication: Cell phones in Jamaican transnational social fields', *Global Networks* 6(2): 143–59

Horst, H.A. and D. Miller (2006) *The Cell Phone: An Anthropology of Communication*, Oxford: Berg

House of Commons, International Development Committee (2004) 'Migration and Development: How to make migration work for poverty reduction', London: The Stationery Office

Howe, D. (2006) 'Tebbit's loyalty test is dead', *New Statesman*, 3 July

Hutheesing, M.O.L.K. (1983) 'The Thiratee Kalyanam ceremony among South Indian Hindu communities of Malaysia', *Eastern Anthropologist* 36: 131–147

IFAD/International Fund for Agricultural Development (2007) *Sending Money Home: Worldwide Remittance Flows to Developing Countries*, Rome: International Fund for Agricultural Development

Ignatieff, M. (1993) *Blood and Belonging: Journeys into the New Nationalism*, London: Vintage

ILO/International Labour Organization (2000) 'Making the best of globalization: Migrant worker remittances and micro-finance', Geneva: International Labour Organization, Social Finance Unit, Workshop Report

Intelecard (2003) 'One hot country', *Intele-CardNews*, Staff Report, January <www.intelecard.com>

IOM/International Organization for Migration (2005) *World Migration 2005: Costs and Benefits of International Migration*, Geneva: International Organization for Migration

Ireland, P. (1994) *The Policy Challenge of Ethnic Diversity: Immigrant Politics in France and Switzerland*, Cambridge, MA: Harvard University Press

Itzigsohn, J. and S. Giorguli-Saucedo (2002) 'Immigrant incorporation and sociocultural transnationalism', *International Migration Review* 36(3): 766–98

—— (2005) 'Incorporation, transnationalism, and gender: Immigrant incorporation and transnational participation as gendered processes', *International Migration Review* 39(4): 895–920

Itzigsohn, J., C. Dore Cabral, E. Hernández Medina and O. Vázquez (1999) 'Mapping Dominican transnationalism: Narrow and broad transnational practices', *Ethnic and Racial Studies* 22(2): 316–39

Iyer, P. (2001) *The Global Soul: Jet Lag, Shopping Malls and the Search for Home*, London: Vintage

Jackson, P. and E. Nesbitt (1993) *Hindu Children in Britain*, Stoke-on-Trent, UK: Trentham

Jackson, P., P. Crang and D. Dwyer (eds) (2004) *Transnational Spaces*, London: Routledge

Jacobson, M.F. (1995) *Special Sorrows: The Diasporic Imagination of Irish, Polish, and Jewish Immigrants in the United States*, Cambridge, MA: Harvard University Press

Jain, P. and M. Moore (2003) 'What makes microcredit programmes effective? Fashionable fallacies and workable realities', Brighton, UK: Institute of Development Studies Working Paper 177

Jayawardena, C. (1968) 'Migration and social change: A survey of Indian communities overseas', *Geographical Review* 58: 426–49

—— (1980) 'Culture and ethnicity in Guyana and Fiji', *Man* 15: 430–50

Jayaweera, H. and T. Choudhury (2008) *Immigration, Faith and Cohesion: Evidence from Local Areas with Significant Muslim Populations*, York, UK: Joseph Rowntree Foundation

Jenkins, R. (1992) *Pierre Bourdieu*, London: Routledge

—— (1996) *Social Identity*, London: Routledge

Jones, W.T. (1972) 'World views: Their nature and their function', *Current Anthropology* 13(1): 79–109

Jones-Correa, M. (2001) 'Under two flags: Dual nationality in Latin America and its consequences for naturalization in the United States', *International Migration Review* 35(4): 997–1029

Joppke, C. (ed.) (1998) *Challenge to the Nation-State: Immigration in Western Europe and the United States*, Oxford: Oxford University Press

—— (1999) *Immigration and the Nation-State: The United States, Germany and Great Britain*, Oxford: Oxford University Press

Joppke, C. and E. Morawska (2003) 'Integrating immigrants in liberal nation-states: policies and practices', in *Toward Assimilation and Citizenship*, C. Joppke and E. Morawska (eds), Basingstoke, UK: Palgrave, pp. 1–36

Jordan, T. (1999) *Cyberpower: The Culture and Politics of Cyberspace and the Internet*, London: Routledge

Kaldor, M. (1996) 'Cosmopolitanism versus nationalism: the new divide?', in *Europe's New Nationalism*, R. Caplan and J. Feffer (eds), Oxford: Oxford University Press, pp. 42–58

Karim, K. (ed.) (2003) *The Media of Diaspora*, London: Routledge

Kasinitz, P., M.C. Waters, J.H. Mollenkopf and M. Anil (2002) 'Transnationalism and the children of immigrants in contemporary New York', in *The Changing Face of Home*, P. Levitt and M.C. Waters (eds), New York: Russell Sage Foundation, pp. 96–122

Kastoryano, R. (2002) 'Türken mit deutschem Pass: Sociological and political aspects of dual nationality in Germany', in *Dual Nationality, Social Rights and Federal Citizenship in the U.S. and Europe*, R. Hansen and P. Weil (eds), Oxford: Berghahn, pp. 158–75

Kearney, M. (1986) 'From the invisible hand to visible feet: Anthropological studies of migration and development', *Annual Review of Anthropology* 15: 331–61

—— (1995) 'The local and the global: The anthropology of globalization and transnationalism', *Annual Review of Anthropology* 24: 547–65

Keck, M. and K. Sikkink (1998) *Activists Beyond Borders: Advocacy Networks in International Politics*, Ithaca, NY: Cornell University Press

—— (2000) 'Historical precursors to modern transnational social movements and networks', in *Globalizations and Social Movements*, J.A. Guidry, M.D. Kennedy and M. Zald (eds), Ann Arbor, MI: University of Michigan Press, pp. 35–53

Kempadoo, K. and J. Doezema (eds) (1998) *Global Sex Workers: Rights, Resistance, and Redefinition*, London: Routledge

Keohane, R.O. and J.S. Nye (eds) (1971) *Transnational Relations and World Politics*, Cambridge, MA: Harvard University Press

King, R.L., J. Connell and P. White (eds) (1995) *Writing across Worlds: Migration and Literature*, London: Routledge

King, R., A.M. Warnes and A.M. Williams (1998) 'International retirement migration in Europe', *International Journal of Population Geography* 4(2): 91–111

Kivisto, P. (2001) 'Theorizing transnational immigration: A critical review of current efforts', *Ethnic and Racial Studies* 24(4): 549–77

—— (2005) 'Social spaces, transnational immigrant communities, and the politics of incorporation', in *Incorporating Diversity*, P. Kivisto (ed.), Boulder, CO: Paradigm, pp. 299–319

Klandermans, B. and D. Oegema (1987) 'Potentials, networks, motivations, and barriers: Steps towards participation in social movements', *American Sociological Review* 52: 519–31

Knott, K. (1986) *Hinduism in Leeds: A Study of Religious Practice in the Indian Hindu Community and Hindu-Related Groups*, Leeds, UK: Community Religions Project, University of Leeds

—— (1991) 'Bound to Change? The religions of South Asians in Britain', in *Aspects of the South Asian Diaspora*, S. Vertovec (ed.), New Delhi: Oxford University Press, pp. 86–111

Knott, K. and S. Khokher (1993) 'Religious and ethnic identity among young Muslim women in Bradford', *New Community* 19: 593–610

Koehn, P.H. and J.N. Rosenau (2002) 'Transnational competence in an emerging epoch', *International Studies Perspectives* 3: 105–27

Koopmans, R. and P. Statham (2001) 'How national citizenship shapes transnationalism: A comparative analysis of migrant claims-making in Germany, Great Britain and the Netherlands', Oxford: ESRC Transnational Communities Programme Working Paper WPTC-01-10

Koser, K. (2002) 'From refugees to transnational communities?', in *New Approaches to Migration?*, N. Al-Ali and K. Koser (eds), London: Routledge, pp. 138–52

Koslowski, R. (2001) 'Demographic boundary maintenance in world politics: Of international norms on dual nationality', in *Identities, Borders, Orders*, M. Albert, D. Jacobson and Y. Lapid (eds), Minneapolis: University of Minnesota Press, pp. 203–23

Kriesberg, L. (1997) 'Social movements and global transformation', in *Transnational Social Movements and Global Politics*, J. Smith, C. Chatfield and R. Pagnucco (eds), Syracuse, NY: Syracuse University Press, pp. 3–18

Kyle, D. (1999) 'The Otavalo trade diaspora: Social capital and transnational entrepreneurship', *Ethnic and Racial Studies* 22(2): 422–46

—— (2000) *Transnational Peasants: Migrations, Networks, and Ethnicity in Andean Ecuador*, Baltimore: Johns Hopkins University Press

Landau, L.B. and I.S.M. Haupt (2007) 'Tactical cosmopolitanism and idioms of belonging: Insertion and self-exclusion in Johannesburg', Johannesburg: University of Witwatersrand Forced Migration Studies Programme, Migration Studies Working Paper Series No. 32

Landolt, P. (2001) 'Salvadoran economic transnationalism: Embedded strategies for household maintenance, immigrant incorporation, and entrepreneurial expansion', *Global Networks* 1(3): 21–41

Landolt, P., L. Autler and S. Baires (1999) 'From "Hermano Lejano" to "Hermano Mayor": The dialectics of Salvadoran transnationalism', *Ethnic and Racial Studies* 22(2): 290–315

Lane, A.D., T. Alderton, M. Bloor, E. Kaveci, B. Obando-Rojas, H. Sampson, M. Thomas, N. Winchester and M. Zhao (2001) *The Impact on Seafarers' Living and Working Conditions of Changes in the Structure of the Shipping Industry*, Geneva: International Labour Office

Lapid, Y. (2001) 'Identities, borders, orders: Nudging international relations theory in a new direction', in *Identities, Borders, Orders*, M. Albert, D. Jacobson and Y. Lapid (eds), Minneapolis: University of Minnesota Press, pp. 1–20

Lapidus, I.M. (2001) 'Between universalism and particularism: The historical bases of Muslim communal, national and global identities', *Global Networks* 1(1): 37–55

Larson, H. (1989) Asian children – British Childhood, Ph.D. Thesis, University of California – Berkeley

Law, J. and J. Hassard (eds) (1999) *Actor Network Theory and After*, Oxford: Blackwell

Lessinger, J. (1992) 'Nonresident-Indian investment and India's drive for industrial modernization', in *Anthropology and the Global Factory*, F. A. Rothstein and M. L. Blim (eds), New York: Bergin & Garvey, pp. 62–82

—— (1995) *From the Ganges to the Hudson: Indian Immigrants in New York City*, Boston, MA: Allyn & Bacon

Levitt, P. (1998) 'Local-level global religion: The case of U.S.–Dominican migration', *Journal for the Scientific Study of Religion* 37(1): 74–89.

—— (2001a) *The Transnational Villagers*. Berkeley, CA: University of California Press

—— (2001b) 'Transnational migration: Taking stock and future directions', *Global Networks* 1(3): 195–216

—— (2002) 'The ties that change: Relations to the ancestral home over the life cycle', in *The Changing Face of Home*, P. Levitt and M.C. Waters (eds), New York: Russell Sage Foundation, pp. 123–44

—— (2003) 'Keeping feet in both worlds: Transnational practices and immigrant incorporation in the United States', in *Toward Assimilation and Citizenship*, C. Joppke and E. Morawska (eds), Basingstoke, UK: Palgrave, pp. 177–94

Levitt, P. and R. de la Dehesa (2003) 'Transnational migration and the redefinition of the state: Variations and explanations', *Ethnic and Racial Studies* 26(4): 587–611

Levitt, P. and N. Glick Schiller (2004) 'Conceptualizing simultaneity: A transnational social field perspective on society', *International Migration Review* 38(3): 1002–39

Levitt, P. and B.N. Jaworsky (2007) 'Transnational migration studies: Past developments and future trends', *Annual Review of Sociology* 33: 129–56

Levitt, P. and N.N. Sørensen (2004) 'The transnational turn in migration studies', Global Migration Perspectives No. 6, Geneva: Global Commission on International Migration

Levitt, P. and M.C. Waters (2002) 'Introduction', in *The Changing Face of Home*, P. Levitt and M.C. Waters (eds), New York: Russell Sage Foundation, pp. 1–30

Levitt, P., J. DeWind and S. Vertovec (eds) (2003) 'Transnational migration: International Perspectives', special issue of *International Migration Review* 37(3)

Light, I., M. Zhou and R. Kim (2002) 'Transnationalism and American exports in an English-speaking world', *International Migration Review* 36(3): 702–25

Lobel, O. (2003) 'Family geographies: Global care chains, transnational parenthood and new legal challenges in an era of labour globalization', in *Law and Geography*, J. Holder and C. Harrison (eds), Oxford: Oxford University Press, pp. 156–78

Logan, P. (1988) Practicing Hinduism: the experience of Gujarati adults and children in Britain, Unpublished report, Thomas Coram Research Unit, University of London Institute of Education

Louch, H., E. Hargittai and M.A. Ceneno (1999) 'Phone calls and fax machines: The limits to globalization', *The Washington Quarterly* 22: 83–10

Lowell, B.L. and R.O. de la Garza (2000) 'The Developmental Role of Remittances in U.S. Latino Communities and in Latin American Countries', Washington DC: Inter-American Dialogue, Final Project Report

Lux, S.J. (2006) 'The nature of transnational networks: Wild and complex', *International Studies Review* 8: 349–51

Mahler, S. (1998) 'Theoretical and empirical contributions toward a research agenda for transnationalism', in *Transnationalism from Below*, M.P. Smith and L.E. Guarnizo (eds), New Brunswick, NJ: Transaction Publishers, pp. 64–100

—— (2000) 'Migration and transnational issues: Recent trends and prospects for 2020', Hamburg: Institut für Iberoamerika-Kunde, CA 2020 Working Paper No. 4

—— (2001) 'Transnational relationships: The struggle to communicate across borders', *Identities* 7: 583–619

Mahler, S.J. and P.R. Pessar (2001) 'Gendered geographies of power: Analyzing gender across transnational spaces', *Identities* 7(4): 441–59

Maira, S. Marr (2002) *Desis in the House: Indian American Youth Culture in New York City*, Philadelphia, PA: Temple University Press

Mandaville, P.G. (1999) 'Digital Islam: Changing the boundaries of religious knowledge?', Leiden: *ISIM* [International Institute for the Study of Islam in the Modern World] *Newsletter* 2, pp. 1, 23

—— (2001) *Transnational Muslim Politics*, London: Routledge

Marienstras, R. (1989) 'On the notion of diaspora', in *Minority Peoples in the Age of Nation-States*, G. Chaliand (ed.), London: Pluto, pp. 119–25

Marques, M.M., R. Santos and F. Aranjo (2001) 'Ariadne's thread: Cape Verdean women in transnational webs', *Global Networks* 1(3): 283–306

Martin, P.L. (2003) 'Managing labor migration: Temporary worker programs for the 21st Century', Geneva: International Institute for Labour Studies (International Labour Organization)

—— (2005) 'Migrants in the global labour market', Geneva: Global Commission on International Migration

Martin, S.F. (2001) 'Remittance flows and impact', paper at the Regional Conference on Remittances as a Development Tool, Multilateral Investment Fund, Inter-American Development Bank, Washington, DC.

Mason, P. (2007) 'From Matatu to the Masai via mobile', <www.news.bbc.co.uk>

Massey, D. (1993) 'Power-geometry and a progressive sense of place', in

Mapping the Futures, J. Bird, B. Curtis, T. Putnam, G. Robertson and L. Tickner (eds), London: Routledge, pp. 59–69

—— (1999) 'Imagining globalization: Power-geometries of time-space', in *Global Futures, Migration, Environment and Globalization*, A. Brah, M.J. Hickman and M. Mac an Ghaill (eds), Basingstoke, UK: Macmillan, pp. 27–44

Massey, D.S. (1987) 'Understanding Mexican migration to the United States', *American Journal of Sociology* 92(6): 1372–1403

Massey, D.S. and K.E. Espinosa (1997) 'What's driving Mexico–U.S. migration? A theoretical, empirical and policy analysis', *American Journal of Sociology* 102(4): 939–999

Massey, D.S., R. Alarcón, J. Durand and H. González (1999) *Worlds in Motion: Understanding International Migration at the End of the Millennium*, Oxford: Clarendon Press

Massey, D.S., L. Goldring and J. Durand (1994) 'Continuities in Transnational Migration: An Analysis of Nineteen Mexican Communities', *American Journal of Sociology* 99: 1492–533

Mau, S., J. Mewes and A. Zimmermann (2008) 'Cosmopolitan attitudes through transnational social practices?', *Global Networks* 8(1): 1–24

McAdam, D., J. McCarthy and M. Zald (1996) 'Introduction: Opportunities, mobilizing structures, and framing processes – Toward a synthetic, comparative perspective on social movements', in *Comparative Perspectives on Social Movements*, D. McAdam, J.D. McCarthy and M.N. Zald (eds), Cambridge: Cambridge University Press, pp. 1–20

McCarthy, J. and M. Zald (1977) 'Resources mobilization and social movements: A partial theory', *American Journal of Sociology* 82: 1212–41

McClure, E. (2000) 'Language, literacy and the construction of ethnic identity on the internet: The case of Assyrians in diaspora', Paper presented at the Conference on "Writing Diasporas – Transnational Imagination", University of Wales, Swansea.

McDonald, M. (1987) 'Rituals of motherhood among Gujarati women in East London', in *Hinduism in Great Britain*, R. Burghart (ed.), London: Tavistock, pp. 50–66

Menjívar, C. (2002) 'Living in two worlds? Guatemalan-origin children in the United States and emerging transnationalism', *Journal of Ethnic and Migration Studies* 28(3): 531–52

Mensah, I.L. and J. Reed Smith (2002) 'Distributors rule ... or do they? Finding success in the volatile prepaid market', *Intele-CardNews*, April, <www.intelecard.com>

Metcalf, B. (1996) 'Introduction: Sacred words, sanctioned practice, new communities', in *Making Muslim Space in North America and*

Europe, B. Metcalf (ed.), Berkeley, CA: University of California Press, pp. 1–27

Meyer, B. and P. Geschiere (eds) (1999) *Globalization and Identity: Dialectics of Flow and Closure*, Oxford: Blackwell

Meyer, J.-B. and M. Brown (1999) 'Scientific diasporas: A new approach to the brain drain', Paris: UNESCO-MOST Discussion Paper No. 41

Meyers, D. Waller (1998) 'Migrant remittances to Latin America: Reviewing the literature', Washington, DC: Inter-American Dialogue and the Tomás Rivera Policy Institute, Working Paper

Michaelson, M. (1987) 'Domestic Hinduism in a Gujarati trading caste', in *Hinduism in Great Britain*, R. Burghart (ed.), London: Tavistock, pp. 32–49

Miller, B. (1994) 'Political empowerment, local-central state relations, and geographically shifting political opportunity structures', *Political Geography* 13(5): 393–406

Miller, D. and D. Slater (2000) *The Internet: An Ethnographic Approach*, Oxford: Berg

Miller, D., A. Skuse, D. Slater, J. Tacchi, T. Chandola, T. Cousins, H. Horst and J. Kwami (2005) Final Report: Information Society, Emergent Technologies and Development Communities in the South, Information Society Research Group, <www.isrg.info>

Mitchell, J.C. (1966) 'Theoretical orientations in African urban studies', in *The Social Anthropology of Complex Societies*, M. Banton (ed.), London: Tavistock, pp. 37–8

—— (1969) 'The concept and use of social networks', in *Social Networks in Urban Situations*, J.C. Mitchell (ed.), Manchester: Manchester University Press, pp. 1–50

—— (1974) 'Social networks', *Annual Review of Anthropology* 3: 279–99

—— (1987) *Cities, Society, and Social Perception: A Central African Perspective*, Oxford: Clarendon

Mitchell, K. (1997a) 'Different diasporas and the hype of hybridity', *Environment and Planning D: Society and Space* 15: 533–53

—— (1997b) 'Transnational discourse: bringing geography back in', *Antipode* 29: 101–14

Modrzejewski, J.M. (1993) 'How to be a Jew in Hellenistic Egypt?', in *Diasporas in Antiquity*, J.D.C. Shaye and E.S. Frerichs (eds), Atlanta, GA: Scholars Press, pp. 65–91

Mohan, G. (2002) 'Diaspora and development', in *Development and Displacement*, J. Robinson (ed.), Milton Keynes, UK: Open University Press, pp. 77–139

Mohan, G. and A.B. Zack-Williams (2002) 'Globalisation from below:

Conceptualising the role of the African diasporas in Africa's development', *Review of African Political Economy* 92: 211–36

Morawska, E. (1999) 'The new-old transmigrants, their transnational lives, and ethnicization: A comparison of 19th/20th and 20th/21st C situations', Florence, Italy: European University Institute Working Papers EUF No. 99/2

—— (2003) 'Immigrant transnationalism and assimilation: A variety of combinations and the analytic strategy it suggests', in *Toward Assimilation and Citizenship*, C. Joppke and E. Morawska (eds), Basingstoke, UK: Palgrave, pp. 133–76

—— (2004) 'Exploring diversity in immigrant assimilation and transnationalism: Poles and Russian Jews in Philadelphia', *International Migration Review* 38(4): 1372–412

Morgan, G. (2001) 'Transnational communities and business systems', *Global Networks* 1(2): 113–30

Morley, D. and K. Robins (1995) *Spaces of Identity: Global Media, Electronic Landscapes and Cultural Boundaries*, London: Routledge

Motomura, H. (1998) 'Alienage classifications in a nation of immigrants: Three models of "permanent" residence', in *Immigration and Citizenship in the Twenty-First Century*, N.M.J. Pickus (ed.), Lanham, MA: Rowman and Littlefield, pp.199–222

Mountz, A. and R.A. Wright (1996) 'Daily life in the transnational migrant community of San Agustín, Oaxaca, and Poughkeepsie, New York', *Diaspora* 5(3): 403–28

Mukta, P. and C. Bhatt (eds) (2000) 'Hindutva Movements in the West: Resurgent Hinduism and the Politics of Diaspora', special issue of *Ethnic and Racial Studies* 23(3)

Murdoch, J. (1998) 'The spaces of actor-network theory', *Geoforum* 29(4): 357–74

Naficy, H. (2001) *An Accented Cinema: Exilic and Diasporic Filmmaking*, Princeton, NJ: Princeton University Press

Nohria, N. (1992) 'Introduction', in *Networks and Organizations*, N. Nohria and R.G. Eccles (eds), Boston, MA: Harvard Business School Press, pp. 1–22

Nonini, D.M. (1997) 'Shifting identities, positioned imaginaries: Transnational traversals and reversals by Malaysian Chinese', in *Ungrounded Empires*, A. Ong and D.M. Nonini (eds), London: Routledge, pp. 203–27

Nonini, D.M. and A. Ong (1997) 'Chinese transnationalism as an alternative modernity', in *Ungrounded Empires*, A. Ong and D.M. Nonini (eds), London: Routledge, pp. 3–33

Nye, J.S. and R.O. Keohane (1971) 'Transnational relations and world politics: An introduction', in *Transnational Relations and World Politics*, R.O. Keohane and J.S. Nye (eds), Cambridge, MA: Harvard University Press, pp. ix–xxix

Nye, M. (1995) *A Place for Our Gods: The Construction of an Edinburgh Hindu Temple Community*, Richmond, UK: Curzon

Olds, K. and H. W-C. Yeung (1999) '(Re)shaping "Chinese" business networks in a globalising era', *Environment and Planning D: Society and Space* 17: 535–55

Ong, A. (1999) *Flexible Citizenship: The Cultural Logics of Transnationality*, Durham, NC: Duke University Press

Orellana, M.F., B. Thorne, A. Chee and Wan Shun Eva Lam (2001) 'Transnational childhoods: The participation of children in processes of family migration', *Social Problems* 48(4): 572–91

Orenstein, M.A. and H.P. Schmitz (2006) 'The new transnationalism and comparative politics', *Comparative Politics* 38(4): 479–500

Orozco, M. (2000a) 'Latino hometown associations as agents of development in Latin America', Washington DC: Inter-American Dialogue, Final Report

—— (2000b) 'Remittances and markets: New players and practices', Washington, DC: Inter-American Dialogue and the Tomás Rivera Policy Institute, Working Paper

—— (2001) 'Globalization and migration: The impact of family remittances in Latin America', paper at Inter-American Foundation/UN ECLAC/World Bank conference on Approaches to Increasing the Productive Value of Remittances, Washington, DC

—— (2002) 'Attracting remittances: Market, money and reduced costs', Washington, DC: Multilateral Investment Fund of the Inter-American Development Bank, Report

Østergaard-Nielsen, E. (2001) 'Turkish and Kurdish transnational political mobilisation in Germany and the Netherlands', *Global Networks* 1(3): 261–82

—— (2003a) *Transnational Politics: Turks and Kurds in Germany*, London: Routledge

—— (2003b) 'Sending countries and international migration: Key issues and themes', in *Sending Countries and International Migration*, E. Østergaard-Nielsen (ed.), Basingstoke, UK: Palgrave, pp. 3–33

Panagakos, A.N. and H.A. Horst (eds) (2006a) 'Return to Cyberia', special issue of *Global Networks* 6(2)

—— (2006b) 'Return to Cyberia: Technology and the social worlds of transnational migrants', *Global Networks* 6(2): 109–24

Parekh, B. (1994) 'Some reflections on the Hindu diaspora', *New Community* 20: 603–20

Parreñas, R. Salazar (2005) *Children of Global Migration: Transnational Families and Gendered Woes*, Stanford, CA: Stanford University Press

Pattie, S.P. (1997) *Faith in History: Armenians Rebuilding Community*, Washington, DC: Smithsonian Institution Press

Pessar, P. (1999a) 'Engendering migration studies', *American Behavioral Scientist* 42(3): 577–600

—— (1999b) 'The role of gender, households, and social networks in the migration process: A review and appraisal', in *The Handbook of International Migration*, C. Hirschman, J. Dewind and Philip Kasinitz (eds), New York: Russell Sage Foundation, pp. 53–70

Pessar, P. and S. Mahler (2003) 'Transnational migration: Bringing gender in', *International Migration Review* 37(3): 812–46

Pickus, N.M.J. (1998) 'Introduction', in *Immigration and Citizenship in the Twenty-First Century*, N.M.J. Pickus (ed.), Lanham, MA: Rowman and Littlefield, pp. xvii–xxxiii

Piracha, M. and R. Vickerman (2002) 'Borders, Migration and Labour Market Dynamics in a Changing Europe', Final Project Report, Economic and Social Research Council (UK)

Pocock, D.F. (1976) 'Preservation of the religious life: Hindu immigrants in England', *Contributions to Indian Sociology* 10: 341–65

Poros, M. (2001) 'The role of migrant networks in linking local labor markets: The case of Asian Indian migration to New York and London', *Global Networks* 1(3): 243–59

Portes, A. (1995) 'Economic sociology and the sociology of immigration: A conceptual overview', in *The Economic Sociology of Immigration*, A. Portes (ed.), New York: Russell Sage Foundation, pp. 1–41

—— (1998a) 'Social capital: Its origins and applications in modern sociology', *Annual Review of Sociology* 24: 1–24

—— (1998b) 'Globalisation from below: the rise of transnational communities', Oxford: ESRC Transnational Communities Programme Working Paper WPTC-98-01 1

—— (2001a) 'Introduction: the debates and significance of immigrant transnationalism', *Global Networks* 1(3): 181–93

—— (2001b) 'Transnational entrepreneurs: The emergence and determinants of an alternative form of immigrant economic adaptation', Oxford: ESRC Transnational Communities Research Programme Working Paper WPTC-01-05

—— (2003) 'Conclusion: Theoretical convergences and empirical evidence in the study of immigrant transnationalism', *International Migration Review* 37(3): 874–92

Portes, A. and R. Bach (1985) *Latin Journey: Cuban and Mexican Immigrants in the United States*, Berkeley, CA: University of California Press

Portes, A. and P. Landolt (2000) 'Social capital: Promise and pitfalls of its role in development', *Journal of Latin American Studies* 32(2): 529–47

Portes, A. and M. Mooney (2002) 'Social capital and community development', in *The New Economic Sociology*, M.F. Guillén, R. Collins and P. England (eds), New York: Russell Sage, pp. 303–29

Portes, A. and R. Rumbaut (2001) *Legacies: The Story of the Immigrant Second Generation*, Berkeley, CA: University of California Press

Portes, A. and J. Sensenbrenner (1993) 'Embeddedness and immigration: Notes on the social determinants of economic action', *American Journal of Sociology* 98: 1320–50

Portes, A. and M. Zhou (1993) 'The new second generation: Segmented assimilation and its variants', *The Annals of the American Academy of Political and Social Science* 530: 74–96

Portes, A., C. Escobar and A.W. Radford (2007) 'Immigrant transnational organizations and development: A comparative study', *International Migration Review* 41(1): 242–81

Portes, A., L. E. Guarnizo and P. Landolt (eds) (1999a) 'Transnational Communities', special issue of *Ethnic and Racial Studies* 22(2)

—— (1999b) 'The study of transnationalism: Pitfalls and promises of an emergent research field', *Ethnic and Racial Studies* 22(2): 217–37

Portes, A., W. Haller and L.E. Guarnizo (2002) 'Transnational entrepreneurs: The emergence and determinants of an alternative form of immigrant economic adaptation', *American Sociological Review* 67: 278–98

PR Newswire (2006) 'Two billion GSM customers worldwide', <www.prnewswire.com>

Pries, L. (ed.) (1999) *Migration and Transnational Social Spaces*, Aldershot, UK: Ashgate

—— (ed.) (2001) *New Transnational Social Spaces: International Migration and Transnational Companies in the Early Twenty-First Century*, London: Routledge

Puri, S. and T. Ritzema (1999) 'Migrant worker remittances, micro-finance and the informal economy: Prospects and issues', Geneva: International Labour Organization, Social Finance Unit, Working Paper 21

Putnam, R.D. (1995) 'Bowling alone: America's declining social capital', *Journal of Democracy* 6: 65–78

Rai, A.S. (1995) 'India on-line: Electronic bulletin boards and the construction of a diasporic Hindu identity', *Diaspora* 4(1): 31–57

Rajagopal, A. (1997) 'Transnational networks and Hindu nationalism', *Bulletin of Concerned Asian Scholars* 29(3): 45–58

Rampton, B. (1995) *Crossing: Language and Ethnicity among Adolescents*, London: Longman

Rapport, N. and A. Dawson (eds) (1998) *Migrants of Identity: Perceptions of Home in a World of Movement*, Oxford: Berg

Rayaprol, A. (1997) *Negotiating Identities: Women in the Indian Diaspora*, Delhi: Oxford University Press

Rex, J., D. Joly and C. Wilpert (eds) (1987) *Immigrant Associations in Europe*, Aldershot, UK: Gower

Riccio, B. (1999) Senegalese Transmigrants and the Construction of Immigration in Emilia-Romagna (Italy). DPhil. Thesis, University of Sussex

—— (2001) 'From "Ethnic Group" to "Transnational Community"? Senegalese Migrants' Ambivalent Experiences and Multiple Trajectories', *Journal of Ethnic and Migration Studies* 27(4): 583–99

Rice, X. (2007) 'Kenya sets world first with money transfers by mobile', *The Guardian*, 20 March

Richardson, D., R. Ramirez and M. Haq (2000) 'Grameen Telecom's village phone programme: A multi-media case study', Hull: Canadian International Development Agency, Final Report

Robbins, B. (1998) 'Introduction Part I: Actually existing cosmopolitanism', in *Cosmopolitics*, P. Cheah and B. Robbins (eds), Minneapolis: University of Minnesota Press, pp. 1–19

Robbins, J. (1998) 'On reading "world news": Apocalyptic narrative, negative nationalism and transnational Christianity in a Papua New Guinea society', *Social Analysis* 42(2): 103–30

Robertson, R. (1992) *Globalization: Social Theory and Global Culture*, London: Sage

Robins, K. (1991) 'Tradition and translation: National culture in its global context', in *Enterprise and Heritage*, J. Corner and S. Harvey (eds), London: Routledge, pp. 21–44

—— (1998) 'Spaces of global media', Oxford: ESRC Transnational Communities Programme Working Paper WPTC-98-06

Robins, K. and A. Aksoy (2004) 'Parting from phantoms: What is at issue in the development of transnational television from Turkey', in *Worlds on the Move*, J. Friedman and S. Randeria (eds), London: I.B. Taurus, pp. 179–206

Robinson, M.S. (2001) *The Microfinance Revolution: Sustainable Finance for the Poor*, Washington, DC: The World Bank and the Open Society Institute

Robinson, S.S. (2001) 'Rethinking telecenters: Knowledge demands, marginal markets, microbanks, and remittance flows', *On the Internet* March/April, <www.isoc.org/oti>

Robinson, W.I. (1998) 'Beyond nation-state paradigms: Globalization, Sociology and the challenge of transnational studies', *Sociological Forum* 13(4): 561–94

Rogers, A. (1999a) 'Capture of PKK leader causes worldwide Kurdish protest', *Traces* 5, <www.transcomm.ox.ac.uk/traces/issue5.htm>

—— (1999b) 'Voting from abroad: Airlifts and Internet', *Traces* 6, <www.transcomm.ox.ac.uk/traces/issue6.htm>

—— (1999c) 'Remittances and underground banking in Asian economies', *Traces* 6, <www.transcomm.ox.ac.uk/traces/issue6.htm>

—— (2000) 'Mexico's historic elections spill over into the USA', *Traces* 10, <www.transcomm.ox.ac.uk/traces/issue10.htm>

—— (2001a) 'Competition over wire transfer business in N. America and Asia', *Traces* 13, <www.transcomm.ox.ac.uk/traces/issue13.htm>

—— (2001b) 'Gujaratis overseas respond to earthquake disaster', *Traces* 13, <www.transcomm.ox.ac.uk/traces/issue13.htm>

—— (2001c) 'Latin America: migrants flow out, remittances flow in', *Traces* 14, <www.transcomm.ox.ac.uk/traces/issue14.htm>

—— (2001d) 'Pakistan's government promotes formal channels for remittances', *Traces* 15, <www.transcomm.ox.ac.uk/traces/issue15.htm>

—— (2001e) 'The Philippines debates dual citizenship', *Traces* 16 [www.transcomm.ox.ac.uk/traces/issue16.htm]

—— (2002) 'Latin America: contrasting fortunes in a region dependent on remittances', *Traces* 17, <www.transcomm.ox.ac.uk/traces/issue17.htm>

Rogers, A. and S. Vertovec (1995) 'Introduction', in *The Urban Context*, A. Rogers and S. Vertovec (eds), Oxford: Berg, pp. 1–33

Rogers, A., R. Cohen and S. Vertovec (2001) 'Editorial statement', *Global Networks* 1(1): iii–vi

Ros., A., E. González, A. Marín and P. Sow (2007) 'Migration and information flows: A new lens for the study of contemporary international migration', Barcelona: Internet Interdisciplinary Institute Working Paper WP07-001

Rosenau, James N. (1980) *The Study of Global Interdependence: Essays on the Transnationalization of World Affairs*, New York: Nichols

—— (2003) *Distant Proximities: Dynamics beyond Globalization*, Princeton, NJ: Princeton University Press

Roudometof, V. (2005) 'Transnationalism, cosmopolitanism and glocalization', *Current Sociology* 53(1): 113–35

Rouse, R. (1991) 'Mexican migration and the social space of postmodernism', *Diaspora* 1(1): 8–23

—— (1992) 'Making sense of settlement: Class transformation, cultural struggle, and transnationalism among Mexican migrants in the United States', *Annals of the New York Academy of Sciences* 645: 25–52

—— (1995) 'Questions of identity: personhood and collectivity in transnational migration to the United States', *Critique of Anthropology*, 15(4): 351–80

Rudolph, S. Hoeber and J. Piscatori (eds) (1997) *Transnational Religion and Fading States*, Boulder, CO: Westview Press

Rudolph, S. Hoeber (1997) 'Introduction: Religion, states and transnational civil society', in *Transnational Religion and Fading States*, S. Hoeber Rudolph and J. Piscatori (eds), Boulder, CO: Westview Press, pp. 1–24

Ruhs, M. (2005) 'The potential of temporary migration programmes in future international migration policy', Geneva: Global Commission on International Migration

Runnymede Trust/Commission on the Future of Multi-Ethnic Britain (2000) *The Future of Multi-Ethnic Britain [The Parekh Report]*, London: Profile Books

Safran, W. (1991) 'Diasporas in modern societies: Myths of homeland and return', *Diaspora* 1(1): 83–99

Salaff, J.W., E. Fong and W. Siu-lun (1999) 'Using social networks to exit Hong Kong', in *Networks in the Global Village*, B. Wellman (ed.), Boulder, CO: Westview, pp. 299–329

Salih, R. (2002) 'Shifting meanings of "home": Consumption and identity in Moroccan women's transnational practices between Italy and Morocco', in *New Approaches to Migration?*, N. Al-Ali and K. Koser (eds), London: Routledge, pp. 51–67

—— (2003) *Gender in Transnationalism: Home, Longing and Belonging among Moroccan Migrant Women*, London: Routledge

Sana, M. (2005) 'Buying membership in the transnational community: Migrant remittances, social status, and assimilation', *Population Research and Policy Review* 24: 231–61

Sassen, S. (1996) *Losing Control? Sovereignty in an Age of Globalization*, New York: Columbia University Press

—— (1998) 'The *de facto* transnationalizing of immigration policy', in *Challenge to the Nation-State*, C. Joppke (ed.), Oxford: Oxford University Press, pp. 49–85

—— (2000) 'New frontiers facing urban sociology at the Millennium', *British Journal of Sociology* 15(1): 143–59

—— (2001) 'Cracked casings: Notes towards an analytics for studying transnational processes', in *New Transnational Social Spaces*, L. Pries (ed.), London: Routledge, pp. 187–207

—— (2002) 'Global cities and diasporic networks: Microsites in global civil society', in *Global Civil Society 2002*, H. Anheier, M. Glasius and M. Kaldor (eds), Oxford: Oxford University Press, pp. 217–38

Schiffauer, W. (1988) 'Migration and religiousness', in *The New Islamic Presence in Europe*, T. Gerholm and Y.G. Lithman (eds), London: Mansell, pp. 146–58

—— (1999) 'Islamism in the diaspora: The fascination of political Islam among second generation German Turks', Oxford: ESRC Transnational Communities Programme Working Paper WPTC-99-06

Schiffauer, W., G. Baumann, R. Kastoryano and S. Vertovec (eds) (2003) *Civil Enculturation: State, School and Ethnic Difference in Four European Countries*, Oxford: Berghahn

Scholte, J.A. (2000) *Globalization: A Critical Introduction*, London: Palgrave

Schuck, P.H. (1998) 'Plural citizenships', in *Immigration and Citizenship in the Twenty-First Century*, N.M.J. Pickus (ed.), Lanham, MA: Rowman and Littlefield, pp. 149–91

Schuerkens, U. (2005) 'Preface: Transnational migrations and social transformations', special issue of *Current Sociology* 53(4): 533–4

Schweitzer, T. (1997) 'Embeddedness of ethnographic cases: A social networks perspective', *Current Anthropology* 38: 739–60

Secretary of Defense, United States (1996) *Proliferation: Threat and Response*, Washington, DC: U.S. Government Printing Office

Shain, Y. (1999) *Marketing the American Creed Abroad: Diasporas in the U.S. and Their Homelands*, Cambridge: Cambridge University Press

Shaye, J.D. Cohen and Ernst S. Frerichs (1993) 'Preface', in *Diasporas in Antiquity*, J.D.C. Shaye and E.S. Frerichs (eds), Atlanta, GA: Scholars Press, pp. i–iii

Sheffer, G. (1986) 'A new field of study: modern diasporas in international politics', in *Modern Diasporas in International Politics*, G. Sheffer (ed.), London: Croom Helm, pp. 1–15

Sheptycki, J.W.F. (ed.) (2000) *Issues in Transnational Policing*, London: Routledge

Shohat, E. and R. Stam (1996) 'From the imperial family to the transnational imaginary: media spectatorship in the age of globalization', in *Global/Local*, R. Wilson and W. Dissanayake (eds), Durham, NC: Duke University Press, pp. 145–70

Skeldon, R. (1997) *Migration and Development: A Global Perspective*, Harlow, UK: Longman

Sklair, L. (1995) *Sociology of the Global System*, London: Prentice Hall, 2nd ed.

—— (1998) 'Transnational practices and the analysis of the global system',

Oxford: ESRC Transnational Communities Programme Working Paper WPTC-98-04

—— (2001) *The Transnational Capitalist Class*, Oxford: Blackwell

Smart, N. (1999) 'The importance of diasporas', in *Migration, Diasporas and Transnationalism*, S. Vertovec and R. Cohen (eds), Aldershot: Edward Elgar, pp. 420–29

Smelser, N.J. (1998) 'Social transformations and social change', *International Social Science Journal* 156: 173–8

Smith, J. (1997) 'Characteristics of the modern transnational social movement sector', in *Transnational Social Movements and Global Politics*, J. Smith, C. Chatfield and R. Pagnucco (eds), Syracuse, NY: Syracuse University Press, pp. 42–58

Smith, J., C. Chatfield and R. Pagnucco (eds) (1997) *Transnational Social Movements and Global Politics*, Syracuse, NY: Syracuse University Press

Smith, J.Z. (1978) *Map is Not Territory: Studies in the History of Religions*, Leiden: E.J. Brill

Smith, M.A. and P. Kollock (eds) (1999) *Communities in Cyberspace*, London: Routledge

Smith, M.P. (2001) *Transnational Urbanism: Locating Globalization*, Oxford: Blackwell

Smith, M.P. and L.E. Guarnizo (eds) (1998) *Transnationalism from Below*, New Brunswick, NJ: Transaction Publishers

Smith, R.C. (1998) 'Transnational localities: community, technology and the politics of membership within the context of Mexico and U.S. Migration', in *Transnationalism from Below*, M.P. Smith and L.E. Guarnizo (eds), New Brunswick, NJ: Transaction Publishers, pp. 196–238

—— (2001) 'Comparing local-level Swedish and Mexican transnational life: An essay in historical retrieval', in *New Transnational Social Spaces*, L. Pries (ed.), London: Routledge, pp. 37–58

—— (2002) 'Life course, generation, and social location as factors shaping second-generation transnational life', in *The Changing Face of Home*, P. Levitt and M.C. Waters (eds), New York: Russell Sage Foundation, pp. 145–67

—— (2003) 'Diasporic memberships in historical perspective: Comparative insights from the Mexican and Italian cases', *International Migration Review* 37(3): 724–59

—— (2006) *Mexican New York: Transnational Lives of New Immigrants*, Berkeley, CA: University of California Press

Snel, E., G. Engbersen and A. Leerkes (2006) 'Transnational involvement and social integration', *Global Networks* 6(3): 285–308

Sökefeld, M. (2000) 'Religion or culture? Concepts of identity in the Alevi diaspora', paper presented at Conference on 'Locality, Identity, Diaspora', University of Hamburg

Sørensen, N. Nyberg (2000) 'Notes on transnationalism', paper at the Workshop on Transnational Migration: Comparative Theory and Research Perspectives, University of Oxford

Sørensen, N. Nyberg and K. Fog Olwig (eds) (2001) *Work and Migration: Life and Livelihoods in a Globalizing World*, London: Routledge

Sørensen, N. Nyberg, N. Van Hear and P. Engberg-Pedersen (2002) *The Migration-Development Nexus: Evidence and Policy Options*, Geneva: International Organization for Migration Research Series 8

Soysal, Y.N. (1994) *Limits of Citizenship: Migrants and Postnational Membership in Europe,* Chicago: University of Chicago Press

Spiro, P.J. (2002) 'Embracing dual nationality', in *Dual Nationality, Social Rights and Federal Citizenship in the U.S. and Europe*, R. Hansen and P. Weil (eds), Oxford: Berghahn, pp. 19–33

Spivak, G. (1989) 'Who claims alterity?', in *Remaking History*, B. Kruger and P. Mariani (eds), Seattle, WA: Bay, pp. 269–92

Stalker, P. (2000) *Workers without Frontiers: The Impact of Globalization on International Migration*, Geneva: International Labour Organization

Stares, P. (1996) *Global Habit: The Drug Problem in a Borderless World*, Washington, DC: Brookings Institution

Stark, D., B. Vadres and L. Bruszt (2006) 'Rooted transnational publics: Integrating foreign ties and civic activism', *Theory & Society* 35(3): 323–49

Stark, O. (1991) *The Migration of Labor*, Cambridge, MA: Blackwell

Strange, S. (1996) *The Retreat of the State: The Diffusion of Power in the World Economy*, New York: Cambridge University Press

Suro, R., S. Bendixen, B.L. Lowell and D.C. Benavides (2002) 'Billions in motion: Latino immigrants, remittances and banking', Washington, DC: Pew Hispanic Centre and Multilateral Investment Fund, Report

Swidler, A. (1986) 'Culture in action: symbols and strategies', *American Sociological Review* 51: 273–86

Tarrow, S. (1998a) *Power in Movement: Social Movements and Contentious Politics*, Cambridge: Cambridge University Press, 2nd ed.

—— (1998b) 'Fishnets, Internets and catnets: Globalization and transnational collective action', in *Challenging Authority*, M. Hanagan, L. Page Moch and W. Ph. Te Brake (eds), Minneapolis: University of Minnesota Press, pp. 228–44

—— (2000) 'Transnational contention', San Domenico: European University Institute Working Paper RSC No. 2000/44

—— (2005) *The New Transnational Activism*, New York: Cambridge University Press

Taylor, J.E. (1999) 'The new economics of labour migration and the role of remittances in the migration process', *International Migration* 37(1): 63–88

TeleGeography (2006) *TeleGeography Executive Summary 2007*, Washington, DC: TeleGeography, Inc.

ter Haar, G. (1998) 'Strangers and sojourners: An introduction', in *Strangers and Sojourners*, G. ter Haar (ed.), Leuven, Belgium: Peeters, pp. 1–11

Thomas-Hope, E. (2003) 'Transnational strategies in the readjustment of return migrants to the Caribbean', paper at the Annual Meeting of the American Association of Geographers, New Orleans

Thränhardt, D. (2002) 'Prophecies, *Ius Soli* and dual citizenship: Interpreting the changes in the German citizenship system', paper at the Workshop on Transnational Ties and Identities Past and Present, Netherlands Institute for Advanced Study, Wassenaar

Tilly, C. (1978) *From Mobilization to Revolution*, Reading, MA: Addison-Wesley

—— (1990) 'Transplanted networks', in *Immigration Reconsidered*, V. Yans-MacLoughlin (ed.), New York: Oxford University Press, pp. 79–95

Tölölyan, K. (1991) 'The nation-state and its others: in lieu of a preface', *Diaspora* 1(1): 3–7

—— (1996) 'Rethinking *diaspora(s)*: stateless power in the transnational moment', *Diaspora* 5(1): 3–36

Tromp, J. (1998) 'The ancient Jewish diaspora: Some linguistic and socio-logical observations', in *Strangers and Sojourners*, G. ter Haar (ed.), Leuven, Belgium: Peeters, pp. 13–35

Tweed, T.A. (1997) *Our Lady of the Exile: Diasporic Religion at a Cuban Catholic Shrine in Miami*, New York: Oxford University Press

UN/United Nations (2006) 'Globalization and Interdependence: International Migration and Development', Report of the Secretary General, New York: United Nations General Assembly A/60/871

UNPD/United Nations Population Division (1998) *International Migration Policies*, New York: Population Division, Department of Economic and Social Affairs, United Nations

—— (2002) *International Migration 2002*, New York: Population Division, Department of Economic and Social Affairs, United Nations

Urry, J. (2003) 'Global complexities', *International Studies Review* 5: 250–252

van den Bos, M. and L. Nell (2006) 'Territorial bounds to virtual space: Transnational online and offline networks of Iranian and Turkish-Kurdish immigrants in the Netherlands', *Global Networks* 6(2): 201–20

van der Toorn, K. (1998) 'Near Eastern communities in the diaspora before 587 BCE', in *Strangers and Sojourners*, G. ter Haar (ed.), Leuven, Belgium: Peeters, pp. 77–94 van der Veer, P. and S. Vertovec (1991) 'Brahmanism abroad: On Caribbean Hinduism as an ethnic religion', *Ethnology* 30: 149–166

van Doorn, J. (2001) 'Migration, remittances and small enterprise development', Geneva: International Labour Organization

Van Hear, N.N. (1998) *New Diasporas: The Mass Exodus, Dispersal and Regrouping of Migrant Communities*, London: University College London Press

Vertovec, S. (1992) *Hindu Trinidad: Religion, Ethnicity and Socio-Economic Change*, Basingstoke: Macmillan

—— (1994a) 'Multicultural, multi-Asian, multi-Muslim Leicester: Dimensions of social complexity, ethnic organisation and local government interface', *Innovation: European Journal of Social Sciences* 7(3): 259–276

—— (1994b) '"Official" and "popular" Hinduism in the Caribbean: Historical and contemporary trends in Surinam, Trinidad and Guyana', *Contributions to Indian Sociology* 28(1): 123–147

—— (1997) 'Accommodating religious pluralism in Britain: South Asian religions', in *Multicultural Policies and the State*, M. Martiniello (ed.), Utrecht: ERCOMER, pp. 163–77

—— (1998) 'Three meanings of "diaspora", exemplified among South Asian religions', *Diaspora* 6(3): 277–300

—— (1999a) 'Conceiving and researching transnationalism', *Ethnic and Racial Studies*, 22(2): 447–62

—— (1999b) 'Introduction', in *Migration and Social Cohesion*, S. Vertovec (ed.), Cheltenham: Edward Elgar, pp. xi–xxxvii

—— (2000a) 'Rethinking remittances', Oxford: ESRC Transnational Communities Programme Working Paper WPTC-2K-15

—— (2000b) *The Hindu Diaspora: Comparative Patterns*, London: Routledge

—— (2001a) 'Transnationalism and identity', *Journal of Ethnic and Migration Studies* 27(4): 573–82

—— (2001b) 'Islamophobia and Muslim recognition in Britain', in *Muslims in Western Diasporas*, Y.Y. Haddad (ed.), Oxford: Oxford University Press, pp. 19–35

—— (2002) 'Transnational networks and skilled labour migration', Oxford: ESRC Transnational Communities Programme Working Paper WPTC-02-02

—— (2003a) 'Migrant transnationalism and modes of transformation', *International Migration Review* 38(3): 970–1001

—— (2003b) 'Migration and other forms of transnationalism: Towards conceptual cross-fertilization', *International Migration Review* 37(3): 641–65

—— (2004a) 'Cheap calls: The social glue of migrant transnationalism', *Global Networks* 4(2): 219–24

—— (2004b) 'Religion and diaspora', in *New Approaches to the Study of Religion*, P. Antes, A.W. Geertz and R. Warne (eds), Berlin & New York: Verlag de Gruyter, pp. 275–304

—— (2006) 'Is circular migration the way forward in global policy?', *Around the Globe* 3(2): 38–44

—— (2007) 'Super-diversity and its implications', *Ethnic and Racial Studies* 30(6): 1024–54

Vertovec, S. and R. Cohen (eds) (1999a) *Migration, Diasporas and Transnationalism*, Cheltenham, UK: Edward Elgar

—— (1999b) 'Introduction', in *Migration, Diasporas and Transnationalism*, S. Vertovec and R. Cohen (eds), Cheltenham, UK: Edward Elgar, pp. xiii–xxviii

—— (eds) (2002) *Conceiving Cosmopolitanism: Theory, Context and Practice*, Oxford: Oxford University Press

Vertovec, S. and C. Peach (1997) 'Introduction: Islam in Europe and the politics of religion and community', in *Islam in Europe*, S. Vertovec and C. Peach (eds), Basingstoke, UK: Macmillan, pp. 3–47

Vertovec, S. and A. Rogers (1998) 'Introduction', in *Muslim European Youth*, S. Vertovec and A. Rogers (eds), Aldershot, UK: Avebury, pp. 1–24

Vickerman, R. (2002) 'Migration myths', *The Guardian*, 10 December

Voigt-Graf, C. (2002) The Construction of Transnational Spaces: Travelling between India, Fiji and Australia, Ph.D. Thesis, Geography, University of Sydney

Waardenburg, J. (1988) 'The institutionalization of Islam in the Netherlands', in *The New Islamic Presence in Europe*, T. Gerholm and Y.G. Lithman (eds), London: Mansell, pp. 8–31

Wakeman, F.E. (1988) 'Transnational and comparative research', *Items* 42(4): 85–7

Waldinger, R. and C. Feliciano (2004) 'Will the new second generation experience "downward assimilation"? Segmented assimilation reassessed', *Ethnic and Racial Studies* 27(3): 376–402

Waldinger, R. and D. Fitzgerald (2004) 'Transnationalism in question', *American Journal of Sociology* 109(5): 1177–96

Walton-Roberts, M. (2004) 'Transnational migration theory in population geography: Gendered practices in networks linking Canada and India', *Population, Space and Place* 10: 361–73

Warner, R.S. (1998) 'Immigration and religious communities in the United States', in *Gatherings in Diaspora*, R.S. Warner and J.G. Wittner (eds), Philadelphia, PA: Temple University Press, pp. 3–34

Wasserman, S. and K. Faust (1994) *Social Network Analysis: Methods and Applications*, Cambridge: Cambridge University Press

Waters, M. and T.R. Jiménez (2005) 'Assessing immigrant assimilation: New empirical and theoretical challenges', *Annual Review of Sociology* 31: 105–25

Webber, J. (1997) 'Jews and Judaism in contemporary Europe: Religion or ethnic group?', *Ethnic and Racial Studies* 20(2): 257–79

Wellman, B. (1999) 'Net surfers don't ride alone: Virtual communities as communities', in *Networks in the Global Village*, B. Wellman (ed.), Boulder, CO: Westview, pp. 331–66

Werbner, P. (1990) *The Migration Process: Capital, Gifts and Offerings among British Pakistanis*, Oxford: Berg

—— (1996) 'Stamping the Earth in the name of Allah: Zikr and the sacralizing of space among British Muslims', *Cultural Anthropology* 11(3): 309–38

—— (1999) 'Global pathways: Working class cosmopolitans and the creation of transnational ethnic worlds', *Social Anthropology* 7(1): 17–35

Werbner, P. and T. Modood (eds) (1997) *Debating Cultural Hybridity: Multi-Cultural Identities and the Politics of Anti-Racism*, London: Zed Books

Wessel, D. (2002) 'Banking on technology for the poor', *Wall Street Journal*, 2 May

Widgren, J. and P. Martin (2002) 'Managing migration: The role of economic instruments', *International Migration* 40(5): 213–29

Wilding, R. (2006) '"Virtual" intimacies? Families communicating across transnational contexts', *Global Networks* 6(2): 125–42

Willford, A. (1998) 'Within and beyond the state: Ritual and the assertion of Tamil-Hindu identities in Malaysia', Paper presented at the conference on 'Globalization from Below', Duke University

Williams, P. and E.U. Savona (eds) (1996) 'The United Nations and Transnational Organized Crime', special issue of *Transnational Organized Crime* 1(3)

Williams, R.B. (1984) *A New Face of Hinduism: The Swaminarayan Religion*, Cambridge: Cambridge University Press

—— (1988) *Religions of Immigrants from India and Pakistan: New Threads in the American Tapestry*, Cambridge: Cambridge University Press

—— (1992) 'Sacred threads of several textures', in *A Sacred Thread*, R.B. Williams (ed.), Chambersburg, PA: Anima, pp. 228–57

—— (1998) 'Training religious specialists for a transnational Hinduism: A Swaminarayan sadhu training center', *Journal of the American Academy of Religion* 66: 841–62

Willis, K. and B. Yeoh (eds) (2000) *Gender and Migration*, Cheltenham: Edward Elgar

Wilson, R. and W. Dissanayake (1996) 'Introduction: tracking the global/local', in *Global/Local*, R. Wilson and W. Dissanayake (eds), Durham, NC: Duke University Press, pp. 1–18

Wilson, S.M. and L.C. Peterson (2002) 'The anthropology of online communities', *Annual Review of Anthropology* 31: 449–67

Wiltshire, K. (2001) 'Management of social transformations: Introduction', *International Political Science Review* 22(1): 5–11

Wimmer, A. and N. Glick Schiller (2002) 'Methodological nationalism and beyond: Nation-state building, migration and the social sciences', *Global Networks* 2: 301–34

Winkler, K.J. (1999) 'Historians explore questions of how people and cultures disperse across the globe', *Chronicle of Higher Education*, 22 January

Wolf, D. (2002) 'There's no place like "home": Emotional transnationalism and the struggles of second-generation Filipinos', in *The Changing Face of Home*, P. Levitt and M.C. Waters (eds), New York: Russell Sage Foundation, pp. 255–94

Wolfe, D. (2002) 'Card usage climbs', *Intele-CardNews*, January, <www.intelecard.com>

World Bank, The (2001) 'Migrants' capital for small-scale infrastructure and small enterprise development in Mexico', Washington, DC: The World Bank

—— (2006) *International Labor Migration: Eastern Europe and the Former Soviet Union*, Washington, DC: The World Bank, Europe and Central Asia Region

Xiang, B. (2001) 'Structuration of Indian information technology professionals' migration to Australia: An ethnographic study', *International Migration* 39: 73–88

Yeung, H. W-C. (1998) *Transnational Corporations and Business Networks: Hong Kong Firms in the ASEAN Region*, London: Routledge

—— (2000) 'Organizing "the firm" in industrial geography I: networks, institutions and regional development', *Progress in Human Geography* 24(2): 301–15

Young, I.M. (1990) *Justice and the Politics of Difference*, Princeton: University of Princeton Press

Zabin, C. and L.E. Rabadan (1998) 'Mexican hometown associations and Mexican immigrant political empowerment in Los Angeles', Washington, DC: The Aspen Institute, Nonprofit Sector Research Fund Working Paper 98–042

Zachary, G.P. (2000) *The Global Me: New Cosmopolitans and the Competitive Edge*, New York: Public Affairs

Zaimoglu, F. (2008) 'Ich habe dieses Podolski-Gefühl', *Die Zeit*, 26 June

Zhou, M. (1997a) 'Segmented assimilation: Issues, controversies, and recent research on the new second generation', *International Migration Review* 31(4): 975–108

—— (1997b) '"Parachute kids" in Southern California: The educational experience of Chinese children in transnational families', *Educational Policy* 12: 682–704

INDEX

actor-network theory (ANT) 33
Africa 55, 57, 106, 112
Alevism 144
analytic competence 70
Annan, Kofi 121, 158–9
Appadurai, Arjun 6, 7, 11, 12, 74
Armenians 130, 131, 151, 153, 154
assimilation 17, 77–9, 80, 88, 162

Bangladesh 58, 67–8, 104–5, 109,
    117–18, 149
behavioural competence 71
border controls 89, 119
borders 86–90, 96, 100
Bourdieu, Pierre 25, 36, 66
'brain drain' 120, 121
Brazil 56, 119
Breckenridge, Carol 6, 7
Britain, see United Kingdom
business networks 45–8, 51

Canada 56, 62, 65, 91, 124–5, 149
capital 8–9, 37
Castells, Manuel 4–5, 23, 35, 159
Castles, Stephen 22, 82, 126
Catholicism 145, 146
Central Europe 105
charitable activities 94, 98, 99, 111
childcare 62
China 31, 56, 106
circular migration 119–27
citizenship 88, 96; dual 11, 15, 25,
    90–3, 100, 121, 124; nationality
    distinction 89–90
code-switching 73
Cohen, Robin 6, 9, 10–11, 41, 132–3, 135,
    136

Colombia 56, 79, 96, 98
communication 14–15, 48–9; cultural
    competence 71; telephone 54–61
community cohesion 78, 81–2
Comparative Immigrant
    Entrepreneurship Project (CIEP)
    79–80
consciousness 5–7
cosmopolitanism 25, 69–74, 85, 87, 155,
    156, 163
creative competence 71
credit unions 117
crime 5, 34
Croatians 95
cultural competence 69–72
culture 20, 44, 162; cultural
    reproduction 7–8, 83; religion
    relationship 143–5; 'toolkit'
    72–3
cybercommunities 48–50, 51–2

developing countries: micro-finance
    118; migration norms 75;
    remittances 105; telephone
    communication 55, 58, 59
diasporas 4, 5, 8, 34, 128–37, 154;
    consciousness 5–7; economic
    objectives 9; 'homeland' politics
    93–100; political activities 10–11,
    150–1; religion 26, 133–7, 141–5,
    150, 152
disaster relief 99, 112
domestic workers 31
Dominican Republic 44, 56, 58, 96,
    106, 153
dual citizenship/nationality 11, 15, 25,
    90–3, 100, 121, 124

Eastern Europe 105, 121
economic development: circular migration 121, 122, 123; hometown associations 111–12, 113–14; micro-finance 114–18; policies 120; remittances 8–9, 109–11, 119, 125
economic transformations 26, 101–27
'economics of synergy' 46, 47
Ecuador 55, 102, 106, 110
education 139, 140
Egypt 15, 110
El Salvador 11–12, 55, 96, 103–4, 106, 112
embeddedness 37–8, 39–40, 45, 46, 51
emigrants: government outreach programmes 15; 'homeland' politics 11, 97; Hong Kong 39; see also migrants
emotional competence 70–1
entrepreneurship 102, 120
Ethiopia 95, 149
ethnicity: diasporas 4, 133; media 8; telephone card use 57; units of analysis 20–1
European Commission 122

families 61–4, 74
Favell, Adrian 31, 50, 52
framing 44–5
France 91, 156
functional adroitness 71

gender 64–6; see also women
Germany 42, 91, 126, 156–7; Alevism 144; diasporas 143; telephone calls 56, 57–8
Global Commission on International Migration (GCIM) 121, 159
globalization 2–3, 25, 54, 159, 161; 'identities-borders-orders' triad 87, 89; impact on the nation-state 85–6, 100; migrant transnationalism 15; telephone calls 59; transformation 22, 23
Grameen Bank 58, 117–18
Granovetter, Mark 35, 37, 46, 47

Great Britain see United Kingdom
Greek diaspora 130, 131
Guarnizo, L.E. 53, 61, 63, 67, 94, 95–6, 101–2
Guatemala 62, 112

'habitats of meaning' 77
habitus 25, 64, 66–70, 74, 76, 83
Haiti 11, 106, 146
Hannerz, Ulf 22, 30, 32, 50, 72, 77
hawala 106
healthcare 110
Held, David 23, 100
Hinduism 135–6, 138, 147, 148–9, 152–3, 155; culture 143–4; nationalist 151; religious pluralism 140; ritual practice 142
home 68
'homeland' politics 11, 14, 15, 25, 80, 93–100
hometown associations (HTAs) 14, 15, 26, 94, 111–14, 119, 120, 161
Hong Kong 39, 56
Horst, Heather 60–1, 105, 108
human capital 37, 80, 96, 123, 124

identity 7, 45, 76–7, 154–5; diasporic 131–2, 141–2; 'homeland' politics 99; 'identities-borders-orders' nexus 86–90, 96, 100; male 65; multiple identities 6, 83, 93, 142, 148; religion 144, 145, 148–9; second-generation youth 139–40
identity politics 16
'imagined community' 20
India 9, 76, 99; Hinduism 135–6, 142, 151; telephone calls 55, 56; women 65
information and communications technologies (ICTs) 60–1, 159–60; see also technology
integration 25, 77–82, 91–2, 125
Inter-American Development Bank 106–7, 115–16, 118
'international' activities, definition of 3, 29, 160

International Labour Organization (ILO) 115, 116
international non-governmental organizations (INGOs) 10
International Organization for Migration (IOM) 121
International Remittance Network (IRNet) 117
Internet 7, 60, 148–9, 159; cybercommunities 48–50, 51–2; Islamism 151–2; remittance pooling 117; transformation 22
investment 102, 105, 111–12
Ireland 96
Irish Americans 94
Islam 136, 139, 148, 150, 151–2, 154–5; diasporic space 143; Muslim 'Other' 140–1; religious travel 134–5; universalization 149; women 144–5
Israel 69, 95
Italy 68

Jamaica 56, 105, 106, 108
Japan 106
Jews 69, 95, 111, 129–30, 131, 132, 135

Kenya 55, 108
Keohane, Robert 28
Koehn, Peter 28, 53, 70, 72, 77, 158, 163
Kurds 42, 95

Landolt, Patricia 23–4, 39–40, 74, 102, 103–4, 112
Latin America 8–9, 55, 57, 106–7
legal status 43, 78, 89, 124
linguistics 73
locality 12
loyalty 98, 99–100, 157–8

media 7–8
Mexico 44, 56, 58, 75, 96; Canadian Seasonal Workers Programme 124–5; hometown associations 113, 114; micro-finance 116; remittances 104, 106, 117, 119

micro-finance 114–18, 119
Middle East 55, 57
migrants 13–21, 25, 38–9, 158–9; business networks 47–8; categorization of 19; circular migration 119–27; cosmopolitanism 163; cultural forms 20, 162; diaspora distinction 136, 137; domestic workers 31; dual citizenship/nationality 90–3; economic activities 8–9, 26, 101–27; families 61–4; framing 44–5; gender 64–6; globalization 161; habitus 66–9, 83; 'homeland' politics 11, 80, 93–100; 'identities-borders-orders' triad 87–90; impact on the nation-state 86; information and communications technologies 159–60; integration 25, 77–82, 91–2, 125; norms 74–5; political opportunity structures 42–3; religion 26, 137–41, 145–55; second-generation youth 76; telephone calls 55–61; transformation 23–4
Miller, Daniel 48–9, 60–1, 105, 108, 148–9
Mitchell, J. Clyde 29–30, 33, 34, 36
mobile (cell) phones 55, 58, 60–1, 108–9, 161
mobilizing structures 43–4
Morocco 68
Mourides 31, 39, 146–7
M-PESA 108
multiculturalism 17, 88, 131–2, 158, 162
'multinational' activities, definition of 29
multiplicity 25, 72, 73–4
Muslims see Islam

national identity 87, 93
nationalism 11, 151
nationality: citizenship distinction 89–90; dual 11, 90–3, 100
nation-building 97–9

nation-state 2, 3, 17, 25, 85–6, 100, 162; deterritorialized 96; dual citizenship 93; 'identities-borders-orders' triad 89; postmodern project of resistance 132; sovereignty 97
Netherlands 42, 56, 81
networks 4–5, 13, 30; business 45–8, 51; cybercommunities 48, 50; embeddedness 37, 38; family 63; migrants 14, 23, 38–9; religion 146–8; social movements 41; social network analysis 32–6, 38, 39–40, 50–1; transformationalism 23
'nexus of competences' 47, 48
Nicaragua 106
non-governmental organizations (NGOs) 2, 3, 28, 41; micro-finance 115; networks 34; remittances 107, 110
norms 74–5
Nye, Joseph 28

opportunity structures 42–3
'order' 86–90, 96, 100
outreach policies 15, 98

Pakistan 8–9, 15, 39, 55, 56, 106, 109
'peoplehood' 88
Philippines 8–9, 15, 56, 63, 65, 109
place 12, 142
pluralism 83, 133, 140–1
policy: circular migration 119–21, 123, 125–7; 'diaspora engagement' 25, 98; dual citizenship/nationality 91, 92; expatriate 97
politics 10–12, 42–3; dual citizenship 93; 'homeland' 11, 14, 15, 25, 80, 93–100; nation-state 86; religious activity 150–2; social movements 42
Portes, Alejandro 9, 12, 16, 18, 24, 28–9; CIEP 79–80; embeddedness 37; entrepreneurship 102; hometown associations 112; migration 39; political participation

94; social capital 36; transformation 160
postmodernism 11, 132
power 37–8
Puerto Rico 65

recognition 138–9
refugees 11–12, 44
religion 26, 128; diasporas 133–7, 141–5; migrants 137–41; transnationalism 145–55
remittances 8–9, 14, 26, 101, 103–9, 118–19; CIEP analysis 80; circular migration 120, 123, 124–5; demand created by 160; development 109–11; government outreach policies 98; 'homeland' politics 97; hometown associations 111–14, 119; micro-finance 114–18, 119; migration research 13; scale of 15; technological changes 108–9, 161; transfer fees 107–8
resources 35, 41, 43, 44
Riccio, Bruno 39, 51, 146–7
rights 11, 92, 93, 97, 98, 138–9
ritual practice 142, 144
Rosenau, James 2, 22, 28, 53, 70, 72, 77, 158, 163

Schweitzer, Thomas 50–1
second-generation youth 76, 139–40, 154, 161
self-organization 146
Slater, Don 48–9, 148–9
Smith, Jonathan Z. 134, 142–3, 152
social capital 36–7, 39–40, 46, 49, 51, 74, 153
social change 21, 50
social morphology 4–5
social movements 2, 10, 34, 40–5, 51
social network analysis 32–6, 38, 39–40, 50–1
socialization 63–4, 65–6
solidarity 5, 6, 87, 133
Somalis 112, 151–2
South Korea 96, 106

sovereignty 85, 86, 87, 97
space 143
Sri Lanka 95, 99
Sylhetis 67–8, 153

tacit knowledge 47, 48
Tamils 95, 99
Tarrow, Sidney 40, 41, 48
technology 2, 3, 10, 22, 159, 161;
    communication 14–15; Grameen
    Bank 118; networks 5; religious
    transnationalism 145, 148;
    remittances 108–9; telephone
    54–61
telephone calls 25, 54–61, 118, 157, 159
television 8
territoriality 89
terrorism 5, 34, 95, 99–100, 151
Thailand 106, 109
trade 102
transformation 21–4, 158, 160–1, 162
'transnational' activities, definition of
    3, 29, 137, 160
transnational corporations (TNCs) 8,
    34, 45–8
Transnational Social Movement
    Organizations (TSMOs) 10
trust 36, 39, 46

Turkey 56, 96, 119, 144, 156–7

Ukraine 69
United Kingdom (UK) 39, 56, 81–2,
    157–8; circular migration 122–3;
    diasporas 143; dual citizenship 91;
    migrant religion 138, 140, 147, 149,
    153
United States of America (USA): border
    control 89; children sent to 62–3;
    CIEP 79–80; circular migration
    126; dual citizenship 91; migrants'
    participation in homeland politics
    95–6; Muslims 149; political
    opportunity structures 42; religion
    138; remittances 101; telephone
    calls 56, 57, 58, 59

voting 92, 95

war 95, 99
Wellman, Barry 49–50
women: domestic workers 31; migrants
    64–6; motherhood 61–2; Muslim
    144–5; religion 139; rights 10, 41
World Bank 113, 115, 121–2

youth 7, 76, 139–40